TALES OF BOWDOIN

Some Gathered Fragments and
Fancies of Undergraduate Life
in the Past and Present

TOLD BY BOWDOIN MEN

Collected by

JOHN CLAIR MINOT, '96
DONALD FRANCIS SNOW, '01

ILLUSTRATED

Barry Mills
3/25/10

NEW PREFACE BY BARRY MILLS,
PRESIDENT OF BOWDOIN COLLEGE

Arthur McAllister Publishers
Harpswell, Maine

Publisher's Note

The book contains stories of the life of Bowdoin College undergraduates and graduates during the second half of the Nineteenth Century. It provides a rare look into college life in an era long past and is a kind of primary source for the history of student life.

Because the book is unedited, it reflects the language and values of its time. To the reader many years later, a few passages will seem unusual or simply wrong – even hateful, racist or sexist. We can read it now with more enlightened understanding.

As a whole, this book provides much light and enjoyable reading, not only to Bowdoin people, but to those interested in a slice of American life more than a century ago.

This volume contains a new preface by Barry Mills, the 14th President of Bowdoin College. His preface gives this volume a valuable and new quality and firmly places it in the course of Bowdoin College history.

This edition of the *Tales of Bowdoin* is a reproduction of the text of the volume as it was published in 1901. While it is not exactly the same, it maintains the style of the original. The illustrations are exactly as in the original.

> Gordon L. Weil, Bowdoin 1958
> Publisher

Tales of Bowdoin

Preface by Barry Mills,
President of Bowdoin College

As Bowdoin College was about to enter its second century, John Clair Minot of the Class of 1896 and Donald F. Snow of the Class of 1901 published a collection of stories about undergraduate life at the College – historical reminiscences, works of fiction, and tales from a broad middle ground of embellished history and factually-grounded fiction.

A number of the authors achieved fame and recognition. Thomas Brackett Reed served as Speaker of the U.S. House of Representatives, C.A. Stephens, wrote for *The Youth's Companion* for 60 years, and a newly-minted alumnus, Kenneth C. M. Sills '01, would later become Bowdoin's eighth president.

There are aspects of the College in 1901 that are familiar to us in 2009, but much belongs to days gone by. The Bowdoin Quad has served as the "heart" of the College for generations and it remains one of the most beautiful places on any college campus in America. However, for the authors of these stories, the College library was located in the Chapel, baseball was played on "the Delta" where Sills Hall now stands, and trolleys and horse-drawn wagons plied Maine Street.

After all, when *Tales of Bowdoin* was published the authors stood closer in time to the opening of the College in 1802 than to the present day. Bowdoin was much smaller then, with an all-male student body drawn largely from the State of Maine (accounting for 229 of the 252 undergraduates and 86 of the 104 students in the Medical School of Maine in 1901).

By the beginning of the 20th century there had been no African-American undergraduates at Bowdoin since John Brown Russwurm graduated in 1826; a few African-Americans had received degrees from the medical school in the 19th century.

Although the College was non-denominational, there were few students at Bowdoin in 1901 whose faith was not grounded in a Protestant religious tradition. At the beginning of the 20th century the history department offered three courses each in English history, European history, and American history – fewer courses than were offered in either Greek or Latin.

In his preface to the first edition of *Tales of Bowdoin*, President William DeWitt Hyde acknowledged a delicate balance between undergraduate high-spiritedness and "cruel and lawless self-assertion." The hazing of freshmen by sophomores, the subject of several tales, is a tradition of the past, and students no longer need to seek its remedy – risking serious injury or death by hanging a hat or class flag from one of the Chapel spires. Other stories give glimpses of events and contexts, such as the firing of blank cartridges from dorm rooms by military drill students in 1861, putting President Woods and Professor Joshua Chamberlain "under fire." I don't know if the "borrowing" of the bust of President Cheney of Bates College ever occurred in 1867, but it certainly makes for a good story. These tales remind us that this College has always understood the value of a sense of humor.

Bowdoin has a long history as one of the oldest colleges in America, and this volume reminds us in serious and humorous ways of our heritage. We have, over the course of our history, remained steadfastly committed to our mission of educating young people in the liberal arts tradition and serving the common good. We value the four-year residential experience and the quality of learning from peers and faculty.

It is our responsibility as stewards of this great history and these traditions to continue our mission in confident and ambitious ways. We as a College must chart a course for the future that respects and honors our past, but also ensures our strength, vitality, and excellence into the future, given the challenges and opportunities of the 21st century.

We owe a debt of thanks to Gordon Weil of the Bowdoin Class of 1958 for allowing a new generation of readers to take ownership of a shared history. Bowdoin College in 2009 is an extraordinary and exciting place to be – an inclusive community enriched by the diverse experiences and perspectives of its students and faculty, committed to academic excellence and service to the common good, and mindful of its own remarkable history. If the authors of these tales could see the College today, I am sure that despite all the changes of the last century, they would find it to be a great source of pride.

Barry Mills, Class of 1972
President of Bowdoin College

THE CENTRAL PATH.

TALES OF BOWDOIN

Some Gathered Fragments and
Fancies of Undergraduate Life
in the Past and Present

TOLD BY BOWDOIN MEN

Collected and Published by

JOHN CLAIR MINOT, '96
DONALD FRANCIS SNOW, 'oi

ILLUSTRATED

———

AUGUSTA, MAINE
PRESS OF KENNEBEC JOURNAL
1901

TO THE MEMORY OF
ELIJAH KELLOGG,
A LOYAL AND REVERED SON OF BOWDOIN,
WHO
CELEBRATED HIS ALMA MATER IN STORY,
HONORED HER BY A LIFE OF PRACTICAL PIETY,
AND WON THE HEARTS OF HER BOYS, HIS BRETHREN,
THIS VOLUME
IS GRATEFULLY INSCRIBED.

PREFATORY NOTE

T O those in whose hearts Bowdoin College holds a place the publication of this volume requires little excuse or explanation. To others its existence can be but a matter of small concern. We give it to its readers in the confident hope that no Bowdoin man of any time can read its pages without finding much to interest him, to stir the memories of his own undergraduate days and to bind him closer to his Alma Mater. Many of the contributions are truthful reminiscences ; some are stories based upon actual happenings, and a few are woven by the shuttle-play of the imagination around scenes familiar and dear to us all. Some are long and some are short ; some serious and others in lighter vein. But all are tales of Bowdoin, with something of the college color and something of the college atmosphere which can only be fully appreciated by those who have known those halls and campus paths and who have heard the whispering of the pines.

It is not to be claimed that this book is complete or exhaustive. Many and many a theme of great possibilities is not touched upon in its pages and many a Bowdoin storyteller is as worthy a place in such a work as are any of the thirty whose contributions herein appear. It may be that this volume is but a beginning, and that other collections of Bowdoin tales will be published, finding a place in the library of every Bowdoin man and giving pride and pleasure to every Bowdoin heart.

The collection of these stories and sketches and their publication have been to us a source of much enjoyment. Encouragement has met us on every hand and the most sympathetic assistance uniformly has been given us. We take this opportunity to express our deep appreciation of the generous interest taken in the work by those whose contributions to its pages have made the volume what it is. Only their loyal cooperation made its appearance possible. And we wish to express our gratitude to the great body of alumni and undergraduates and the many friends whose cordial support made the undertaking a success. We wish particularly to acknowledge our obligation to Roy Leon Marston, '99, who drew the cover design which adds so materially to the attractiveness of the volume.

JOHN CLAIR MINOT, '96,
Augusta, Me.
DONALD FRANCIS SNOW, '01,
Bangor, Me.

June 1, 1901.

CONTENTS

PAGE

CHUMS AT BOWDOIN 1
    Edward A. Rand, '57
THE BORROWING OF PRES. CHENEY'S BUST 17
    A Phi Chi of '67
A TALE OF TWO FRESHMEN 27
    Henry Smith Chapman, '91
ST. SIMEON STYLITES 51
    Kenneth C. M. Sills, '01
WHEN THE SELF-SENDER WALKED HOME 63
    C. A. Stephens, '69
TOLD AGAIN 75
    Arlo Bates, '76
THE HAZING OF STUMPY BLAIR 87
    Fred Raymond Marsh, '99
THE MAY TRAINING 95
    Thomas B. Reed, '60
LOST : LOVE'S LABOR 103
    Webb Donnell, '85
IN THE PRESIDENT'S ROOM 117
    Henry S. Webster, '67
THE STORY OF A BOWDOIN STORY-TELLER 129
    Wilmot B. Mitchell, '90
THE EDUCATION OF JACOB SHAW 149
    Franklin C. Robinson, '73
A SMOKE TALK IN NO. 7 171
    Clarence B. Burleigh, '87
HOW TRIANGLE WON 189
    Thomas Littlefield Marble, '98
AT THE ALTAR OF TRADITION 197
    George Brinton Chandler, '90

TALES OF BOWDOIN

PAGE

INDIAN PUDDING. 209
    John Alexander Pierce, '01
A HISTORY AND THE REASONS FOR IT 217
    Edward C. Plummer, '87
THE OLD DELTA 227
    Albert W. Tolman, '88
BOWDOIN UNDER FIRE 239
    Charles A. Curtis, '61
AN INQUISITION OF 1835 251
    James Plaisted Webber, '00
RANDOM RECOLLECTIONS OF 1871-5..259
    Christopher H. Wells, '75
JOHN FERRIS, GRADUATE 271
    Edgar O. Achorn, '81
DIOGENES 279
    Henry L. Chapman, '66
THE RIVAL FULLBACKS 291
    Henry A. Wing, '80
BOWDOIN'S FIRST GREAT BOAT-RACE 305
    D. A. Robinson, '73
A COLLEGE GIRL'S BELATED IDEAL..321
    Frank Warren Hawthorne, '74
ONE NIGHT IN JUNE 339
    John Clair Minot, '96

ILLUSTRATIONS

PAGE

The Central Path..*Frontispiece*

Phi Chi, '73 19

The Campus on a Winter Morning.....................................36

Memorial Hall 54

The Summer Foliage 89

The Great American Traveler..119

Elijah Kellogg ... .144

The Searles Science Building..155

The Interior of the Chapel 179

In the Fall of 1888 202

The Old Delta...231

Massachusetts Hall 254

The Abode of Diogenes...281

An End Play on the Whittier Field 295

A Class Race on the Androscoggin....................................310

The Walker Art Building...343

INTRODUCTION

B OWDOIN College has been preeminent, not as a writer of books ; not even as a trainer of scholars; but as the mother and maker of men : men of personality and power and public leadership. The secret of this marvellous productivity is not to be discovered in laboratory or library ; it is not printed in the Catalogue, or published in the President's Report ; it was never formulated in a faculty vote, or betrayed to the listener by the whispering pines. The story of student life must tell it if it is ever told at all. The college, therefore, welcomes the present volume as a revelation of the spirit which here has been at work to make her sons the men they have become. That spirit is the spirit of freedom.

We have had two distinct theories of college life : one that of Presidents McKeen, Appleton, Allen and Harris, and the great Professors Packard, Smyth, Newman, Cleaveland and Upham, which treated students as boys under parental discipline. This theory was never an entire success, according to the standards and expectations of its advocates. The seven other devils, worse than the first, were always forthcoming to occupy the chambers which were swept and garnished by "the Executive Government."

Yet, these founders of our academic tradition builded better than they knew ; for in the grotesque aspect of policemen, patrolling the campus by day and chasing miscreants by night ; and in the more dubious rôle of detectives scenting out deviltry in Sodom and Gomorrah, as the ends of Winthrop Hall used to be called ; sifting the evidence in solemn conclave at Parker Cleaveland's study ; and meting out formal admonitions and protracted rustications to the culprits ; these grave professors were lending to mischief just that dash of danger which served to keep the love of it alive.

President Woods, whose administration was contemporaneous with the latter stages of this boisterous boyhood of the college, was wise enough to appreciate the worth of this then deprecated side of student life.

In his mild and charitable eyes, robbed hen-roosts, translated live stock, greased blackboards and tormented tutors, were indeed things to be perfunctorily deplored ; but they were not deemed specimens of total depravity, or cases of unpardonable sin : nor was he as insistent upon meting out a just recompense of reward to the culprits, as his more strenuous colleagues thought he ought to be. This mingling of austerity on the part of the faculty which made mischief of this sort worth doing, with extreme leniency on the part of the President, which insured immunity from serious penalty, made the college from 1839 to 1866 probably the best place there ever was in the world for boys to be boys, and to indulge that crude and lawless self assertion which was the only available approach which the colleges of that day afforded to manly courage and ordered independence. With such a stimulus, what wonder that here were reared Hawthorne, Longfellow, Abbott, Pierce, Cheaver, Stowe, Prentiss, Hamlin, Bartol, Smith, Hale, Evans, Andrew, Abbott, Frye, Fuller, Howard, Chamberlain, Smyth, Webb. Reed, Hubbard and Putnam. Elijah Kellogg was the consummate flower of such a régime ; and "Phi Chi" gives it appropriate immortality in song.

In later years, the improved laboratory facilities and increasing use of the library ; the introduction of the elective system, and the advent of athletics ; have given the students a free life of their own. Hence the sphere of artificial freedom which they formerly carved out for themselves, and which all save the genial Woods so deeply deplored, is no longer an educational and spiritual necessity to them. The students to-day are as free as they ever were ; but it is a freedom in the life of the college, rather than against it. Resistance is as necessary to the development of character, as friction to the motion of a railway train ; but the student now finds his resistance in the generous rivalry of fraternities ; in the difficulties of self-chosen and congenial studies ; and the prowess of athletic teams from other institutions.

Faculty and students now sing "Phi Chi" together, with a common reverence for the boyhood of the college, and a common consciousness that, for the most part, childish things are put away. To be sure, the faculty still occasionally is obliged to appeal from Philip drunk to Philip sober ; from passing student caprice to the permanent student aims and ideals. Yet, even in the rare cases where serious discipline is necessary, the student's class-mates or fraternity friends are consulted ; and almost invariably their honest judgment either modifies the faculty action, or else acquiesces in the faculty decision. Students have become more mature and manly as a greater sphere of freedom has been placed within their reach ; and the professors, instead of exercising lordship over their private affairs, are rather, as St. Paul says, "helpers of their joy."

These stories happily bind together the old life and the new by the common bonds of youthful enthusiasm, hearty good fellowship, and true academic freedom, running through them all.

As the graduates of former years here refresh their memory of what the college did for them, I am sure they will offer anew the tribute of Henley's "Matri Dilectissimae:"

"The stars shine as of old. The unchanging River,
Bent on his errand of immortal law,
Works his appointed way
To the immemorial sea.
And the brave truth comes overwhelmingly home :—
That she in us yet works and shines,
Lives and fulfils herself,
Unending as the river and the stars.

"Dearest, live on
In such an immortality
As we, thy sons,
Born of thy body and nursed
At those wild, faithful breasts,
Can give—of generous thoughts,
And honorable words, and deeds
That make men half in love with fate !
Live on, O brave and true,
In us, thy children."

TALES OF BOWDOIN

CHUMS AT BOWDOIN

EDWARD A. RAND, '57

CHUMS AT BOWDOIN

Chapter I.—In College

W HAT a marvel was that night ! It was a February evening when Goodwin Smith, at the close of a winter's school, reached the college yard again. The snow was deep. One dead mass of white was before him. Down upon it, the moon that seemed to be more than at the full, poured a flood of silver. A "dead mass," did I say ? Where the moonlight fell, it kindled death into life. Upon that silvery whiteness, all the trees had left the impress of their forms as if in a wonderful rivalry of effort to get the most distinct shadow possible. Not a twig but left its black print upon the snow. Not a breath of wind stirred the trees to confuse the fine tracery of these shadows. Overhead, the stars had swung out their torches for their customary procession, though not so vivid as on moonless nights.

"There is Orion !" said Goodwin. Yes, the hunter was out with his dogs, while timid Lepus was trying to shrink away in the vivid moonlight. One almost expected to hear a blast from the hunter's horn, and would Sirius bark in faithful response, and Procyon bay in the distance ? "There is Regulus !" said Goodwin. This brilliant gem that for centuries had been upon the handle of Leo's silver sickle, was still faithfully ornamenting it. Not far away, the white bees that Pliny watched, were clustered in Praesepe, refusing to let go their ancient hold upon the ancient hive.

Below this wonderful beauty, rose out of the snow in prosaic stiffness the old college buildings, Massachusetts Hall, Winthrop Hall, Maine Hall, Appleton Hall, so many in their very name declaring that they were of a beloved Massachusetts origin and so closely akin to Harvard. In form, they were sugar-boxes, but whether their contents were saccharine, time alone could show.

Box succeeded box, structures that were monotonous masses of length, breadth and height, but what a breaking of the stiff, prosy line there was in the upward climbing roof, the upspringing, soaring towers of the new King Chapel, that noble expression of Christian aspiration, that strong symbol of a faith that has foundations.

"I must go there and stand on the Chapel steps !" thought Goodwin.

The slender, beshawled figure tugged along a big, old- fashioned carpet bag that would bump against his slender legs. He puffed by the motionless black shadows on the white snow, each seeming to say, "Look this way !" No, he wanted to see something else. He stood on the Chapel steps and looked up.

Orion was still out in the silent, silver chase. Leo curved his gemmed sickle, and around the hive in Cancer clustered the white-winged bees. Between those starry heights and the snow, was the flow of glorious moonlight. The soul of the student was thrilled. He shivered in the cold but he could not leave the spot. He did not forget that behind him was the Chapel of granite. He had never seen such a structure before his student life at Bowdoin. He had lately read Ruskin's "Seven Lamps of Architecture," and was never tired of an attempt to interpret the symbolism of this Chapel of stone, whose towers pierced the infinite blue and whose foundations went down to the Immutable. Some of the windows were pieces of brilliant shading. He had been accustomed to the small squares of colorless glass in the old New England meeting houses, and their only duty was to stand as receivers and let the glare of the sunshine through. These panes of rich staining, to his sensitive imagination, not only received but flamed into scrolls of fiery prophecy, or poetry, and they always had a message. While not remarkable as pieces of art-work, they marked him. His friend Paiseley Gore, the Sophomore, found him one day in the college library facing a window of warm, rich color, and he was saying over a bit of Keats' "Eve of St. Agnes :"

> "And diamonded with panes of quaint device,
> Innumerable of stains and splendid dyes,
> As on the tiger-moth's deep damasked wings."

"You little booby !" said Paiseley the practical. "They won't bring you bread."

Goodwin tried to say these lines that night out on the Chapel steps, his teeth chattering away, but the "t-t-tiger-moths" tripped him up.

Some one passed him, and a second student came up to the first and called out, "Say, Tom, have you seen Goodwin Smith ? He expected to arrive about this time and I have been hunting him up, this hour."

The big carpet bag on the Chapel steps stirred quickly and the Freshman followed it. "Here I am, Paiseley !"

"There, there ! So you be ! Goody, how are ye ?"

The next moment, Goodwin felt gratefully the folds of an immense shawl going about him. In those days, shawls were included in men's furnishing goods. Every student wore a shawl, generally of a light blue or gray shade. The effect was peculiar when they flocked after prayers out of the Chapel, their shawls fluttering in the wind. Had the shawls been red, it would have seemed as if a lot of flamingoes with flapping wings had been let loose into the college yard. If Paiseley's shawl had been red that night, it could not have been warmer.

"Let me take that bag ! There ! Let me have it—mind ! I'm so glad to see you !" Big Paiseley gave him a bear hug. "I've been out twenty times looking for you."

"I—am ever so glad to see you. I—just wanted to get the effect on those steps—effect of the moonlight—"

"Oh, fiddlesticks ! Sentiment ! You'll die of it. It will freeze you. Now you come to my room."

They sat awhile before the open fire in one of those hospitable Franklin stoves of a previous generation.

"I'll just thaw you out first, young man. I got your letters all right. You liked your school."

"Oh, yes."

"And the place where you boarded ?"

"The Fellows', Deacon John Fellows ? Oh, yes. They were very kind to me, as to you when there last winter."

Paiseley wanted to ask about the deacon's daughter, Mattie. His heart—this was the heart of Paiseley, not the deacon—was a heart that was a locket carrying the image of the deacon's daughter, a beautiful girl.

3

He never had confessed it to Goodwin. It was a locket that never had seen the daylight. He did want to say one word about the girl.

He hesitated. He began. He stammered as if in the cold he also stood on the Chapel steps. "Did M—M—Mattie—" He stopped.

He began again and as he began, a warm, guilty, blush overspread his features.

"Did M—Mattie go to—to—school ?"

His ears were also burning. The locket was now open before the returned schoolmaster and Paiseley knew it.

"Oh, yes !" said Goodwin, and he too stammered. "And she was a g-g-good scholar. I—I had a kind of f-fancy she might like—ker—you !"

Goodwin was now blushing. The two guilty men lifted their eyes and for a moment faced one another.

"What a botch I've made of it I" thought Goodwin. "Paiseley loves that girl. How red he is !"

"He is dead in love with that girl," thought Paiseley, eying the Freshman's heat. "Well, I won't interfere."

Paiseley was glad to rise, glad to drop the whole tribe of "Fellerses," as people in that town called them, and he said to Goodwin, "Now we will have a change. First, I'll lock up."

He went to the door and carefully sprung the lock. Then he drew a big screen before the door. Thin indeed was the screen, but it looked thick as the Chinese wall sketched upon it, and the world seemed far away as the twentieth century from Old Cathay. He went to the windows, and let the heavy folds of the red curtains cover the old-fashioned panes. He went to the wood-closet. Ah, what old time treasures were in it !

"Goodwin," called out Paiseley, "I have a splendid bed of red oak coals already there, and now will you have some rock maple—sound to the core and heavy—or birch covered with Californy gold ?"

"It's a cold night. Bring out both kinds."

"There," said Paiseley, "I like to see it burn."

"Yes, the rock maple has white wings of flame and the yellow birch wings of old gold, say a little tawny."

"Sentiment !"

"And it talks, an open wood fire does. The maple purrs softly like a cat, and the red oak sobs and weeps like Niobe."

"Sentiment agin ! You mean 'tis wet and it sizzles. Now we'll have something practical. Have you been to supper ?"

"N-no. I've got some c-c-crackers." Goodwin was one who sometimes for economy's sake "boarded himself." A cracker looked more cheerful than a landlady's bill, or a club demand.

"Young man, if you say crackers again, I'll crack you. See here ! A little legerdemain ! What will you have, chicken for two? That means two chickens. Presto !"

He lifted a table cloth froth a tin kitchen before the fire.

"There, I got my landlady, to fix these for me, tender and sweet, you know, and I've been trying to keep them warm—just roasted—and I thought you never would come—"

"Paiseley, the Magnificent, but—Paiseley ! Did you abstract these from a Bunganock roost ?"

"No, sir ! We call that stealing at home, and it ought to be called stealing in college. I believe in one code of obligations for home and college, one code for man and woman, one code for Sophomores and Freshmen, and so we will waive all class distinctions and eat together. And another thing, young man, I want you to stay in Gomorrah to-night and be my guest."

"Oh, I must go to my room. You know my fire is built, as you kindly said you would build it."

"I—I—know I did, and I went round to Sodom and looked into your room and it did look so cold—"

He might have added "so poor and bare and homesick." Goodwin was poor, and he had not reached the level of Montaigne's philosophy so as to appreciate any advantage from indigence. Life with him was Huxley's "struggle for existence." It was evident in the scant furnishings of that room. In comparison, how full of luxurious comfort was Paiseley's room in the other end of the college, Gomorrah. Paiseley was the son of a wealthy farmer and his furniture had cost enough to equip half a dozen rooms like Goodwin's. Besides this, Freshman housekeeping is an experiment. It never can equal the ease and comfort of the Sophomore's furnishings that show a stage of completeness always accompanying prolonged good housekeeping.

But Paiseley was speaking again and in reply to Goodwin's plea that he had no Livy with him and must go to his room to study that classic and the time of recitation would be that barbarism, the hour before breakfast.

"See here, young man ! Thoughtful as ever, I brought your Livy over here. So you can get your lesson here. Then in the morning, an agreeable surprise will be furnished Uncle Tommy.[*] There will be a recitation from his promising pupil, Goodwin Smith—"

"Nonsense !"

"No interrupting remarks, young man ! All out of place here ! Let me smother that tongue with more chicken. There ! Now you keep quiet and be comfortable. You will have a good night's rest and be up in time for prayers before recitation. Old Di[†] will wake us."

"You have him now ?"

"Yes, or he has me. He came in, this morning. He built my fire and bowed his stovepipe hat to it as if worshiping some Persian divinity. I was awake and saw him. Thinking I was asleep, he came to wake me up, and tapped on my bedpost with a bunch of keys and got off a lot of doggerel about a command from Neptune and his mermaids to wake me up. I yawned and said I would throw my boots at his stovepipe if he did not leave, which he did. Now see how well everything will turn out if you stay here."

It was so good to be taken care of, to be warm, to have a hearty supper, to go to rest in so luxurious a bed as Paiseley's.
Goodwin could see in the snug bedroom where the oak coals hung over the furniture the drapery of their warm, crimson glow. He heard the wind mildly purr and mew like a cat anxious to get in, and the noise drowsily diverted him and coaxed him down, down, down Slumber's stairs into the chambers of forgetfulness. After a while, the crimson drapery vanished from the furniture. The hot coals sobered to ashes and went out.

---

[*] The beloved Prof. Thos. C. Upham.
[†] Diogenes, the nick-name of Curtis, the gray haired hermit who served the students.

In the yard, though, the light went on. The white moon showered its sparkling pearls on the white snow. Orion kept up the chase after Lepus all the while, and Praesepe's bees hung poised and motionless on their white wings. The winter night was so glorious in the old college yard. It was such a silent glory unless interrupted by the vigorous singing " 'Tis the way we have at Old Bowdoin" by a party of Sophomores from a secret society meeting, or the lackadaisical music of "Annie Laurie" from an old time Senior just going into society and at an early hour strolling home alone from a church sociable.

CHAPTER II.—OUT OF COLLEGE.

The cloud burst at last. As a threat it had been lying upon the horizon of American life for long years. It might be only a threat but it was not a thin mist today, to be blown away tomorrow ; it lived on. It was not always of the same size. It might alarmingly tower one year and then would subside, but it disappeared never. "The irrepressible conflict" was coming nearer. In 1860, the cloud mounted the sky again, black with threat. "War between the North and the South is coming," said the watcher of the heavens. The cloud darkened all the sky at last, and the red bolts of war tore down through its folds and struck in every direction. Few were the homes North and South that in some way did not feel the jar of the tempest. In many households it was more than a jar. It was a shattering of the family life. Bowdoin's sons with heroic manliness went to stand by the colors of Union and Freedom, imperiled in the fight. How little did some I used to see in the old happy college paths, imagine that there would ever be opened a path to a Memorial Hall and their consecration would be inscribed on any bronze tablets there !

Among my classmates, did Edward Thurston Chapman in the quiet of his honorable student-seclusion hear the thud of that distant gunboat explosion on the James River, fatal as if sullen Stromboli had suddenly lifted its ashy furnace-door ? Could John Barrett Hubbard, so manly and undaunted, have possibly caught the flash of those roaring guns at Port Hudson before which his consecration and courage would be swept away like the harvest straw before the October gust ? And there was "Bob"

Spearing from New Orleans. Doubtless he followed his conscience and he stood in the strife on the side of the South. When he saw the sun of college winter days crimson the morning snow, did he once think that his young blood would redden the snows of Fredericksburg ? I turn the page here and close the chapter of personal reminiscence.

It was the summer of 1863. Gettysburg was not far away, but nobody saw the tragedy. Least of all, did the anticipation of it come to the farmers who looked complacently at the corn fields of that town that would soon be torn by War's reckless plow driven in every direction. People only knew there were movements of armies but those that listened in Pennsylvania caught not as yet the sound of a hostile footfall.

It was that summer of 1863 that an officer in our army was going along a street of one of our large cities. It was a chilling morning and his rank was concealed by his army cape. He was not a person of graceful carriage, but he had a stout, sturdy build and a resolute air that commanded respect. This was apart from his uniform that always compels attention.

"What's the matter ?" he said when he had passed a big brick building labeled "hospital." There was a group at a corner, looking down upon an object on the sidewalk.

"Oh, what's the matter with the man ?" asked the officer.

"He's drunk," said a burly fellow whose red face suggested that he ought to know from experience.

The officer pushed aside the crowd, bowed and exclaimed, "Heavens, this is Goody ! why, you poor fellow !"

He lifted the head tenderly as if a mother had found a child, and then folding him close to his breast, stroked gently the white forehead and brushed aside the tresses of black hair from a face of classic beauty.

"He's drunk," said a shabby but wiry fellow. "Him and me," and he nodded toward the burly man, "him and me are going to take him to the station. It is the thing to do for him."

"No, you don't !" growled the officer. "Drunk ! He abhorred liquor in college. He never touched it, and he hasn't touched it since. I know all about him. This is a fever-stroke, overwork or something."

"What are you goin' to do 'bout it ?" said the burly man. "Leave him be !"

"You touch him, if you dare," said the officer.

He looked around.

"I wish I had a squad of soldiers here."

"You needn't think because you are an hosafer, you can boss us. Leave him be, I say."

The burly man held a dirty fist insultingly near the officer's face.

"Is there somebody here—" He looked around again.

"I'm not a soldier, only a woman, but I b'lieve in standin' by the flag. I'll help ye."

It was a woman. Her air was that of patriotism going to the battle-front, as if she would say, "Which one of these shall I take?"

"You just hold on to *him*," he replied, relinquishing his burden to the woman.

"Poor feller !" she murmured. "I know ye. Who'd-er thought it ? There, there, keep still !"

She tenderly hushed the sick man, who had begun to moan. "I'll be a mother to ye ! There, there ! Hush-sh-sh ! Make b'lieve ye're down in dear old Maine among friends."

The two men had laid hands upon the officer. He was getting ready for a grapple that would tax his powers. The sight of Goodwin Smith had awakened out of sleep old college memories. He saw the ropes and the rings suspended in the primitive gymnasium amid the old murmuring pines where he could outswing and outjump every other student. He thought of the "hold ins" when in the Sophomore arch he had tossed back every heavy Freshman that had dared assault it. The thrill of the old muscular excitement swept through him. He laid aside his cape.

"You needn't think you can draft us for the war !" said one of the objectors.

"The war has no place for imps like you !" said the officer, and gripping each brute by the collar he led them both to the curbstone, and flung them as if carrion out into the street. They could only mutter and stare at him in astonishment. Then he went back, took up Goodwin Smith and beckoning to the woman, went toward the hospital steps.

9

"You belong in here ?" he said to the woman, noticing sonic peculiarity of dress.

She nodded her head.

Together, they went up the steps.

"You don't know me," she said. "You came from Brunswick and taught school at Crawford Centre down in Maine, and Goodwin Smith taught after you, and you boarded at Deacon Fellerses'. You forgotten Mattie ?"

Forgotten ! Her face had been glowing like a sweet evening star among his remembrances, but evening stars are not accessible. He had never married, but he had hoped that Goodwin and Mattie would be sensible enough to take that step. Out of the seed of separation, marriages do not grow. The two had cherished an interest in each other at one time, but they had not met for years, and no one could say whether under memory's gray ashes there might be any spark of mutual interest alive.

Paiseley Gore did not tell the woman whether he remembered or had forgotten Mattie, but as they entered the superintendent's office, he said, "See here ! You are not 'Ann' ? Bless me !"

The calling of her name pleased her.

"I am Ann Stevens, the hired woman at the Fellerses' !"

But the superintendent was waiting for a communication from Capt. Paiseley Gore, having rung a bell for "bearers" as soon as he had caught sight of the officer and the man in his arms.

Capt. Gore bowed. "This man, sir, I want you to look after. He's one of God's great princes, an old college chum. Take the best care of him and I'll foot the bill."

"Oh, that will be all right."

"But I want extra care of him. He has been using himself up, studying for the ministry, working in the slums, teaching to pay his way—an old trick of a college student—and he has broken down. I happened to be on a furlough and was going through the city and found him. My furlough is up tomorrow and I must get back to my regiment. You see Lee's army has broken loose and I must get to our army, but I will write you. If anything should happen to me—I have remembered him in my will. Don't forget

10

that he is one of God's great heroes though a little fellow. I knew him in college, and a fellow that knows another fellow in college, feels tender—"

"I won't forget," said the superintendent, smiling. "I've been there."

"You see, he wanted to be a soldier and he couldn't pass the examination, but really he is a great man. God, when He measures big souls, doesn't go by feet and inches."

"You're right," said the superintendent.

A few minutes later, Ann Stevens was alone in her room. She went to the looking glass, a way she had when she wanted to tell a secret and leave it in a safe place. "Now, Ann!" she exclaimed, contemplating a rather homely but very sensible face, homeliness and good sense often being wedded in this life. She called again, "See here !" The Ann in the looking glass nodded to the Ann before it, as if to say, "Go ahead. You can trust me." "I want to tell you what is goin' on. The superintendent says I may git the nuss for the patient. Who's a better one than the gal in Maine I worked for and that I have followed to this place because she wanted to do some good for her country, hoping they would put soldiers here ? That's all ! Don't tell ! We'll see how it comes out."

In a little while there was a woman standing over a patient's bed in a quiet room, a woman in the garb of a nurse. She bent low her sweet face, out of which shone the hope and courage of youth.

"Ann says I know him," murmured Mattie, and then her eyes grew bigger and bigger, as if some fuller wave of light, of discovery, of resolution, were sweeping into her soul. She said nothing. She made no outcry, though here was one who as the teacher of the little village school, had made a change in her life. He had left an emptiness in her soul, a hunger that had never yet been satisfied. So hungry, and he was in this very room ! He was the patient that she, as the hospital nurse, must tend ! Hark, he was saying something ! "I hear the old pines talking." He opened wide his eyes. "They're talking. Once at Brunswick, when I went into the old cemetery back of the college, I thought I caught the sound, the roar of the sea. It was all around me. No, it was only the wind talking up in the tops of the pines. Lovely !"

"Yes, yes, it's lovely," said the nurse. "Now I will try to make a noise like that and you go to sleep. I want you to be very quiet."

He smiled and closed his eyes. That wandering mind, though, was not at rest yet.

He spoke again : "Say, are you my sister ?"

"I must humor him," she said, and replied, "Yes, yes ! Now I want you to go to sleep."

"Are you my wife ?"

"He will forget this. He's out of his head," she thought, and replied, "Yes, I am your wife. Now go to sleep and I will make the wind in the pines."

That always hushed him, the thought of the sound that seemed to come up from the stretching shores of Harpswell Neck and old Bunganock, and breathing its music across miles of sandy plain and reaching the big stretches of pine-growth back of the colleges, started up all the harpers and players on organs in the treetops ! What a soft, luxurious dream of melody in gentle June days, and in the winter storm what vigor, as if Neptune's band had just come to town and were playing back of the colleges!

One day, a convalescent was sitting on a balcony and the sweet-faced nurse was beside him.

He asked, "Have you heard from Paiseley Gore yet ?"

"He—I'll tell you the news some time. He went to his regiment, you know. It was Gettysburg."

"You need not tell me. He is very near me. He came to me in a dream and a beautiful smile was upon his face, and I said, 'Paiseley, what a look of life you have, so bright.' 'Yes,' he said, 'they could not hurt me.' It's a beautiful thought that death is not less but more life, and that this fuller life is about us, God caring for us in the old tender way, but caring for us too through those—you know what I mean—I was thinking of Paiseley."

His head drooped and his lips quivered.

"I wouldn't say anything more now, for you're weak. You have many dreams, don't you ? You had one about the wind in the pines, and —"

"Yes, and one day I—I must tell it—I dreamed you said you were my wife."

Her's was the drooping head now.

"You said it ?"

12

"Yes—but —"

"Are you weak and so you can't think of it ? You won't take it back?"

"N-no."

THE BORROWING OF PRESIDENT CHENEY'S BUST

A Phi Chi of '67

THE BORROWING OF PRESIDENT CHENEY'S BUST

A T the time I entered Bowdoin, near the middle of the 60's, the leading Greek-letter society there was, in some respects, the Phi Chi. This society, let me say for the reader who may not be familiar with college organizations and nomenclature, should not be confounded with the Phi Beta Kappa, for notwithstanding the similarity in their names, the two societies had *some* points of difference. In general the Phi Beta Kappas affected scholarship, or book learning, while the Phi Chis were the more aggressive, and inclined to achievements that required and developed greater originality, self-reliance and executive ability. It justified, too, its right to a Greek name rather more, it seems to me, than any other of the Greek-letter societies then at Bowdoin ; for besides having its headquarters in the attic[*] of Winthrop Hall, its members strenuously endeavored to live up to some of the practices of the ancient Spartans, if history tells the truth about them, acceding with those notable exemplars to the dogma that there are things not approved, perhaps, by theorists, which it is nevertheless justifiable to do, provided one doesn't get caught. I am not defending the doctrine, but merely recording the fact. Stated accurately, Phi Chi life was a year of experimentation with certain ethical theories ; a year devoted to testing and learning morals by the laboratory method as it were.

I had better perhaps say here for the information of "yaggers," "oudens," and older graduates, that Phi Chi was a Sophomore society founded by the illustrious class of '66, which, to use the metaphorical language of a eulogist of the day, "placed its standard from the very

---

[*] A friend of mine who is a profound Greek scholar from having devoted his whole life to the study of that language, informs me that the word attic is derived from Attica, and so means pertaining to Attica or Athens. He has written a lengthy monograph on this matter, which he intends to give to the public as soon as he can find a publisher who will publish it at his own risk. My friend expects to get a Ph. D. for this.

17

beginning high up on a lofty eminence," (see unpublished speeches of Wilson of '67) ; which, being interpreted, means that its founders started the society off at a rattling pace. But it can be truthfully stated, I think, that the standard was not lowered, or the pace was not slackened, whichever, metaphor is preferred, by '67, into whose keeping it of course passed next.

Yet the pranks performed by the Phi Chis of '67 were with one exception, for which a few hot heads were to blame, reasonably innocent. One of them, for example, was what I have called "the borrowing of President Cheney's bust."

It was well known to several members of the class of '67 that President Cheney of the then nascent college at Lewiston, had a fine bust of himself, a present, it was said, from one of his classes. That he should have a strong affection for the bust, therefore, seemed reasonable and right, but it was reported that he idolized it. Now if Phi Chi ever believed that she saw the index finger of duty unmistakably pointing out the way, it would be when an opportunity was presented to remove from the land a cause for idolatry. But there were other motives that prompted to the deed I have undertaken to narrate, and one was the feeling that the bust of an eminent and intellectual man of high character, with its continual inspiration to noble thoughts and honorable deeds, would be a desirable ornament for the headquarters of the society. These quarters were not without souvenirs, but they had nothing in the bust line, and fed by the knowledge that this lack could be remedied, the desire to remedy it grew steadily till at length three members of the society, who may be designated as Alpha the Sly, Beta, his lieutenant, and Gamma, an assistant, volunteered to form a party to procure the coveted prize.

The expedition set out from Brunswick in a carriage at early candle-light. The night was dark and cloudy, and later it began to rain, dampening everything but the ardor of the adventurers. Lewiston was reached about the "wee short hour ayont the twal," and the youthful Bates College was found fast asleep. Leaving the team at a discreet distance in care of Gamma, Alpha the Sly and his lieutenant manoeuvred their way to the college buildings. By cutting out a pane of glass, an entrance

PHI CHI, '73.

A. L. Crocker, A. G. Ladd, A. J. Boardman, F. S. Waterhouse, G. E. Hughes, W. A. Blake, J. E. Badger. R. C. Gould, F. H. Fassett, J. F. Elliot, A. P. Wiswell, F. M. Hatch, F. W. Hawthorne.

was effected and in a space of time that was not needlessly prolonged, the bust, carefully wrapped to keep it from injury, was on its way to the carriage. As soon as it was safely bestowed therein, the expedition faced for home in a pouring rain.

When a mile or two of the return journey had been covered, Alpha the Sly discovered that his pocket handkerchief was missing. The last he could remember of it was that he had it out when the pane of glass was cutting. It had his initials on it, and must be recovered *quocumque dispendio temporis*. So back they turned and found the lost article under the window by which entrance had been effected. Notwithstanding this delay, the adventurers were able by a little forcing to reach Brunswick and land the bust safely in the society's headquarters, in ample time for morning chapel.

That evening there was a grand convocation of Phi Chi. The bust was on exhibition, of course, and was duly admired ; the story of the expedition was related in full detail, and enthusiastically cheered. There was also the usual amount of atrocious punning, such as "that bates all," "it is too bad to rob Bates College of all her Cheney-ware," and "I wonder how long it will take President Cheney to get over his bust this time." Finally all gathered around the bust and joined in singing "Do they miss me at home, do they miss me ?" after which they retired to their rooms to prepare themselves for their early morning recitation in Greek.

At all subsequent meetings of Phi Chi during the year the bust was on exhibition with other trophies, but in the intervals, it was thought best to conceal it. There were various devices for doing this, but sometimes it was hidden in a large pile of feathers. How those feathers came there I never knew, but should surmise that for a long time after Winthrop Hall was built, all the chickens, turkeys, ducks and geese eaten by the college faculty, must have been taken up there to be plucked.

As soon as the loss of the bust was discovered, President Cheney, it was reported, began vigorous efforts to recover it. His suspicions first very naturally felt on his own Sophomores. He called them together and with tears in his eyes, charged them with the crime, and threatened to expel the whole lot of them unless the bust was returned. They on their part, with tears in their eyes, protested their innocence, and so, though he didn't half believe them, he forgave them, we were told.

He then came to Bowdoin and reported his loss to President Woods, with the request that diligent search and inquiry be made to ascertain whether the lost had not found its way thither. President Woods, deeply sympathetic, though he was unable to believe that his Sophomores would do such a deed, made the investigation as requested, but without avail. He was furthermore able to prove an alibi for Bowdoin on the ground that on the evening before and the morning after the bust was taken, every member of the class of '67 was present at chapel except one who was proven, however, to have spent the entire night in his bed at his home in Bath.

It was reported that President Cheney made the same request at Waterville and Dartmouth and, indeed, at all the New England colleges, and theological seminaries, and other institutions where he thought that by any possibility the bust might turn up, but the search of course was fruitless.

But meanwhile the Sophomore year of '67 began to draw to its close, when Phi Chi with all its opportunities and responsibilities must be transferred to '68. I will restrain myself from all sentimentality over this farewell to prank and frolic, and I only allude to it, to say that as the day for it approached, the question, what to do with the bust, became a matter of considerable deliberation. It was not thought best to leave it to the Phi Chis of '68, partly for fear they would not take as reverent care of it as it deserved, but chiefly because there appeared to be no secure way of concealing it. In the annual change and repairing that took place in the summer vacation, it would be safe in no student's room unless he staid to watch it, and as for the attic of Winthrop Hall,—well, there was no certainty that the President, or Prof. Packard, or even Prof. Upham might not take it into his head to climb up there, since there would be no students around to catch them at it. They were not considered by Phi Chi as trustworthy. But even if they refrained, it was more than probable that the college carpenter would come prowling around. He had found things up there before, and might try it again.

A good many suggestions were made as to the disposal of the bust, but none of them seemed worthy. It may be asked why it was not sent back to President Cheney. Well, I can best explain why by relating the story of the Kentucky colonel who reported to his friends one morning that a wonderful feat of legerdemain had been performed at his club the evening before, by a guest from Vermont, "We put a glass of water in his hand," explained the colonel, "and covered him over with a blanket ; when at the end of two or three minutes we took the blanket off, the glass was empty, but we couldn't find a sign of water on his clothing, or on the blanket, or anywhere about. Now, what did he do with it ?" At last some one suggested that perhaps he drank it. "By George !" exclaimed the colonel slapping his thigh, "none of us ever thought of that."

But at last a plan was hit upon that met with general approval; it was to send the bust to Barnum, who was then fitting up his second museum in New York city, his first having been burned a short time previously. The bust was accordingly packed carefully in a strong box to keep it from all injury, and properly marked with its destination and "to be handled with care." As it was seen that it would hardly do to ship the package by express from Brunswick, it was taken to Portland by private conveyance and sent from there, the expressage to be paid by the receiver. Then for a time all knowledge of the bust was lost. Whether indeed it reached its destination in safety could only be guessed, because for obvious reasons no receipt had been asked for.

It did, however, as was afterwards learned, reach Barnum's safely, but as none of his people knew whom it represented, or who had sent it, it was placed on a shelf among other curiosities.

It came about perchance a few years later that a son of President Cheney found himself in New York with a little leisure on his hands, and decided to "take in Barnum's." As he strayed from ward to ward, looking at the various curios and phenomena, behold the lost bust of his father, marked "Sophocles," and claiming to have been made from a death mask of that worthy by an eminent artist, and obtained by the "Great Showman" at a cost of $25,000.

Young Cheney, as you may surmise, lost no time in reporting the discovery to his father, and also in bringing the matter to the attention of

Barnum. As the bust was neither a freak nor a fraud, Barnum was willing to part with it, and thus at length the lost found its way back into the possession of its owner ; and I may add in conclusion, that none were more pleased over the final outcome than the ex-members of Phi Chi of the class of '67.

A TALE OF TWO FRESHMEN

HENRY SMITH CHAPMAN, '91

A TALE OF TWO FRESHMEN

I

W HEN Dexter Morgan first appeared on the campus, there was much felicitation in athletic circles. Johnny Moore, the captain of the foot-ball team had seen him at the station, and remarked to a companion, with an enthusiasm rarely displayed by a public character weighed down by such momentous responsibilities, that there was one Freshman at least who seemed to have been put together with special reference to the game of foot-ball. Kip White, moreover, who held a similar position of authority in the track-team, observing the stranger from the window of his room, where he lounged in the lazy autumn sunshine, was moved to declare him the most hopeful raw material he had seen since he first wore running-breeches.

"He looks as if he could do anything from the hundred yards to the hammer-throw, and do 'em all equally well," was the flattering sum of his critical judgment.

The young Freshman certainly offered very unusual physical recommendations. His frame was at once sturdy and supple, his breadth of chest and length of limb were equally admirable, while a certain grace and pliability of movement showed the perfect balance of his strength. A well-featured fellow he was, too, with a straightforward eye, and a mouth which clearly bespoke firmness and will power. When it was learned that beside all this, he was the son of Col. Morgan whom everyone knew as one of the ablest lawyers in New York, and therefore in the country ; a faithful alumnus, moreover, and a trustee of the college, it needed no occult power of divination to fortell his early eminence in his class.

But somehow things failed to turn out according to expectation, and in proportion as Dexter's rise in the estimation of his college-mates had been swift, so was his fall headlong. The first shock was administered to Johnny Moore who hurried around to Morgan's room in South Maine as soon as he could find a few moments to spare from his arduous duties with the awkward squad on Whittier Field. He was cordial almost to the point of condescension, but Morgan who might better have appreciated the captain's friendly intentions, if he had ever seen the haughty manner in which he ordered other Freshmen into canvas jackets and moleskins, froze him with distant politeness.

He was very glad to be honored by a call from Mr. Moore; the courtesy was appreciated, but he was sorry it wouldn't be possible for him to oblige Mr. Moore by joining the foot-ball squad. He didn't care to play.

Johnny was not used to this sort of talk from a Freshman, and still less prepared for the air of cool self-possession with which it was accompanied. He stared incredulously at Dexter, and asked him if he didn't know the game, "because if you don't," he added, patronizing once more, "you ought to, with such a build as yours."

Mr. Morgan, it appeared, had had some experience with the game in preparatory school, but didn't care to pursue it further. No, his parents had no objection that he knew of, to the game, but he thought he would better keep out of it, and he imperturbably bowed the astonished captain out at the door. Johnny did not surrender so easily, however, for he could not think with patience of so much rare strength and agility going, as it were, to waste, but though he bombarded the inexplicable boy with arguments until he fairly lost his own temper, he failed to move the quiet and polite determination with which Dexter held him off.

Of course the big Freshman fell irretrievably, in the opinion of most, when this state of affairs became known. He followed it up by declining with the same air of indifference, the invitation to organize his own class team, and even remained away from the class-meetings whereat the newcomers became better acquainted with one another, and discussed the plan of campaign to be directed against the arrogant Sophomores.

As a crowning piece of indiscretion, he snubbed the upper-classmen who came to dangle fraternity badges before him. His own father had belonged to a society long since defunct so far as Bowdoin was concerned, and he was therefore "fair game." Half a dozen invitations to fraternity chapter-houses and dining-clubs were extended to him ; almost any society would have pledged him willingly, but he was shy. Every invitation was declined with cool courtesy, and he made it no secret that he did not propose to become a fraternity man.

Thus from being in a fair way to become a college hero, Dexter Morgan became first a college mystery and then an object of general suspicion and reproach. He never failed to be polite, and could not fairly be charged with freshness or sullenness. He merely held everyone at arm's length and neither had nor wanted intimates. He roomed alone and was never known to call on any of his classmates. In the class-room he did well enough and when he was not studying or reading he was most likely to be ranging alone over the country about Brunswick, gaining by long hard walks the exercise his vigorous body required. It was not unusual for him to cover fifteen miles in an afternoon, and before many weeks had passed there was hardly a picturesque fringe of the rugged shore of the bay, or a sparkling reach of the broad river which he did not know as well as if he had lived in the old town all his life.

His class-mate Charley Marryat was the only one who seemed able to establish any relations whatever with him. Charley did not come to college that fall until late in October,—there was some trouble or other with his eyes,—and by the time he arrived every room in the dormitories was taken. But he brought with him a letter from his father, an obscure minister in some little town up the State, but who had been a class-mate and friend of the great Col. Morgan. His letter was addressed to Dexter Morgan, who when he had read it hastened to ask its anxious bearer to share his rooms with him, an offer which was gratefully accepted.

Perhaps Charley's appearance had as much to do with the matter as the contents of the letter, for Dexter was a softhearted fellow in spite of his dignity, and no one could look at Charley without feeling a little sorry for him. He was a frail, almost puny little fellow, with pale straw-colored hair and large china-blue eyes. With this ensemble went an appropriately timid, appealing manner, which was not exactly sapless either. It simply called your attention to his extreme youth and delicate health, and without complaining about them at all, nevertheless urged you to do whatever you could to make things easier for him.

So Charley moved an old second-hand desk, a couple of chairs and some other necessaries into Morgan's room, which was already furnished about to its limit with the nicest things that good taste could select and abundant money could buy. He also erected a shrine to his big roommate in the recesses of his heart and worshipped him there as few men have the fortune to be worshipped by one of their kind. It was not strange that this should be so, for Dexter had every advantage which the other lacked, and combined with them a kindliness and gentleness of manner toward his new friend which would alone have won Charley's susceptible heart. Their's was the attraction of opposite natures, which, when it really manifests itself, is more powerfully magnetic than any other.

It was a welcome change for Dexter, to have someone with whom he must live in relations of the closest intimacy. He was neither reserved nor sulky by nature, and though by his deliberate choice he had cut himself off from the companionship of his college-mates, he had already begun to find the life of a solitary decidedly irksome. But though Charley, in his affection and admiration for his new friend, set himself at once both to find out the cause of his unaccountable behavior and to induce him to alter it, he made little headway. Dexter was willing to be as cheerful and companionable as possible with him, but he was not to be allured from his lofty, attitude toward everyone else. It was not merely a disappointment, but a grief to Charley that this was so. He could not bear that his room-mate should be anything else than the leader he was born to be, the conspicuous figure first of his class, and then of the whole college. It worried him to hear Dexter called stiff, and proud, and conceited and priggish, when he knew what a charming fellow he could be when he chose, and it hurt him that Dexter would not give him his confidence and explain conduct so incomprehensible. But through it all he was loyal and against the all but unanimous verdict of practical ostracism which the college democracy passed against his friend, his shrill voice was raised in unending protest.

The snow came late that winter, and all through December Dexter Morgan found it possible to take the long, hard walks from which he drew so much solace. Now and then the faithful Charley, if he felt more energetic than common, accompanied him, though both pace and distance had to be modified to suit his strength. One bright Saturday, near the close of the term, the two boys made a joint expedition to the old shipyard on the road to Harpswell. The yard, once as busy as any along the New England coast, in the days of wood and canvas, when the Yankee clipperships were mistresses of the sea, was deserted now, though the last vessel had left the stocks only a few years before. The road which led in from the four-barred gate, over the hill and under the pine trees to the water side, was overgrown with grass, the shops and sheds were rotting in idleness, the ground where once great ships had proudly risen was littered with decaying timbers, and the odds and ends of iron and rope which the workmen had not thought it worth while to take away. On the slope of the hill overlooking these ruins of a once great industry, and giving prospect of the waters of the Cove, and the rocky shores and evergreen heights of Prince's Point opposite them, the boys sat down to drink in the picturesque beauty of the scene. The tide—fortunately—was full, and the steel-blue water sparkled frostily in the bright sunlight, with the cold brilliance of a northern sea in winter.

"Br-r-r ! It makes my teeth chatter to look at it," said Dexter, burlesquing a shiver as he spoke. "Doesn't it look icy, Kid ?"

Charley agreed absently. He was nerving himself to speak more openly to his friend than he had yet dared, and hardly knew to what he was assenting. At last he found his courage and spoke:

"Dexter, will you mind it, if I ask you to tell me why you wouldn't try for the team this fall ? You know as well as I do that you could have made it, and what's more you knew they needed you. They wouldn't have lost the Amherst game and come so confoundedly near dropping to Bates, with you at tackle in place of that mark, Weeks."

Dexter did not answer at once, and Charley watched him anxiously.

"There isn't any reason which would have kept you out of the game if you had been in my place, is there, Kid ?" he said at length.

"Of course there isn't. I wouldn't see Bowdoin put out anything but the best in any line, if it lay with me to help it," replied Marryat, flushing indignantly.

"Ah that's the difference, you see," said Morgan. "I haven't gotten to feel that way yet. I doubt if I ever do. We don't look at things the same way, Kid."

Charley regarded him hopelessly. "You don't need to tell me that," he said. "What I want you to do is to tell me your point of view. You understand mine well enough, but I can't make yours out. The fellows say you are—well, I won't say what—but I know better. There's something back of it all, and I wish you'd tell me what it is. Why wouldn't you join any of the fraternities either ? Oh, you see I'm going to have it out with you now I've begun. You'll feel better for telling me, anyway, old man. It's worth while giving your confidence to somebody."

There was another pause when Charley stopped speaking, as though the other were considering whether it was best, after all, to be equally frank. But in reality Dexter was glad of the chance to speak what was in his mind. His hesitation was more the effect of his fear that if he spoke he would inevitably fall in the estimation of the only friend he had in college—he who had always had so many friends and admirers.

"You won't think any the more of me if I tell you," he said finally ; "but I'll do it all the same. The fact is I never wanted to come here anyway. All my friends in New York and most of the fellows I knew at school have gone to Yale, and I wanted to go with them. Father insisted on my coming to Bowdoin. I came, of course, but I've never pretended to be glad I came. What's the use ? If I could make the Yale team now, it would be worth while, but I don't care the snap of my finger for foot-ball here. What does it amount to anyway ? There's no name to be made in games with a lot of small college teams—no one hears of you up here. And I've no call to work myself half to death for a college I didn't want to go to, and don't want to stay in. I can see you're looking sour, Kid, but I'm telling you my point of view. You don't like it, but you asked for it."

"I'm not looking sour, Dexter, and I'm ever so much obliged to you for speaking. It's hard for me to understand, you know, for I've been brought up all my life to look forward to coming to Bowdoin, till I've come to think it about the best luck a man can have, to be here. I didn't realize how you felt. I never heard you speak of Yale."

"No, you haven't. Why should I ? It wouldn't help things to growl over them in public."

"I'm sorry, old man." Charley's voice was very sympathetic ; he had a genius for sympathy. "I wish you could get around to my point of view—or else I wish we could change ours about. You could do so much for the college if you had mine, and I couldn't do any less for it if I had yours."

Dexter's answer was gruff in tone, but kindly in undertone. "Shut up, Kid !" he said. "Don't talk nonsense. You will do more for anything you're fond of than I could with all my muscle. You've got things that count for more than all the athletic records a man can make. You've got brains for one thing, and common sense, and a bit of honest sentiment, and, by George, I think sometimes I haven't a particle of any of them. But 'I'm made the way I'm made,' as the old darkey said, and 'it look like it'll take a mighty outpourin' of grace to save me.' "

Charley smiled merrily. "No one can say you're not modest as to your own merits," he said. "You'll come around in time, old man. You've been disappointed, but you'll find the old college a pretty good place after all. Your father loves it, and so does mine, and what is good enough for them can't be much beneath their sons."

"I'm an obstinate brute though, Charley," returned Dexter, "and when I'm started in one direction, it's awfully hard to make me change my course. So far I've done the best I could to spoil my course here, and I guess I've made a pretty thorough job of it. The fellows have me sized up pretty well—and mind you, I don't say I'm sorry either. I can rub along all right if it's my luck to stay, and if I can induce the Colonel to relent next year, why, I shan't regret having stuck it out the way I began. There's one thing I won't do, and that is—pretend. I didn't want to come here, and I don't want to stay."

"I shan't give you up, though," returned Charley, rising to his feet. "You're just the sort of fellow who will be at home at Bowdoin, when you're ready to look at things more reasonably, and all you've got to do is to be your real self to bring the whole push around to you, whenever you'd rather have them friends than enemies. You're on the wrong track now, and down at the bottom of your heart you know it. You're getting to like the old college, in spite of yourself, and you do not mean half you say. By spring you won't mean any of it and then you'll stop saying it. There's some missionary work to be done with you, my boy, and I'm appointed to do it. Now let's go home. It's cold sitting here."

II

The winter passed at last, as all Maine winters do if one only has patience with them, and Charley was still at his missionary work. Dexter yielded slowly, indeed at times it seemed that he had not yielded at all, and fits of discouragement often depressed the spirits of his ardent little friend. He did come to know some of his class-mates better, however. They came to see Charley, and Dexter, who was only a big boy, in spite of his stubbornness, could not help laughing and joking with them, and so getting to like them. But though he made in this way a few personal friends, who one by one came to admire him almost as much as Charley did, he stood as much aloof from the college at large as ever, and displayed no sort of interest in any of the student activities of the institution.

His long walks had at length to be given up, for the snow made them more laborious than enjoyable, and Dexter's abundant energy next turned itself upon gymnasium work. He spent no less than two hours a day in the building performing with enthusiasm what most of the college endured as drudgery, and finishing his daily employment of every appliance on the floor with a run of several miles around the gallery-track. At which sight the track-men groaned, for it was evident that this contrary, inexplicable Freshman was by long odds the best distance man in college—and he would not consent to train.

When the first chill days of Spring came round, the roads being still so deep in slush and mud that tramping was out of the question, the cinder-track on Whittier field offered good footing and fresher air than was to be found under the gymnasium roof. So it was there he took his exercise, a stiff three-mile run at the close of every afternoon—rain or shine. And at sight of his swinging, tireless pace the track-men gnashed their teeth afresh and declared that the sulky Freshman ought to be hazed till he knew his place and saw his duty. Perhaps he should have been, but no one cared to undertake the task. Charley Marryat's methods were more likely to prove effective with Dexter Morgan's kind of stubbornness.

Charley was really producing his effect ; for Dexter was already heartily ashamed of his peevishness. He found the fellows he knew

THE CAMPUS ON A WINTER MORNING.

companionable and manly, and those who cut him on the street (of whom there were a few) had, as he admitted to himself, what he should consider ample justification. He was sometimes surprised that he had not been sent to Coventry long ago by the united action of the fellows. Little by little, too, he began to recognize the atmosphere of the college, and to like it, and to understand why his father loved it, and why his classmates loved it too. The spirit of the place, as well as the admonitions of Charley Marryat, was beginning to work within him, and though he knew himself to be outside the hearty and wholesome life of the college, he felt that he was being drawn into it even against his will, as a strong swimmer is drawn into the vortex of a whirlpool. Gradually, through Charley, his circle of acquaintances was widening. Gradually he was getting to know the fellows he met, better, and as the barrier of suspicion and reserve between them was broken down, he found in them fresh sources of contagion from which the infectious Bowdoin spirit might be caught. All this he would hardly admit even to himself, but when he found himself unconsciously humming "Phi Chi" as he rubbed down in the gymnasium after his daily run, he could not deny that he was failing to maintain his pose of indifference with entire success. Of course he still wanted to go to Yale—there was no doubt about that, but he was beginning to understand how he might be very happy at Bowdoin—if he had started in right, and how he might in time grow really fond of the college.

He was in one of these "melting" moods, when Kip White, already introduced to the reader, appeared at his room to make a last appeal in behalf of the track team. Kip was a tall, rangy youth, with hair which blazed aggressively, and eyes which snapped when they did not twinkle.

"The Worcester meet is only three weeks off, Morgan," he began pathetically, "and we've got a team which will give a good account of itself from top to bottom. Jack Stillings is good for a place in the dashes—perhaps for a win Stump Grattan and myself will attend to the hurdles and the long jump. There's Forster and Bemis in the weights, Berny Sweeney in the pole vault, and Phip Douglass and Skinner Jones in the middle distance. But we haven't a single good long distance man. I don't know what else you can do, but I know you can run the mile and the two-mile in pretty near record time. I held a watch on you the other day, from behind the stand—you won't mind, will you ? and with you to hold up our end there, we'll have the best- rounded team the college has ever had. If you won't we'll have to depend on Dietrich, and he can't get even a third, unless everybody else sprains an ankle going the first lap. What do you say ?"

Dexter was very near to saying "Yes" at once. It seemed a lucky chance that he should have so apt an opportunity to purge himself of sullenness and indifference without having to make the first advances himself. But a stubborn spirit still possessed him. He would not give in too easily.

"You give my running more credit than it deserves," he said. "I only run for exercise."

"Whatever you run for, you can beat any man in college at a distance," asserted Kip. "I think you're sure of points at Worcester, too. At any rate you ought to try, for the sake of the college."

Dexter smiled a little bitterly, but he only said : "I haven't been training properly, you know. I was smoking when you knocked on the door, and I haven't followed training rules of diet by a good deal."

"There's time enough for that yet," argued Kip. "Your condition is near perfect anyhow, and a couple of weeks' good training will put you right on edge. And even without strict training you can run. I've seen you."

While the two were talking Charley Marryat had been listening nervously, his eyes fixed on his room-mate. Now he broke in eagerly :

"Say you'll do it, Dex ! It's a chance I'd give a farm for ! Do it like a good fellow, won't you ?"

Dexter did not answer at once, and when he did he spoke hesitatingly. "I can't answer tonight, White," he said. I really don't want to, you know. It means work and bother and the end doesn't count for much with me, I'll admit. But perhaps I shall come around to it."

White's eyes snapped warningly, for the Freshman's coolness annoyed him.

"The boys all said you wouldn't do it," he said, getting up. "But I told them you would if it was put before you right. You think it over. It means more to you, as I look at it, than it does to the team."

It wasn't a fortunate thing to say, for it pricked Dexter's obstinacy awake again. He said nothing but, "All right, I'll think it over ;" but to himself he grumbled, "If he thinks he can work me that way, he's mistaken. If I do run, it won't be because I want him and his crowd to jolly me along. I can get along all right without them, I guess."

As White left the room Charley got up and followed him into the hall.

"Kip," he said, "when the entries go in—you enter Morgan for the mile and the two-mile. Never mind what he says beforehand. It won't do any harm, and I think I can get him to run, if you'll let me manage it."

"All right. I'll enter him," replied the track-captain.

"But he might as well understand that if he stays out of this, there'll be no notice taken of him in the future. He can do the college a good turn now, and if he won't, why, we don't have to get down on our knees to any self-important, conceited prig of a Freshman, whether he's the son of Colonel Morgan of New York or of the President of the United States!"

Kip spoke with some asperity, and he did not realize that his voice, somewhat shrill by nature, rose in pitch as he spoke. The door was closed, to be sure, but his final words pierced it. Not wholly intelligible when they reached Dexter's ears, they still conveyed their sense and froze his uncertain purpose into determination. He would see Kip White elsewhere before he'd run for his team.

He had cooled off by morning, but the decision he had reached had become inflexible in the process. Charley found it harder than ever to move him, though he could not discover why it was so.

"Dex, old man," he said finally, as near losing his patience as it was possible for him to come, "I don't like to put it on this ground, but I wish you'd do it for me. You know how much I want to do something for the old college, now, while I'm here. Perhaps because it's the thing I can do least of all I feel especially so about athletics. Of course there's nothing I can possibly do myself, but if I could persuade you to run at Worcester, it would lead to so much else, and I should feel that I had done a real service, both to you and to the college. Why won't you, old man?"

"Well, well, Kid, perhaps I will," responded Dexter snappishly. "You'll nag me to it, if there's no other way, I suppose." At which unkind remark, poor Charley, who had the sensitive man's fear of making himself a bore, flushed and was silent.

It was only a few days after this that Charley came in from recitation to find his room-mate hastily throwing his things into an open suit-case. He looked pale and anxious, and his smile as he looked up was a haggard affair.

"Your good counsel is all for naught, Kid," he said, nodding toward an opened telegram lying on the center table. "The Worcester meet will have to go on without me this spring. The Colonel's sick—something sudden and serious, they tell me and perhaps I shan't ever come back again."

He spoke with laborious self-command, but there were tears in his eyes. He loved his father dearly and just now he was thinking how little he had done to make the last few months happy for him. Charley, with a sympathy subtle beyond his years, understood him, and silently pressed his hand. Almost without words, they parted at the station ; but they had never been so close to one another as they were then.

The college heard of Dexter's departure without emotion. The track-men lamented the final disappointment of the hopes they had entertained of him, but otherwise no one seemed much concerned about him. There were a few perfunctory words of regret and that was all. Never before had Charley realized how completely his friend's conduct had alienated the ready sympathy of all except himself.

III

The day of the Worcester meet that year was as nearly perfect as a day in May can be—which means a good deal. The pretty oval was flooded in sunshine, and the fresh, cool green of grass and trees formed a rich setting for a scene of life and color which glowed and shifted in fascinating complexity. The stand was full to overflowing and the bright spring gowns and blossoming hats of the pretty girls who had flocked to watch and applaud their brothers and friends—or more than friends— gave it the various hues of a huge but incoherent kaleidescope. A romantic glamour surrounds those great athletic meets of antiquity—the

Olympic games. But after all, what tame affairs they must have been, since no women were allowed to witness them ! Whether the ancient records are beaten now-a-days or not, no one can say, and no one much cares. But what a pity the old Greek champions could not have had the supreme pleasure of winning their victories in the very sight of the girls for whose good opinion they cared as much, no doubt, as do their modern successors !

Among the soberer groups of dark-clothed youths who thronged the track and field, shone an occasional white-clad athlete, while on every hand, in knots and flags and streamers, waved and floated the colors of the rival colleges the dark green of Dartmouth, the rich purples of Amherst and of Williams, the sober brown of the Rhode Island college, the steel gray and cardinal of Tech, the gleaming white of Bowdoin.

One young fellow who sat far back in the stand, an inconspicuous knot of white in his buttonhole, watched it all with a strange blending of enjoyment and unhappiness. It was Dexter Morgan, who, on his way back to Brunswick, found himself entirely unable to resist the temptation to leave his train at Worcester and follow the crowds out from the city to the oval. It was perhaps the instinct of the born athlete, who never willingly misses a public contest in the sports he loves, though there was at bottom another reason, too, a newborn interest in his own college and its team.

He had found his father very ill, but not, as he had feared, dying. He had waited until the doctors declared him well on the road to recovery and had a few serious talks with him as he sat by the bedside. What passed between them Dexter never told. Whatever it was, it was the final influence in the process of effecting a good and permanent amendment in his disposition. Now as he sat by himself in the stand, he wished heartily that he might be down there with the rest, wearing his "Bowdoin" proudly across his bosom, and ready to do what he could for the honor of his college. The snap of the referee's pistol as the hundred-yard trials began, broke in upon his revery, and he found himself suddenly upon his feet. watching long-legged Jack Stillings romp away from his field, and shouting lustily as he breasted the tape five yards in the lead. A few moments later he was cheering Kip White, whose ruddy shock of hair rose and fell as hurdle after hurdle was cleared, and finally, though hard pushed in the flat by a big Williams runner, flashed by the judges in first place. "Skinner" Jones he saw draw a second in the quarter-mile, and Stump Grattan in spite of his short legs attained a similar distinction in the low hurdles. Over in the field he could see Bemis and Forster hurling the discus with encouraging strenuousness, while the staccato yell of a small but earnest band of Bowdoin rooters further down the stand set his blood to tingling with the thrill of the occasion.

He could not sit still, and paced up and down at the back of the stand, eager to join the other wearers of the white, but not sufficiently sure of the reception which would be accorded him to make the venture. On every hand he could hear surprised comments on the strength of the team the Maine college had sent out and confident predictions that the race would lie between Bowdoin, Dartmouth and Brown. Then he had to watch the mile run drag its slow length along, the single Bowdoin entry, poor old Dietrich, falling further and further behind at every, stride.

"Oh, why don't you *run ! run !* you lobster !" he growled to himself. "Put your head back and climb ! Confound him ! he's stopping ! My soul, what an exhibition !" and he clenched his fists in fierce indignation.

He heard a man wearing the green laugh sarcastically. "They don't train 'stayers' up in Maine," he was saying to a pretty girl who sat beside him. "They'll never beat us out without a point or two in the distance events. Look at Symmes spurt ! There's five more points for old Da-di-di-Dartmouth Wow !"

Suddenly as he listened, irritated unreasonably by the man's enthusiasm, Dexter was struck by a bold idea. To think was generally to act with him, and a few moments later he was pushing his way across the track and through the crowd to Kip White's side. The captain was watching the pole vaulting, and coaching Berny Sweeney, who was struggling for third place with two other unfortunates, red in the face with the violence of his efforts at levitation. Dexter touched him on the arm.

"Hullo, Morgan," was White's cool greeting. "Where are you from ?"

Dexter did not think the obvious answer needed to be made. He plunged at once into more important matters. "What's the outlook ?" he inquired.

White looked at him with some surprise. "Well, we've got a fighting chance," he said. "We've got seventeen points sure, and a few more to come.—Now, Berny, don't try to jump it. This is no high jump. Keep cool and push like hell with your arms. Don't get rattled. You've got that Amherst man winded now. You can last him out. Every point counts, you know." Then turning again to Morgan he went on : "You saw 'em run old Dutchy off his feet, I suppose ? Well, we haven't anything else up our sleeve. Bemis will collect a point or perhaps three in the shot, and Berny here will get a third, I think, but I can't figure out more than twenty-three anyhow. Dartmouth will do twenty-five anyway, and so will Brown— perhaps more. We're still in the ring, but I guess about third will have to do us."

"Have you got some running clothes at the dressing rooms that I could wear ?" asked Dexter quietly. "We'll have to be quick about it, I suppose the two-mile will be on before very long."

White wheeled sharply and looked the Freshman straight in the face. "Morgan," he said, "if you pull us out of this, we'll never forget it."

When the entries for the two-mile run lined up before the stand, the afternoon sun was hanging low, but the excitement of the day was at its height. Bowdoin had twenty-two points, Dartmouth and Brown each twenty-three. Nothing else except the high jumping remained unfinished, and that, as it happened, could not seriously affect the standing of the leaders. The two-mile run must decide the result, and the event was held to lie between Symmes who had gallantly won the one-mile for Dartmouth, and Wallis of Brown. The new runner in Bowdoin's colors attracted the attention of expert observers by his splendid build, but he was only an inexperienced Freshman and could not be expected to do better than third. Bowdoin's supporters, already hoarse with vociferous endeavors, were moreover stricken dumb with surprise at the sight of Morgan the irreconcilable, actually there on the track, ready to run for his college. While they debated whether or not their organs of vision were to be relied on, the pistol cracked and the race began without a single cheer for their representative. Only in his ear resounded White's whispered words :

"Go in and win, old man. You can do it. We won't forget this."

For seven of the eight laps the race as usual lacked every element of dramatic effectiveness. The pace-makers capered out in front and ran themselves into exhaustion without disturbing the serenity of the real contestants ; the young Freshman from Bowdoin, was not as they had hoped, even momentarily flighty. He stuck doggedly to Wallis's heels, for he felt that this was the man to watch. Symmes had already run a bruising race, and was not fresh. As the gong rang at the commencement of the final lap the pent-up excitement broke loose in cheers and yells, and among them Dexter heard a snappy "B-o-w-d-o-i-n," and then in a clamorous shout his own name—"Morgan !" His pulse quickened instinctively.

And now Symmes and Wallis moved out away from the other runners who had laboriously kept within a dozen yards or so of them—but close behind them, not to be dislodged, was Morgan. He was surprised to find how easily he ran ; the training he had had was so irregular and insufficient that he had feared a collapse. But he was not in the slightest distress. He had been running greater distances than two miles all the winter and all the spring, and was well within himself. Symmes was spurting now, trying in vain to draw away from his two pursuing shadows. Dexter could see his elbows laboring with the stimulated pace. But the gap did not widen. On the contrary Wallis and Morgan closed up steadily. Symmes had shot his bolt. His spurt had been made too early, and he lacked the stamina to prolong it. Dexter wondered dimly as he ran what the man whose contemptuous laughter at poor Dietrich's expense had so exasperated him, thought about "stayers" now.

Round the back stretch they went, the confused shouts of the crowd remote in a seemingly infinite distance. Now they were passing Symmes, who was done for, but struggled gamely on, and Wallis in turn was trying by a burst of speed to shake off his only dangerous competitor. It was not to be done. Dexter was breathing hard, his head, overcharged with blood, spun dizzily, his legs seemed moving in erratic defiance of his will, but he had not lost an inch. Round the turn into the home stretch they swung— they two,—with the championship hanging on the issue.

Dexter had run more than one hard race in his schooldays, but never such a race as this. The sprint had been continuous for nearly a quarter of a mile and with his irregular training he felt the strain badly. His lungs seemed bursting ; it hurt to draw each panting breath. Things blurred before him, his blood hammered thunderously in his ears. He felt that he was exhausted, that he must give up, and yet so long as that other bobbing automaton a yard in front of him kept on running, so must he.

Suddenly, as if by some trick, he found himself side by side with Wallis, who had swerved toward the rail. Again a few strides, and he could only see his rival out of the tail of his eye. He could not understand at first. It seemed too much to believe that the other had weakened, that he himself was actually winning. Before he could settle the thing in his puzzled brain, he was aware of a dim blur of shouting people on either side of the track, and straight ahead among a group who faced him he saw a tall youth with bright red hair who leaped up and down, and waved his arms in the air.

Then across his chest he felt the soft, yielding pressure of the tape, and stumbling blindly on, he lay at last closely enfolded in Kip White's embrace, while around them danced a score of demented young gentlemen, who howled without intermission a refrain which seemed to consist of a selected portion of the alphabet, varied by something which sounded very much like his own name. It was an agreeable occasion, he felt, though he would have appreciated it more if he had not been so tired.

"Kip," he said between long breaths, as they led him, still the center of the bounding group, to the dressing room, "I've been several sorts of a fool this winter. Do you think the fellows will forget it, and give me a fresh start ?"

"Don't you worry, Colonel," replied White, knighting him, as it were, upon the field of victory, with the intimate name he was to bear among his college fellowship ; "You've earned the right to be any kind of a fool you like."

IV

On Monday evening, a great bonfire roared gloriously before King Chapel, its flickering blaze throwing the massive granite front and the graceful twin spires in golden relief against the sombre darkness of the sky. Upon the steps of the historic building stood the victorious team, self-conscious and embarrassed by their conspicuous position, while all the college sang and danced and shouted in their honor. Moreover, that the tribute of noise might never slacken, a band hired for the occasion executed martial music with more spirit than harmony, in the background.

Least demonstrative, yet perhaps most joyful of all, was Charley Marryat, who had been going about in a daze of incredulous bliss since the news of Morgan's share in the great result had come. The limit of his capacity for sheer ecstasy of happiness was reached when his idolized friend was called on for a speech amidst the frenzied acclamations of the fellows, who but a few days before would have had but the coldest of nods for him had they met on street or campus.

Dexter was pale with excitement and fatigue, but his fine presence and dignified manner, inheritances from his distinguished father, made him in spite of his youth and embarrassment, a genuinely commanding figure.

"I have done nothing to call for this honor," he said when the cheers at last had died away. "You all know how foolishly I have behaved since I came to college. I'm glad if I have been able to do anything which may help to repair the mistakes I have made, and testify to my present love for old Bowdoin. Henceforth, if it lies in me, I am going to be as good a Bowdoin man as any of you. Some of the boys have complimented me by saying the race I was fortunate enough to win brought the championship to Bowdoin. If it did, I want to tell you that it's not me you have to thank, but the man who showed me what the college was, and what I owed to it. If it hadn't been for him, there wouldn't have been any Bowdoin man in the two-mile event, and perhaps, therefore, there wouldn't have been any championship to celebrate tonight. You all know who I mean, I think,— Charley Marryat."

There was another roaring cheer, for Morgan and Marryat together this time, and here through the crowd came a band of dishevelled Freshmen bearing on unsteady shoulders, Charley's feebly struggling form. Up to the steps they staggered, and there in the midst of the heroes of the day they deposited him—a blushing, boyish little figure, who could not yet make out what it was all about. But Dexter Morgan's big, friendly hand reached out of the confusing half-darkness and drew him close, while amidst the tumult of the shouting men and the blaring band he heard Dexter's voice in his ear :

"There, Kid, are you satisfied now ? Don't ever let me hear you say you can't do anything for the college, for you've brought the championship to Bowdoin."

ST. SIMEON STYLITES

KENNETH C. M. SILLS, '01

ST. SIMEON STYLITES

"ALL ready, fellows ! Remember I'll say one, two, three, forward ! Start on the left. Left ! Right ! Left! Right ! Left ! Keep in step, Si ! Hat on straight, Tom ! All ready. One ! Two ! Hulloa, where's St. Simeon ?" And the marshal looked about searchingly.

The long line of Juniors, capped and gowned, patiently marked time. Half way down on the right there was a vacancy. Two or three minutes later St. Simeon came in and took his place seriously ; but as he was always serious his fixed stare passed by unnoticed. Jack Bryant, the marshal, signalled to the orchestra on Memorial stage, raised his white and green decked baton. "Left ! Right ! Left ! Right ! One, two three, forward !" and the line went slowly thudding up the aisle.

Memorial Hall had its usual Ivy Day crowd—the expectant mothers, the passive fathers, the pretty sisters. And of course each proud Junior on his way to the stage hoped to see his own friends. As the slowly-marching class reached the center of the hall, one maiden whispered loudly to another : "That's St. Simeon there, isn't it ?" The man designated nearly blushed ; for he had never been prominent in any way during his college course. He had never been pointed out in his life. For three years so quietly, so much to himself had he lived that when the class got to studying Tennyson in English Lit, someone had dubbed him "St. Simeon Stylites," and the hastily bestowed nickname had stuck.

The girl who knew him was uncommonly pretty—else what were the use of this tale ?—slight and tall with dark hair and brown eyes, and a big picture hat. She wore a simple white frock. She must be the cousin of Ted Briggs, Kathleen North, whom St. Simeon was booked to take to the dance that evening. It seemed a pleasant prospect but St. Simeon gave just the slightest semblance of a sigh as the line passed on. At the stage it separated and wound its slow way up over the steps and sat down as one man.

Soon the Ivy Orator was holding forth. His words sounded sing-song; for it was hard to see the relation of the Philippines to a Bowdoin Ivy Day. St. Simeon began to ponder over other things. Only half an hour ago he was hunting his room over for his cap—he was always looking for his cap. Then long after the starting time he bounded down the End stairs. There was need of hurrying. Just as he was running down the stone steps the Western Union messenger boy rode up on his wheel.

"Telegram for any one ?"

"Yes, Gordon Fox."

"Hulloa ! That's for me. Probably an Ivy message from dad. He knew I was to have a part today." And St. Simeon tore the yellow envelope open jaggedly. The cablegram was dated from Rome that morning and read :

"Dr. Fox died of fever here Thursday. Burial Friday.
                    T. H. JOHNSTON,
                              U. S. Consul."

St. Simeon quickly signed the messenger's book, then staggered back. His father—gone—and way, way off in Rome. His father who had always seemed so young to him,—who was looking forward to his son's doing well on this very Ivy Day,—who knew what it all meant, for he was a Bowdoin man himself. Everything seemed terribly black to the poor boy. He opened his gown and crumpled the yellow paper into his pocket. He stood there on the steps thinking for a moment or two. It would not be plucky to give up his part now. Yet it was not clear that he could get through. He walked towards Memorial very slowly. A squirrel by the side of the path looked up curiously. The little fellow was trundling a big nut ; and, as St. Simeon passed, he covered it with a huge leaf and scampered blithely away.

The next instant St. Simeon somehow or other found his mind made up. Try to forget that missive he must, and go on with his response. His father would not have willed him to falter. He hurried on and joined the line just as Ted Briggs was starting after him. As he saw Ted he determined to say nothing to any of his friends on that day for fear of marring their pleasure.

MEMORIAL HALL.

The orator was drawing on to the end of his part. In his peroration he spoke of a soldier's pluck. St. Simeon braced himself involuntarily. The poem which followed was a dreary affair ; the exercises seemed predestined to failure. The president, a close friend of St. Simeon's, looked worried. As the poet went on with gushing lines about Spring Summer and Autumn and Winter, St. Simeon's thoughts again strayed. He looked down at the pretty girl in the audience with the big hat and the brown eyes. Almost a week before Ivy, Ned Briggs had come to St. Simeon for help. He was overwhelmed with two girls who had both unexpectedly accepted ; and St. Simeon must take one. He had chosen Miss North whom he had seen for a few moments at a Junior assembly. How eagerly he had looked forward to Ivy Hop it was now idle to think.

When the poet had finished the orchestra played some movement that sounded much like a dirge. St. Simeon pulled at his watch ; as he did so he felt the crumpled telegram. He wondered if his father had been buried yet, if perhaps his body was that very hour being borne down the aisle of the English church at Rome. People asked why such solemn music was chosen for Ivy Day ; but to St. Simeon it seemed very natural.

The president got up to give the customary class history and then to make the Ivy presentations. The first two responses fell absolutely flat. The exercises were evidently a failure. St. Simeon trembled. It was his turn now. The president introduced him rather wittily, as "Mr. Gordon Fox, the world renowned, tower-dwelling saint of the class." St. Simeon thought of getting through quickly ; but he threw his whole self into the speech. His wit and quaint cynicism made folks wonder if Bowdoin had ever heard a more brilliant response in all her Ivy days. Some Seniors gasped when the quiet St. Simeon was given a part ; they gasped more as he spoke on. His thrusts at his fellow classmen made them "wood" more than thrice ; his gentle and humorous raillery won over the audience. He was the saving remnant of the afternoon.

When he got through, the people in the crowded hall almost cheered him. He saw Kathleen North dapping mightily. Then he sat down. The whirlwind of applause seemed strange to him. It was not right, he thought. He wished his father were here instead of in Europe with a sick patient. Suddenly a picture stood out before his eyes. There was a bare room with staring white-washed walls, a little shrine in one corner, and in the center a bier with a heavy pall. A man of brown robe anl cowl came in and knelt down crossing himself mechanically. He withdrew instantly; and St. Simeon again saw the hats and colors and dresses of the Ivy crowd.

He began to think deeply. Away off in the distance he heard the Popular Man accepting the wooden spoon. There was some reference to "our St. Simeon ;" and the audience broke out into applause again. A professor whose class had started Ivy Day said to a young girl by his side, "I never heard of anything like that before."

The orchestra struck up another march and the class went out two by two, slowly, rhythmically. St. Simeon's face was flushed ; but he still seemed very serious. Everyone glanced at him now ; Kathleen smiled up brightly. It was hard for St. Simeon not to feel his triumph bitter and hollow.

When the ivy was planted and the ode sung, the class and every one else hurried over to the Chapel. St. Simeon walked quietly with a couple of friends who warmly hailed him. One class-mate who had had a response ran across the campus, tooting a horn merrily, his gown streaming behind him. When the Juniors reached the gallery above the Chapel the bell had stopped ringing and the service had begun. Most of the Juniors looked on impressed. St. Simeon noticed one crouch down and take a drink. He himself felt faint and sick at heart. The Seniors formed their locked-step ranks and marched out slowly. Soon the strains of "Auld Lang Syne" arose. Gordon wondered if they had Seniors' Last Chapel when his father was in college. The next moment he was repeating the graceful lines of a young graduate :

> Should avid acquaintance be forgot,
> Though some stand low and some stand high,
> Though some be rich and some be poor
> And some be early doomed to die ?
>
> To some will fall the victor's crown,
> The honors and the joys of life,
> But some in sorrow must sink down
> And perish in the world's great strife.

A Junior or two had already started down the Library steps. St. Simeon slipped away, ran quickly to the End, and laid aside his gown. He went out past the Gym to the pines by the Whittier Field. He was at last by himself. Throwing himself down on the ground he sobbed as if his heart would break. He just realized that he was all, all alone in the world. He thought he heard someone coming and crept in under some bushes and lay there thinking. His father had ever been a brother to him—a big generous brother—and now he was dead and gone. He would never know of his son's success that afternoon, never say those few words of praise that would mean, oh so much !

Just then St. Simeon became aware of footsteps rustling over the pine needles, and of a girl's voice. "Didn't Gordon Fox do splendidly this afternoon ? I'm going with him to the dance to-night you know. He's a great friend of Ted's." Her companion gave a grudging sort of a reply and the two passed on. Gordon wondered what he should do about to-night ; he must not let Ted know, and mar his fun. He left the question undecided and walked down town. Everyone was at supper. He bought an evening paper with a long account of Ivy Day ; it spoke much of Gordon Fox, the son of the well-known physician. This was the very paper he had counted on mailing to his father. His sorrow was very bitter now ; he almost cursed Fate.

On his way up Maine street a town girl stopped to tell him how well he had done. He thanked her formally and hurried on. He went into the room thinking there might be another cablegram. Instead he found a note from Ted.

"We've all gone down to the Inn. Couldn't find you so took Jordan in your place. Be *sure* to turn up at the dance with Miss North's order.
E. J. B."

It just occurred to Gordon that he had made out the list of Miss North's partners and that it was nearly time for her to have it. He heard a Freshman go whistling his way to his room on the top floor. St. Simeon called him back. "If I'm late at the dance, give this to Ted, will you ? It's Miss North's order." He of the Freshman class gave a long gaze of astonishment. "Are you crazy, Saint ? Late for a dance with Kathleen

North. Why I'd fifty times rather be conditioned in Buck." And the desperate little fellow hurried on.

St. Simeon sat down in his desk-chair and lit his pipe. He looked over the evening paper—not a line about his father. All the words became blurred and the praise of his own response was intolerable. He got up and went into the next room. "Time to get ready for the dance, isn't it, old man ? Don't you forget you promised me one with Miss North, will you?" And Gates stropped his razor nervously. St. Simeon made some daft reply and went out of the End.

It was about half past eight and a warm night. Gordon started to walk through the Longfellow Woods. The air was very soft and crickets innumerable were chirping. He found a log in the woods and sat down smoking. Although he had always been much by himself he never knew before how soothing solitude is. He wondered if at Rome things were as beautiful. It was so still there in the woods that he walked about until midnight. As he passed Memorial on his return he heard a waltz clearly. It was his favorite *"Donauweibchen."* He wondered what Kathleen North thought of him and if Jordan were absolutely filling his place. Then he walked back to the End.

He still felt that he must be alone ; and for fear of Ted's finding him he went into a Freshman's room whose door his key fitted. Towards three o'clock he began to hear fellows coming in from the dance. He looked out the window just in time to see Jordan and Ted pass by. "Where in the world was old St. Simeon?" said Ted. "He must be sick." "Guess not," said Jordan. "You know he's struck on a little girl up at Lewiston, probably he's up there. My, but he's the fool. Kathleen North can dance, boy. I tell you, and —" The two went in and their door slammed. St. Simeon still looked out over the pines ; he was a quiet thoughtful boy ; and, as he gazed at the great stars, he kept asking himself what and where his father was. He pondered on the mystery until it was almost dawn. Four fellows, slightly clad, straggled out to play tennis ; two were young alumni, two Seniors. They laid down the stakes and a queer match followed. Tim Taylor, rather drunk, straddled the net-pole, acting as umpire. St. Simeon watched their antics for awhile ; then heard them discuss the belle of the ball ; three of the five voted for Kathleen North.

The alumni won the set, 6-2 ; and the players and umpire left the court to swallow the prize.

The sun was rising now. St. Simeon looked up the campus towards the Chapel. A peculiar light mist hung about the trees midway from the ground ; just a faint streak of fog. St Simeon went out again for the air seemed to soothe him as a quiet physician. A chickadee or two gave the long drawn note preceded by a short one, a haunting melancholy cry. Soon all the birds began their matins. Gordon felt happier. He wondered if his father had been laid to rest in that beautiful Protestant burial ground at Rome that he had read about where were the graves of Keats and Shelley ; a place he remembered "to make one fall in love with death." The thought gave him some comfort. He started on a long walk through fields and woods. Soon he met a boy driving a herd of cows to the morning's milking. The kine looked at him pityingly from their big, beautiful eyes. There was a sweet smell from their overflowing udders. The boy greeted him and gave him a drink of fresh, foaming milk. It was the first little streak of light in a very dark and dull and lowering horizon. St. Simeon was beginning to see that if he must live out the rest of his life without the help of one who had done everything for him, even milk-boys and squirrels and woods and fields were dear companions. His father had talked to him often of a love for God's out-of-doors. He remembered much being said of Nature when the class was studying Wordsworth and Burns. Now he began to see a little of the much that it all meant.

Before he knew it, he was back near the campus ; and the bell was ringing for morning chapel. He turned in from Maine street thoughtlessly and found himself face to face with Ted and Kathleen and the whole party. Ted was ahead with his other girl and Kathleen turned around to speak to St. Simeon. She held out her hand cordially.

"Good morning, Mr. Fox. Where were you last night, you deserter ?"

St. Simeon still looked serious and care-worn. "If you'll take a short walk with me, I'll tell you all about it," he said. "Ted's too interested to care about me now, but if you want to—"

And the two walked through Longfellow Woods ; and there he told her everything. "I am so sorry, so very sorry" she said ; and St. Simeon knew that Kathleen North was a girl who meant each one of her words.

WHEN THE SELF-SENDER WALKED HOME

C. A. Stephens, '69

WHEN THE SELF-SENDER WALKED HOME

U P to 1880 fully thirty per cent. of all Bowdoin men were "self-senders"—a term that needed no explanation when I was there, late in the sixties.

At the opening of the college year, in September, when the Sophomores and upper classmen were inspecting the new Freshmen, with a view to taking them into the societies, etc., a common question concerning each was, "Who sends him?"—the answer being usually, "His folks," or "Sends himself." There was, it is true, an intermediate caste or grade, in part assisted by parents, or friends ; but the self-senders, pure and simple, were about thirty per cent.

How this runs since 1880 I am not well informed, but believe the per cent. to be less, as it naturally would be, with the increase of wealth in the country. The subject is not wholly pertinent to my present homely narrative, and is introduced merely as a prelude to declaring my own caste there ; I was a self-sender, and at times a wildly distressed one. In truth, the under-graduate whose bills are honored by the paterfamilias and who has only to attend to athletics and the curriculum, has and can have, no idea of the exigent mental attitude of the self-sender ; he is quite another being.

Eminent educators have held, I believe, that more than compensating advantages come to the student who has his own way to make, in the habits of thrift and self-reliance thus fostered; but I have never yet met a bona fide self-sender who would fully endorse this view, much less one who would voluntarily subject himself to such a discipline.

But it is a fine topic for the self-made man and others to expatiate on to the young, thirty years later, when they have all become prosperous, and after a good dinner. It requires about that amount of perspective to be really enjoyable.

My own idea is that the uncertainty, worry, fret, fear, envy and other ignoble emotions that periodically agitate the self-sender's mind, rather more than offset any good that accrues to him from his scrimping and self-reliance. But cases and temperaments differ, no doubt. Some boys have better heads for managing these things ; some bear the pressure of debt with equanimity and a calm confidence in the future. One of my college-mates, I remember, was always smiling, always happy, always whistling and carrolling like a bob-o'-link, though he owed everybody from two old aunties at home, to "Gripus" at the college book store ;— and he who could owe "Gripus" and yet be happy, must needs have been panoplied with more than Horatian armor of triple brass. But the men of later years don't know "Gripus" : we did.

In my own case, the joys of college life were frequently devastated by financial crashes which I had not the skill or the sagacity to forestall and stave off ; or rather, I did stave them off too long, and held on till the bottom fell clean out.

One such overtook me near the end of the Fall term of the Sophomore year. All my small monetary expedients had gone wrong. An incautious expenditure in furnishing my room (No. 2, Appleton Hall) began the trouble. Bad luck with two or three ventures for gain, followed on. I had been agent for an inexpensive sewing machine during the Summer vacation ; a light machine, operated by a crank ; I carried the sample about the country, in a valise. In September, I intrusted my sample and three other machines to a sub-agent who was to sell them on a commission. But now in November—I learned that he had sold the three machines and decamped with the proceeds, and had left my sample machine and valise at Yarmouth railway station. A small speculation, too, in stove-wood and dried apple, at the home farm up in Oxford county, which I had deemed a sure thing, had come to naught from the accidental burning of the building in which it was stored.

In brief, my whole *menage* had collapsed. I was bankrupt. Even my steward and fellow student of the boarding-club was after me, with suspicion on his brow. Him I satisfied by leaving my Sophomore books with "Gripus," on an advance of six dollars. My last dollar was then in ;

and naught remained but to foot it home via Yarmouth, to reclaim the "sample" sewing machine—my only available asset.

Ah, what a bleak morning that was ! Bitterly cold with the ground hard frozen, and beginning to spit snow. Yet even the hard, whitening earth and cold gray heavens were less bleak than my financial sky.

After a last vain effort to mortgage my half of the room furniture to my chum who was a crafty financier, I crossed the campus—not then adorned by the Art Building and Memorial Hall—to Gen. Chamberlain's cottage. The General was then the college President pro tem ; and my object in calling was to obtain his permission to withdraw before term closed and seek the sanctuary of home. Thus the hard-run fox as a last resort seeks refuge in the burrow of cub-hood. I had the promise of the district school, in the home neighborhood ; and the parental farm-house was at least good for a few weeks board, till new schemes could be hatched.

Briefly I recounted my condition to the General's keenly appreciative ear, and having heard it, he made not the least objection to my immediate departure. He agreed with me, *nem con*, that home was the best place for me. With laughter, but a cordial hand-shake, he wished me a pleasant walk up the country and regretted the state of the weather !

Dear, kind old Professor Packard had noted that I was in trouble the day before, and had made it in his way to join me as I left the recitation room. Encouraged too far by his sympathy, I told him how I stood. But when he had grasped the full significance of my revelations, even his warm heart was chilled. In all his experience of indigent Sophomores, he had never met one so utterly devoid of resources. He acknowledged with regret that he knew not what to advise me.

I have a vague faith still that "Billy," (Prof. William Smythe author of the Algebras and Calculus and who, college tradition says once ciphered himself up at midnight from the bottom of the college well into which he had inadvertently fallen) might have figured it out for me, in terms of x. y. and z., if only I could have taken refuge in one of his equations ; but the old arithmetician was ill in bed that week, being now very infirm, and so missed the chance of a lifetime to perform one final, famous feat in those abstruse mathematics which he loved so well and long. Could he have rescued me that morning—and I have always half believed he could—not far below George Washington himself ought he now to be sitting in Miss Helen Gould's new Hall of Fame.

But no help came to me, either from the Chair of Moral Philosophy, Revealed Religion, or Mathematics ; and buttoning up my old overcoat, I set off along the railroad track to face the snowstorm and walk to Yarmouth, thirteen miles, there get my abandoned sample sewing machine, and then walk home, forty-seven miles from Yarmouth, sixty in all.

It soon became hard walking on the ties, for snow was now falling fast ; but I reached Yarmouth by noon and recovering my property, on which, luckily for me, there was no storage charge, I sat down in the station to eat a meager bit in the way of a lunch which, mindful of emergencies, I had privately conveyed to my pocket from the club breakfast table. Then for an hour or two I attempted to do a little sewing machine business in Yarmouth village. I hoped to sell my sample machine and thus be able to take the evening train home. But it wasn't a good day, for it ; the women cut my story short, snappishly ; an "agent" of any sort was persona non grata that bleak afternoon. Later, I tried to dispose of the machine in several stores and at a hardware shop—quite in vain. No one would even look at it ; there did not seem to be a smile, nor a bit of geniality that day, in the whole place.

I had staked a good deal of time on hopes of selling my sample machine in Yarmouth ; and now, at two of the short winter afternoon, found myself face to face with the necessity of reaching home that night, for I had money neither for food, nor lodging.

For three or four miles I plodded along the railroad, then as the snow was deepening on the track, I diverged to a highway off to the left of the line. Here by, good chance, as I at first thought, I was immediately overtaken by a man alone in a large pung, driving a fat, strong horse. He wore a broad-brimmed hat and blue-drab cloak, and he proved to be a Shaker Elder, returning from Portland to the Shaker village at New Gloucester.

"Will thee ride, friend ?" he asked, with grave kindness.

"Thank thee, I will," said I, and immediately conceived rosy hopes of accompanying him home, spending the night with the Shakers, and even selling them my sewing machine. I had heard that these good people do not charge wayfarers for a night's lodging and food. Accordingly, I set myself to beguile the way and amuse the Elder with lively conversation. But I must have overdone it, I think. For some reason which I never quite understood, the Elder suddenly froze to me. Possibly it was from learning that I was a college student. He waxed grim and became as mum as an oyster. I tried him further with two humorous stories ; but he never cracked a smile to them ; and soon after, coming where the road to the Shaker village diverged from the main road, he pulled up for me to get out.

Thereupon I asked him point blank to let me go home with him, overnight. But "Here is where our roads separate, friend," was all the answer he vouchsafed me.

By this time it was dark ; and being both hungry and cold, I applied recklessly, at the first house I came to, for lodging and supper, and then at the next house and the next ; but the people were all inhospitably inclined.

There were eight inches of snow by this time, the footing getting more difficult every hour ; and I resolved to apply at every house till some one took me in.

The next human habitation, however, was fully half a mile farther on. It stood back from the road, and I could see neither tracks about it, nor light within ; but I plodded to the door and knocked. There was no response, but I heard a cat mewing dolefully inside. It was a small, low house, with a shed and a little stable adjoining. I knocked again and yet again, without result ; but still the cat mewed on, piteously. Finally I tried the door. It stuck at the top but was not locked. I pushed it open and shouted, "Hullo ! Anybody at home ?"

All dark and still ; but I heard the patter of the cat's feet. I stepped in. It seemed not very cold inside, but the air was dank and had an odor of household laxity, or senility. I had a match and struck it. The outer door opened into a low room nearly bare of furniture, with soiled, green-figured paper on the walls. There was a fire-place and ashes, but no spark of fire. A little blue tin match safe stood on the mantel shelf, also an iron candle-stick with an inch or two of tallow candle. In the match safe were four or five matches and stubs of matches. When I had lighted the candle, the cat came and rubbed against my legs.

There were three doors opening out of the front room, one to the chamber stairs and one into a little kitchen in the rear. The third I could not open ; it appeared to be stuck fast in its casement, or else buttoned or propped on the other side. I knocked at it and called out again, then came to the conclusion that the house was one from which the inmates had recently moved and taken most of the furniture. The appearance of the kitchen also confirmed this surmise. It contained little save a rusted, much cracked cooking stove, choked with ashes. In one corner stood an empty flour barrel, having a large, white cloth spread over the top of it and a gummy, warped old cake-board on top of that. In the shed leading to the stable were chips, litter and a few sticks of wood.

After several failures, I kindled a fire in the stove and warmed myself a little ; for my feet were wet and it was chilling, bleak weather. Snow drove against the windows ; and altogether the night was so bad that I determined to remain there till morning, if not ordered away, by the proprietor. But hunger was nearly as imperative with me as cold, and after getting the old stove warmed up, I searched the premises again for food stuff, going down cellar—where there was not so much as a frozen potato—also to the shed and stable, and up stairs to the low open chamber. The only edible that could be discovered anywhere was a little husk trace with five small dry ears of sweet corn, hung on a nail in a rafter of the chamber roof. Thus it had escaped the mice, though the small rodents appeared to have been making frantic efforts to reach it.

Appropriating the corn trace, I went back to the kitchen and began parching the kernels for my supper ; and I left the poor cat—a little, lean Maltese tabby, with eyes the largest part of her—shut up in the chamber, to look for the mice. The cat had been tagging my every step, getting under foot, ever after I had entered the house.

Dried sweet-corn kernels, when toasted, swell up to full size and are not very difficult of mastication. My hunger prompted me to roast and eat every kernel of the five ears ; and afterwards I thawed a handful of snow in a tin basin by way of a solvent. Altogether it was as frugal a meal as even a self-sender has ever made, I fancy.

Fatigue, after my long, hard day, exposed to the cold wind and snow, soon asserted itself. There was one old basket-bottomed chair in the front room. Placing this in the warmest corner, I filled the stove with the last of the wood, then took off my damp boots, opened the old oven door and thrust in my feet. Afterwards, drawing my overcoat about me, I leaned back with my head against the wall, to take things easy till morning.

Very soon I was asleep, but voices which sounded like those of boys or youngsters, waked me not long after ; I also heard sleigh bells. A sleigh in passing appeared to have stopped near the house ; I heard the occupants talking low and snickering. Suddenly four or five tremendous blows, as if from an ax or club, were struck on the clapboards of the house near the door, and a voice shouted. "Wake up, Granny ! Wake up !"

For the moment I imagined that the rogues had peeped in at the uncurtained back window of the kitchen and by the faint gleam from the stove had taken me for an old grand-sir, sitting there with my feet in the oven. Presently several missiles, stones it is likely, from the stone-wall near the road, were thrown on the roof and rolled off with a great clatter ; and I could still hear the scamps sniggering.

By way of a counter demonstration, I caught up the big white cloth from the flour barrel, and wrapping it around myself, head and ears, stalked to the outer door which I threw wide open, and uttered a horrible groan ! What with the snow on the ground and a moon under the storm clouds, there was sufficient light to render objects dimly visible. Two of the rogues were standing in the yard near the wall ; and I think that they actually took me for something spookish. One of them uttered an odd sort of exclamation. They beat a retreat to their sleigh and drove off.

It was still snowing and so cold that I made haste back to my warm stove oven and chair. I was apprehensive lest the young roisterers might raise a party and return, bent on investigating the supernatural. My dread of that, however, did not prevent me from soon falling asleep again, my head propped in the angle of the wall, on the chair back, and my feet in the oven as before.

I waked several times, I remember, but my final nap must have been a long one. There was broad daylight when I roused last. Indeed, it was much later than I supposed, being nine or ten o'clock I am sure. The sky was still clouded ; but the storm had ceased. The stove and kitchen were cold as a tomb. I pulled myself together, washed my face in snow at the front door, tidied up and made ready to sally forth from this harbor of refuge. But I was gaunt from hunger and made yet another search for something with which to stay the sense of inner emptiness. I found a squash in the stable and had thoughts of attempting to bake it in the stove, having first cut it into slices.

While canvassing this expedient, however, I heard a noise in the front room and hastily looking in, saw the door—the one I had found fastened—shaking, as if some one were removing a bar or a prop on the other side. Even while I stared, it opened and there issued forth a very tall and wild-looking old female in a long yellow bed-gown ; and it is no exaggeration to say, that the skin of her face and hands was quite as yellow as the flannel of the gown ! But her hair was as white as an Albino's and fully as voluminous. Indeed, there was a most uncanny quantity of it. It frowsed out and hung down her shoulders and in front over her arms, quite to her waist. She had an old tin teapot in her hand and came directly toward the kitchen door where I stood, rooted and dumb with wonder as to how this could be !

What was stranger, I saw that she did not seem to see me, though apparently looking straight at me. Her eyes appeared to have a mottled gray crust on them, which I now presume to have been cataracts. On she came and I backed back into the kitchen, then spoke. "Is this your house, marm ?" I exclaimed, not knowing what else to say. But she paid no heed and came on, I backing away till I was directly between her and the little window. Then she stopped short, having caught sight of something against the light. Turning her head and strange white hair down and to one side, she peeped and peered at me, like a hen in the dark, out of the corners of her nearly sightless eyes.

"I see ye !" she then cackled out. "I kin see ye there. Who be ye ? Be ye Sally Dennett's man, or be ye Bijah Libbey ?"

"No, marm, I'm a stranger," I said. "I thought this house was empty. I came in on account of the storm."

"Whart ?" she bleated. "Be ye Bijah ?"

I repeated that I was a stranger.

"What-a-art ?" she cried, taking a step nearer me.

It was plain now that she was deaf also, as well as blind— deaf as a post.

"Whart ? Whart be ye a-sayin' ?" she cried again, and put out one of those awful skinny, yellow hands to feel me over.

Ah well, I was young then and had had no breakfast and not much supper ; partly for that reason, perhaps, my stomach gave a sudden turn. Snatching up my valise, I bolted out of that house, gained the highway and deep as the snow was, ran for as much as half a mile—till I felt better.

It was an old beldame granny who lived there alone. She had been abed in that room all night, while I was ranging over her house and parching her trace of sweet corn ! The poor, deaf, blind old creature had heard nothing of my invasion. It was too scandalous even for a Sophomore and I never dared tell any of the fellows about it.

My only consolation and hold on self-respect, lay in the thought that I had discomfited the louts who had stopped there at midnight to torment her ; but it is doubtful if she heard even the stones on the roof.

Plodding on drearily enough for an hour or more, my luck took a turn for the better. A woman driving a white horse in a pung, set full of stone pots, overtook me a large, fleshy, comfortable-looking, middle-aged woman with three big brown hair moles on her lip and cheek. I suppose I cast a longing look at the vacant seat and warm buffalo robe ; for she pulled up after passing, looked around and presently asked me if I would like to ride.

I did not keep her waiting while I considered whether I had another engagement, for my feet were already wet again.

Remembering my ill success with the Shaker Elder, I determined to go easy in conversation and did not talk much. Besides I was cold and faint. But conversation did not flag ; this woman was herself a talker ; and before we had gone a mile I had learned that she had been to the "village" that morning ; that she had sold a hundred and twenty pounds of butter ;

that butter was twenty-six cents a pound and eggs twenty cents a dozen ; and that her hens were laying well ; also that she had told "George," her husband, that he was welcome to all the farm crops came to, if she could have the butter and eggs.

But *mox anguis recreatus*. Having gained breath and warmth under her comforting buffalo skin. I took thought and putting my best foot forward, turned the conversation on sewing machines—not then so hackneyed a theme for an agent's eloquence as now.

Unsuspecting woman ! She little imagined how desperate a man she had been warming back to hope and guile under that cozy robe. In twenty minutes I had sold her my sample machine, for seventeen dollars, delivered the goods and got my money !

By good luck, too, her homeward route took me within a mile of the Empire Road railway station, which I reached in time to take the afternoon train home.

Once more on my native heath, I settled to pedagogy for ten weeks, and meantime sold eight sewing machines. So that in March I was able to rejoin my class, in funds again for the rest of the year.

TOLD AGAIN

A𝚁𝙻𝙾 B𝙰𝚃𝙴𝚜, '76

TOLD AGAIN

E VERY alumnus knows the old traditional anecdotes of Bowdoin, but who was ever tired of hearing them repeated ? Told over by one class after another and by one generation to the next, they, keep a perennial interest by being part of the magic time of college life ; and so I may be forgiven for reporting a talk in which all the stories were confessedly old.

The room was what Percy, who was accustomed to jeer at his friend's fondness for luxury, called "a Kensington-stitch bower." Philip Vaughn had innumerable lady friends, whose lives, judging from their fruits, must be devoted chiefly to embroidering tidies, tobacco-pouches ; hangings and rugs for the adornment of the bachelor's bower ; until floor and wall bloomed out in wildly arranged cat-o'-nine-tails, pre-Raphaelite sunflowers, and innumerable other æsthetic devices, constructed upon the conventional plan of making them as impossible as was within the limits of female ingenuity to compass.

Tonight Percy and Phil were seated in those strikingly sprawly attitudes dear to the masculine soul, puffing at fragrant pipes, and staring at the open fire, whose glow brought out with great effect the glories of the Kensington-stitch tokens. The talk somehow turned upon old times at Bowdoin, drifting on into anecdote and reminiscence, as such chats are very apt to do.

"You remember," Percy asked, "the time Prof. W. took the Senior class over into the Topsham woods botanizing, and the boys hired a hand-organ man to follow ? He struck up *Mulligan Guards* just as the Professor had begun a learned discussion on a rare something or other."

"How the Prof. laughed," retorted Phil. "But I think the funniest time was the cuspidors. You were out then, weren't you? Prof. C. got vexed at some of the boys' spitting, and remarked that if it was necessary for them to expectorate, he desired that they would bring cuspidors with them ; and

I'll be hanged if every man Jack didn't get a spittoon and carry it into recitation next morning ! The way we banged them about those tiered seats in Adams Hall was a caution to peaceful citizens !"

"What jolly old days those were," Percy sighed regretfully. "Do you remember how often old Senex used to say, 'I'm having the best time of my life, but I shall never have to regret that I didn't know it as I went along.' That was a bit of philosophy I always admired."

"What a separate world a college is," Phil said. "It wouldn't seem to me very funny anywhere else to hang an old circular saw out of my window and pound it with a junk bottle, but as part of my college life I laugh whenever I think of it. There is a different way of looking at everything inside the college campus, and I always have a secret sympathy for student tricks, no matter how much it is proper to disapprove of them from an outside standpoint."

"Dr. C. told me a story the other day," Percy observed, trimming his pipe, "that pleased me a good deal. Dr. C. roomed on the southwest corner of Maine Hall, and had a very sunny place. Gray, who was just across the entry, came in one day with a lot of pears not quite ripe, and asked to leave them in C.'s windows to ripen. A few mornings after, Professor Packard called on C. to ask something about a library book. After he had done his errand the old gentleman walked up to the window and began to examine the fruit. 'Very fine pears,' he said, 'it is a variety rare about here, too.' 'They look first rate,' Doc. answered, 'though I've not tasted them yet.' 'You'll find them very good, I assure you,' Father Packard observed blandly, as he moved toward the door. 'Very good indeed. I took great pains with that graft ! Good day.' And poor C. never had a chance to explain that he wasn't the man who purloined them !"

"Pretty good !" laughed Phil. "It wouldn't have made any difference, though, if he had denied complicity, I suppose. Circumstantial evidence is too much for most any of us. There is a fine story of Prex. Woods, that a clergyman in Maine told me. You know the President's sympathies were notoriously with the South in the war, and the boys were not slow to comment on it. One morning when Prex. came in to prayers he was astonished—or at least I fancy he must have been—to find every man Jack of the fellows in his place, and all as quiet as stone griffins. He took his chair as usual, and he must have felt a cold chill run down his back from the way in which everybody looked at him."

"He'd feel that," interrupted Percy, "from the Chapel. It is always colder than the tombs."

"He was no sooner seated," resumed the other, "than his eye caught a great sign stretched across the front of the organ-loft on the opposite end of the Chapel, with the words 'PRAY FOR THE COUNTRY' in letters a yard high. He read the Scripture as usual, and then started in on the prayer amid an awful stillness such as never was experienced at college prayers before or since. He got along to the phrases with which he was accustomed to close, and not a word about the country. Then there was a sort of dull murmur among the boys. Nobody made any noise in particular, you know, but there was a kind of stir. The president didn't dare hold out any longer, for the pressure of that body of boys, with all the moral sentiment of the country behind them, was too tremendous for even his will ; he gave in and prayed for the country with the utmost fervor !"

"He must have been sincere !" Percy commented. "There's a Bowdoin hazing story which always pleased me immensely. One day a knot of fellows in the room of X., a gallant Sophomore, were discussing hazing. 'I tell you,' X. said, with emphasis, 'the Freshies like the fun as well as we do. It's part of college life. Why, I'd be ducked myself for ten cents !' 'Here's your ten cents,' returned E., a brawny Junior—you must have seen him. Phil, he was in '67—he was famous for his will and his muscle. 'Now I propose to duck you !' Remonstrance was vain, and as E. was big enough to annihilate X. had he chosen, there was nothing for the unhappy Soph. but to submit, obtaining only the privilege of being allowed to don old clothes. Thus equipped, X. took his seat outside his room door, surrounded by a circle of grinning friends, and E. procured a pail of water. Do you know, instead of making one grand dash of the ducking, and letting X. off with that, that merciless E., who had certain old scores to settle, proceeded to dribble the cold water over his victim by the dipperful. Now he would playfully trickle a small stream down the sufferer's back, then dash a pint full in his face ; again a little cascade would pour upon the Sophomore's head, or an icy streamlet meander down his manly bosom. E. pitilessly held X. to his agreement, and, as he threw the last drop of water into his eyes, poor X., drenched and redrenched, sprang away with a string of oaths so hot they might have dried him ; but it was never noticed that he was anxious to discuss hazing again. By George I'd have liked to see the performance."

"These things are no end funny," Phil said, poking the fire. "I don't know whether they are so to folks outside the ring, but the whole college feeling comes up to me with them. Don't you remember the day we '76 boys were reciting in International Law to Prof. Caziarc, and old H. distinguished himself so ? Unluckily, this wasn't one of the days when H. was prepared, and, as he neglected to read ahead in the class, his answers were of the wildest. 'How long,' asked the Professor, 'does a ship remain liable to seizure after violating a blockade ?' H. gazed at the ceiling, rubbing his chin and changing legs in his inimitable way, but no happy evasion occurred to him. A fellow behind him was prompting in frantic whispers, and at length succeeded in attracting H.'s attention. Old H. was so intent on the ceiling, though, that to do this the prompter had to speak so loudly as to be heard over the whole room. Of course everybody laughed in concert, but no line softened in the grave countenance of H. Taking in the situation in a twinkling, he drawled out, with perfect composure : 'I am told that it is six months !' How the boys applauded !"

"There's a good recitation story they tell of Prof. Chad- bourn," Percy said, taking up the ball in his turn, "though the truth I don't vouch for. They say that he began a recitation in Natural History by asking the first man in the class if he'd ever seen a porpoise. 'No, sir,' was the answer, as prompt as you please. 'The next,' says the Prof., and the next said 'No,' too. And so they went down the class, Chadbourn of course forgetting all about what the question was, before he got half through the row. 'Very well, gentlemen,' he remarked in his most magisterial manner, as the last man added his negative to the rest, 'you may take this lesson again tomorrow and I hope to find you better prepared!' Another story of him is that he asked once if anybody in the class had ever seen a frog in the water. The boys all said no till it came to G., who remarked that he had seen a frog in the water. 'Good.' the Prof. said, 'I am glad there is one man here who is an observer. Now will you tell us, Mr. G., under what circumstances you saw the frog in the water and what he was doing.' 'Oh,' answered G. brightly, 'I put him in, and he was trying to get out !' "

"Then there was S., in '75," went on Vaughn. "Prof. Carmichael was talking of the difficulty of determining the direction from which a sound comes. 'For instance,' he said to S., who was reciting, 'if you are in the depot and hear a whistle you cannot tell whether it is the Bath train coming from one direction or the Lewiston train from the other.' 'Oh, yes, I can,' S. answered. 'I can always tell the direction by the sound, for the Lewiston train whistles twice !' And you remember P.'s answering the question as to the kind of weather in which we have thunder-showers, by saying, 'In stormy weather' ?"

"Some of the Bowdoin boys did a couple of droll things the year after we graduated," Phil said. "The eternal war between Fresh. and Soph. was raging with great violence, and there was no end of sharp-shooting on both sides. I fancy the Freshies were the smarter from the two stories I heard. One night they were laying out for a 'peanut-drunk'—is there anything funnier in college nomenclature than calling a gorge on that arid fruit a 'drunk' ?—and they were told that the Sophs. had found it out and meant to stop it. They went on with their plan, though, and to the usual bushel or so of peanuts they added a can of cider. Of course when their enemies interrupted the innocent festivities, they bore away peanuts and cider, upon which they feasted in high glee. Fancy the feelings of those wicked and wretched Sophs. when, on draining the can of its last glass of cider, five drowned mice dropped into the glass !"

"By Jove ! That was tremendous !" cried Percy. "I wonder a Freshman was left alive to tell the tale !"

"I fancy they weren't very cheeky for a day or two," returned the other. "But their second trick was worse yet. The Sophs. became possessed of a pair of plump chickens."

" 'Became possessed' is a good phrase," interrupted Percy. "I've become possessed of chickens on the Harpswell road myself ! 'Convey,' the wise call it. Go ahead."

"I knew I was touching you in a tender spot," continued the narrator. "Having the chickens, they took them down town to that disreputable Tim Ponson, who used to cook your fowls for you, to have them roasted.

Certain choice spirits—both on two legs and in black bottles—were brought together for the feast, which Tim had promised should be ready by nine o'clock in the evening. But a few audacious Freshmen, Billy M. and Tom Winter among them, in some unexplained way got hold of a knowledge of the Sophomoric plans, and at half-past eight presented themselves at Ponson's door. 'Hallo, Tim,' says Winter briskly, 'are those chickens ready ?' Tim looked a little astonished, but Billy broke in and explained that S., who had delivered the birds to the cook, had sent after them. 'Hurry up,' Winter went on. 'The fellers have got dreadful tired of waiting now.' So old Tim bestowed the chickens, smoking hot, in a basket. 'Will yer take the plates and the taters, too ?' he asked. But having secured the chickens the boys were not inclined to wait, so they told him to follow with the other things, and off they scud with their booty. Saucy knaves ! Perhaps the Freshmen did not have a howl over those birds ! And perhaps the Sophs were pleased at the trick ! But wasn't it clever ?"

"Capital ! I only know one thing which would have been better, and that was the thing some of the '75 boys didn't do to Prof. Z. You know what a little, wizened, dried-up man he was, and how cordially everybody disliked him. The one year he was at Bowdoin he made more enemies than he could unmake in a lifetime. Well, X. and Y., '75 boys, got into the Church on the Hill one Saturday night, when Prof. Z. was to preach on Sunday. They planned to cut a trap-door behind the pulpit, with a spring to be worked by a cord going under the carpet to the students' seats. They meant to pull the door out from under him about the time he got started in the long prayer, and let him down out of sight ! Unfortunately, the sexton came in, and they had to give the thing up !"

"Unfortunately ! you say ?" Phil said, laughing. "That shows where your sympathies are !"

"They are always with the boys in private," Percy retorted. "In public I have to disapprove of anything of this sort as improper ; indeed, as extremely improper !"

The two friends laughed, and smoked, for a few minutes in genial silence. Then Percy went on again, for when once college days are recalled there is not soon an end to the flood of reminiscence.

"I met Dr. B. the other day," he said, "and he told me some droll stories about Professor Cleveland. I dare say they are not more than half true, but even that is a very good portion of verity for this wicked world. Professor Cleveland, it seems, was excessively afraid of lightning. His researches into natural phenomena gave him such an impression of the immense power of the electric force as almost to overcome his courage. The story goes that he had in his cellar an insulated stool, upon which he was accustomed to sit cross-legged like a Turk during every thunderstorm. Once a strong-minded female who was visiting his house felt called upon to remonstrate with him upon his fears. So she made her way down cellar, and began to upbraid him for his timidity. He made no reply, only he drew his legs a little more closely under him as a terrific peal of thunder shook the house. and his visitor became more and more voluble. 'I'm ashamed of you,' she snapped out at last, 'any fool knows enough not to be scared by a thunder-shower !' 'Yes,' the old gentleman returned, drily, 'there are only a few of us who know enough to be frightened.' "

"A great moral truth," Phil commented. "Isn't there some sort of a yarn about Professor Cleveland and an electric battery ?"

"Yes ; they say he was showing his big battery to the class, one day, when he remarked : 'Gentlemen, quiet as this instrument seems, there is energy enough stored up here to cause the instant death of a man. One touch of the finger to that knob would instantly kill an able-bodied man.' Then, turning to his assistant, the Professor beamed benevolently upon him through his spectacles, absent-mindedly and cheerfully saying, 'Mr. Dunning, touch the knob.' "

"The best story of Cleveland I ever heard," Phil said, "was of a rebuke he gave to a noisy class. It was about the time of Brooks' villainous assault upon Charles Sumner in the Senate Chamber, and of course the country was full of talk about that scandal. Professor Cleveland was late to lecture one day, and as the class got into a very riotous state while waiting for him, he had some ado to quell it when he came in. He was a good deal nettled and administered a most scathing rebuke, ending with the words, delivered in so impressive a manner that more than one of his hearers speak of it to this day : 'Gentlemen, in future let such brawls be confined to Congress, and do not disgrace with them these halls consecrated to science and culture.' "

"No doubt !" his friend laughed. "But there's another story of Professor Cleveland that comes to my mind in this connection, chiefly because no earthly connection exists between the two. It seems that he went to church but once on Sunday, it being vaguely suspected that the remainder of his day was spent in unholy toil in his laboratory. A committee of the Faculty was at last sent to remonstrate with the old gentleman, and in the most delicate and politic way they laid the case before him, dwelling upon the evil influence of his course, the injury to him and to the cause of religion, ending with a declaration that there could be no good reason why the Professor should not attend church. 'Gentlemen,' the culprit said, drawing himself up in the haughtiest manner, 'Professor Cleveland goes to church but once on Sunday, and that is reason enough.' And the committee retired in confusion."

"There's a delightful quality of self-poise shown in that story," observed Percy. "Another phase of the feeling was shown by our friend Fall. A military instructor at Bowdoin was very fond of using military terms, and the boys naturally guyed him for it. One day he said to Fall, who was cutting up in recitation, 'Fall, you may go to your quarters.' 'Sir,' answered Fall, saucily but serenely, 'I haven't any quarters to go to.' 'No quarters ?' demanded the instructor, 'what do you mean ?' 'I'm expecting a remittance every day,' Fall said coolly, 'but now I haven't any quar—' 'Sir,' interrupted the other, 'leave the section room instantly !' "

"Impertinent whelp !" Phil said. "Jamie Charles was on the whole the coolest specimen we had in our class. I shall never forget the malicious impudence with which he fumbled and fussed with a loose leaf of his German book, at last dropping it and then cramming it into his pocket with an affectation of the greatest confusion, so that Professor M. had no choice but to call him up and ask for that translation, only to find that he'd been gulled."

"The time that Professor M. had his revenge," Percy returned, "was when Jamie, with a big fish hook and the greatest patience, angled for the Professor's shutters from the attic window. It took him half the afternoon, and just as he was hauling up the last blind, the Professor, who was supposed to be down town, put his head out of the window, and mildly but firmly insisted upon Charles putting the shutters back ; in which pleasant but laborious occupation my young Sophomore spent the rest of the afternoon, not without some jeering on the part of the boys."

"Do you remember," asked Phil, "the fuss we had with Mr. X., whose ministrations at the Church on the Hill used to bore the boys so ? He was the man that said in a sermon that the temperance crusade had been so effective as to lower the price of whiskey several cents on the gallon."

"I remember that day," Percy put in. "We all applauded and got summoned the next morning for disturbance in church."

"The best joke was about the proposed removal of the students from the church. The fuss I spoke of came from Brother X. going to a ministers' meeting or a conference or something else, and berating the college as a nest of infidelity because he had not been appointed Professor of Moral Science. So it was proposed that the students should be taken to the college Chapel for service and the church left to itself. While the matter was being discussed in Faculty meeting—or as the story goes— Professor Z. suggested that another of the Faculty, who is a clergyman, should first preach a farewell sermon to the people of the Church on the Hill. And what do you think was to be the text?"

"I give it up," Percy said. "It is too near morning to guess conundrums, and especially scriptural ones."

"It was to have close reference to their staying behind with X.; it was to be 'Tarry thou here with the ass while I and the lads go up yonder to worship !' "

THE HAZING OF STUMPY BLAIR

FRED RAYMOND MARSH, '99

THE HAZING OF STUMPY BLAIR

"**S**TUMPY" Blair was a Freshman, not so much because it was his first year in college, though as every one will admit, that was reason enough, but because of a certain circumstantial evidence that characterized all his actions. For instance, he seemed instinctively to keep his "weather eye," as it were, open on the balmiest of Autumn days. He was constant in his attendance at gymnasium in all his spare hours, and had been heard to express great pleasure at the prospect of a class in Indian clubs for the Freshmen during the Winter term. It was even rumored that he sat up till the early hours of morning, burning the electric fluid that feebly oozed through his sixteen candle-power light and preparing his Mathematics for the coming day. Of course only Freshmen do all these things and it follows that "Stumpy" Blair was unmistakably a Freshman.

But "Stumpy" Blair had many excellent qualities to offset the misfortune of his class standing. He was a goodhearted fellow, could play the piano to perfection and was immensely popular in the college. He was also as large physically as he was inexhaustible in his unruffled good nature. He was nearly six feet tall, broad shouldered, straight as an arrow, and that is why everybody in Bowdoin called him "Stumpy" Blair.

It is an unwritten law that every Freshman owes the college a living, in the sense of lending a mild excitement to the dull routine of study by the mistakes he naturally makes in his new surroundings. This law "Stumpy" Blair persistently and even arrogantly disregarded. He declared that he enjoyed nothing better than tobacco smoke when a dozen red-eyed upper classmen left his room after a social call one evening. He was even caught one night before retiring in the very act of taking his hair brushes from between the sheets of his bed, where they had been surreptitiously placed by unknown persons. Any well-brought-up Freshman would have crept to bed and set up a yell of astonishment as the stiff bristles raked his shins, just for the benefit of those who might have been listening near. But "Stumpy" Blair was not that kind. He was by far too precocious. He could not understand that there is an infancy in college life as well as in real life, as well as in business life. He desired to assume the dignity and prerogative of a Senior while yet a child. Of course the result was a curious combination. His case took an original form and it demanded original treatment.

There are some, to be sure, who would denounce the fact that there was need of any treatment at all, unless it should be with others outside the Freshman class. However that may be, those who have been in college themselves, or better still have taught in the district schools, cannot class pure mischief as a missing link in the human character. When a number of healthy animals are put together there are sure to be pranks and mischief, generally if not always untainted by any malice in the colleges of the present time. This, however, is not a defence of what happened ; it is merely the reason why something had to be done in the case of "Stumpy" Blair.

A solemn meeting of which no records were kept, was held by a number of upper classmen whose names are not recorded in the Jury's Book of Illustrious Dead and who felt on their shoulders the responsibility of upholding the unwritten law. Several days after this meeting "Stumpy" Blair felt, rather than smelled, a powerful odor on entering his room after his Math. recitation. The place was a veritable Inferno with the taint of rotten eggs. In Physics we are taught that ether is considered to be an impalpable and all-pervading jelly through which the particles of ordinary matter move freely. It was such a substance that "Stumpy" Blair seemed to encounter as he entered his room, though it affected his sense of smell and taste alike. It was certainly original treatment.

Of course the news of "Stumpy" Blair's discovery was soon known and he had no dearth of sympathizers—outside his door. Various expedients were suggested. One fellow was so cruel as to suggest that "Stumpy" count his chickens after they were hatched. The common belief, which "Stumpy" Blair himself held, was that a rat, or rather a colony of rats, had died somewhere in the room, and hence the odor. How to find the rats was the problem.

THE SUMMER FOLIAGE.

"Stumpy" Blair was determined they should be found and his friends encouraged him in his efforts. First he made a careful survey of the premises to see if he could locate the place, but the odor was as strong by the window as by the closet door ; it was an "all-pervading" odor—the stench of decay. Resolved to find the pest, "Stumpy" Blair took each piece of furniture, carefully examined it and carried it out in the hall. The room was bare but the smell was still present. Undaunted, he finally took down the pictures and there, hanging to the cord of one, he found a small, uncorked vial. The vial was about half full of an innocent looking fluid. The label read : "H^2 S. Keep tightly corked," with a death's head underneath.

"Stumpy" Blair drew a sigh of relief as he examined it closely. He fitted a cork tightly in the vial, immersed it in a bottle of his strongest cologne and labelled it "Freshman Year." Several days later President Hyde received an anonymous letter with the polite request that Chemistry be placed on the elective course for Freshmen. That was the end of the hazing of "Stumpy" Blair.

THE MAY TRAINING

Thomas B. Reed, '60

THE MAY TRAINING

I N the archives of Bowdoin College,—meaning by archives, in this case, the garret of Maine Hall,—was long to be seen an old and faded flag. On a ground of white, was a bristling swine, done in dubious brown. Astride this fierce animal, holding on by the ears, was a full-uniformed military officer. Above his head was the awful inscription, "Bowdoin's First Heat." Thereby hangs a tale. Deeming that the history of Maine would be incomplete without the recital, we venture at our peril to take up this story of demi-gods and heroes.

As early as 1820, the students were annually warned to "appear armed and equipped as the law directs." Accordingly, being incorporated into the town company, they, occasionally improved the good nature of the inhabitants by choosing under their astonished noses, students as chief officers. Besides this, they indulged, say excellent old ladies with suitable unction, in other "highly unbecoming and indecorous tricks." It is credible also, judging what is past by what is present, that there was no lack of practical jokes. At last, it being rather too much for the townspeople to endure, the Legislature passed a bill exempting students from military duty. Then did peace, like the dews of evening, settle once more upon Brunswick. Its citizens rejoiced in warlike dignities. They became Corporals and Lieutenants and Captains, and were happy. Unconscious innocence ! Little they knew the future and the bellying cloud of disaster above. But the military spirit was on the increase throughout the State. Valorous individuals talked of slaughter, and of glory won on tented field. "Our people must become citizen-soldiery. It is the only safety for a free people ; the only bulwark of our free institutions." And the valorous individuals went on, as ever, conquering and to conquer. As the result of all this, in 1836 it seemed good to the Legislature of Maine to pass a law requiring students to train. It seemed good to them, also, to make sarcastic remarks indicative of contempt, which was not wise. This act, contrary to custom, went into effect soon after it was passed. Of course there was commotion in college. Stump oratory was rampant. Every man with gift of language and ability to collect together six others, gave vent to sentiment of rebellion in firm and determined tones, and backed them by irrefutable arguments. But it is a singular fact, that even irrefutable arguments do not always hold sway in this world, nor prevent warrants from coming. Every student was summoned ; sick or well, present or absent, it made no difference. For the selectmen were efficient and determined to sacrifice all things to duty—having an eye likewise to the fines. The collegians, finding that stump oratory came to little, held a meeting, heard speeches, passed resolutions of a complimentary nature, and determined to train. From that time it seemed as if college had become a barrack. "Forward March," "Right and Left Oblique," were the only sounds to be heard. At dinner, instead of peaceful request to pass the potatoes, rang the warlike command to march down that detachment of beef-steak, or order out that platoon of potatoes, or squadron of pie. Meantime, active preparation went on behind the scenes. Only sometimes, by glancing at the windows, you might see "hideous forms shrinking from sight," and fancy college had turned menagerie, and all the animals got loose.

At length came on the eventful day. The roll of war-drums and roar of artillery heralded and ushered in the dawn. The rays of the rising sun slanted across the baleful banners flung from the peaceful Halls of Learning. The village spire, forgetting to point heavenward, draped its summit in the folds of a fearful flag, on which you might have read the soul-inspiring, foe-disheartening "BELLUM." The sun reached the zenith. From all quarters the motley crowd poured into the college grounds. Every man was a master-piece. The ingenuity of weeks had not been put forth in vain. Some glowered in painted faces. Masks transformed some into fantastic demons. Gorgeous whiskers, putting to shame all the music teachers for miles around, bristled on the cheeks of the 'mailed minions' of war. Through huge goggles leered the mocking images of old age, and around sides shaking with laughter were tied melancholy badges of despair. The head gear was equally varied. Broad brimmed beavers, smart cocked hats, hats of every size, shape and fashion, from a clown's bag to a general's chapeau, topped heads brimming with wisdom. Plumes of all styles, of old rope feathers, brooms and brushes, waved from tin caps and *chapeaux de bras*. One Peucinian, worthy even of later time, mounted a helmet of bark from which floated down the majestic pine bough,— "*pinos loquentes semper*." For arms they bore claymores and cimeters, iron or wooden, rusty guns rendered trustworthy by padlocks, handspikes, poleaxes, scythes, brooms, bayonets, spears, case-knives, and saws. And had the Calculus been born into the world, that "sublime instrument" would have adorned every hand. As for body equipments, every battle-field from Bannockburn to Queenstown seemed to have stripped its dead and furnished its share. No eye ever before beheld such motley groups. All the nations and tribes, from Lapland to Australia, were mimicked and caricatured to perfection. Thus the crowd stood, each convulsed with laughter at the comical costume of the other. And thus equipped, they were marshaled in order of classes, the Pandean and Pandowdy musical bands marching in the van, beneath a flag inscribed "The De'il cam' fiddlin' through the Town." The medical class followed with a banner bearing an armed skeleton surrounded by the motto, "*Magna est medicina et prevalebit*." The Seniors and Juniors carried the flag we have already described. The Sophomores were cheered on by the goddess of Victory and Death, with the motto "*Dulce et decorum pro patria mori*," and the Freshmen by a jackass rampant, and beneath him, "The Sage ASS, what made the LAW."

Then commenced the march. Slowly swelled the solemn strains from the Pandean and Pandowdy. Standards waved and horns blew most melodiously. Welcome worthy the noble commander, who appeared just then to pluck the fadeless laurels of that fadeless day. He merits particular description, says the ancient chronicler, and so, having materials, we describe him. On his head was a diminutive hat. Over his shoulders drooped the "waving folds" of an ox-tail plume. Wooden goggles bestrode his nose. Behind his back clattered an old hat, a canteen, a tin-kettle, a cigar box, and Heaven knows what else. His horse was a strange animal, "compound of horse and jackass." Price eight dollars, as was afterwards discovered, for he died on the field of glory.

Receiving with shouts of applause their hero, who bowed to the very verge of equilibrium, the troops marched down Maine street, crossed into Back Stand, and proceeded to the place of training behind the Bank, where now a row of quiet cottages, each one just like the other, peacefully rear their roofs,—their commander amusing them meantime with comical remarks, pleasant no doubt then, but unappreciable at this present day. Arrived on the grounds, the deep-mouthed cannon thundered them salute. They were then drawn up before their captain to listen to the roll-call. "Attend," commanded he, "and answer to your names." The whole troop thronged round the affrighted officer. "One at a time" trembled he in terror-stricken tones. The clerk called the first name. "Here !" "Here !" shouted all the posse in a breath. Next name. "Here !" "Here !" from all again. The Colonel as before makes a few jocose remarks which cannot be smiled at now. At last, order was restored and the roll-call went on. Then began the examination of equipments. They stepped forward, one by one. "Mark him down—no equipments," shouted the captain, grown quite valorous now, finding no personal injury intended. The spectators nearly split their sides, while rage was filling the hardened bosom of the man of war. But what could he do, when his officers were "grinning around him like bears at bay ?" This ended, they were ordered to form a line. "We've formed a line, but we can't keep it," mourned the valiant defenders of their country. "Form a line, or march off the field," roared the despairing and discomfited captain, biting his lips.

Loudly swelled the strains of triumph from Pandean and Pandowdy. Wreathed with earliest victory and laureled with latest renown, the conquerors left the field, their swords unsheathed, their guns unfired, but their souls lifted heavenward by the glowing consciousness of battle done for truth and right. So they marched on, through the verdant streets of Brunswick, and the shaded lanes of Topsham, until they reached the college grounds. There, as everywhere, noble tongues were burning to eulogize noble deeds.

"Fellow-students and Soldiers," began the orator, whose speech has come down to our day, "Fellow-Students and Soldiers, you have earned for yourself and your country, never-fading laurels. When dangers and perils thickened around your devoted country, when her *hardy yeomanry* were no longer able to defend her soil and her liberties, *you* have nobly stepped forth to her rescue. You have doffed your Students' gowns and assumed the mailed dress of war. You have exchanged the badges of literary distinction for the toils and dangers of the battle-field. You have extinguished the midnight lamp and lit in its place the fiery torch of Mars. If you have followed Minerva in the flowery paths of literature ; if you have toiled with her up the rugged steps of science ; you have also followed her in the ranks of war and glory. If you have twined about your brows the prizes of poetic distinction, you have also encircled your temples with the wreaths of military glory. Yes, Fellow-Students ! side by side we have followed in the career of literary fame, and shoulder to shoulder will we advance in the cause of liberty, *law*, and our country.

"Soldiers, you have deserved well of your country, and think not but that she will fully discharge the debt. Students and Soldiers, let this be our motto—"War and Science, Military Glory and Literary Distinction, Now and Forever, ONE and INSEPARABLE."

Thus we have endeavored to collect and preserve whatever might be valuable of a scene and action which still lingers in dim tradition about the college walls. Of its consequences, it suffices to say, that it was the prime cause of that utter contempt into which general musters soon sank within the bounds of Maine. As to its immediate effects, no pen can do it justice ; for no pen can bring back the quaint antics of the actors, the jolly laughter of staid professors, or fill again the windows with the giggling groups, or line the sidewalks with the grinning sovereigns.

LOST: LOVE'S LABOR

Webb Donnell, '85

LOST: LOVES LABOR

T HE Freshman class had been unfortunate. On the diamond, the gridiron and in the tug o' war, lacking as it did the united action that comes of long association and practice, it had fallen an easy victim to the doughty Sophomore class. In consequence, naturally, the Freshies to a man felt sore and vindictive.

Even worse was to follow. On All Fools' Day the Sophomores prepared a most stupendous hoax for the lower classmen, who with the buoyant step of childhood walked plump into it, and became forthwith the laughing stock of college, town and State itself. The wounds inflicted by the unfortunate class contests were as nothing to the gaping rents torn in the poor Freshies' feelings by this latest adversity.

Such was the state of things when rumors began to circulate that the Bugle, that lagging annual of the students, was getting ready to be born. The Freshmen, in the light of past experience, began to suffer qualms. Disaster was in the air. And presently premonitions became actualities, for definite rumors went the rounds that a most scathing, most harrowing cartoon, based on the All Fools' Day episode, was already in preparation for the year-book, as the jubilant Sophs' contribution to the "grinds" that publication was wont to contain.

A Bowdoin graduate of the year before had recently obtained a position on one of the great New York dailies and formed a delightful friendship with the paper's most illustrious cartoonist. This artist had an enviable repute for his keen political "take-offs" and more than one public man had writhed under the sting of his sharp-toothed sarcasm. Nast's power in the days of Tweed was small compared with the wide reach of this man's influence. Now, it would seem, it was the turn of the Bowdoin Freshmen to writhe. And how they did it !

The aid of the Bowdoin man in New York had been solicited by the Sophomores, and he had induced the great cartoonist to exert his skill upon the All Fool's incident. The consideration which the Bowdoin man had mentioned as usual for such work had, to be sure, drained the class treasury to its dregs, but it was worth the money. The knowledge of this great deal had been jealously guarded by the Sophomores to give keener zest to the grand finale of its discovery between the covers of the Bugle. But, alas ! one irrepressible Soph. had not been able to withstand the strain. He had gleefully whispered the secret to a young lady down town, and she in turn had imparted it under ban of awful penalty if revealed, to her particular friend. As this latter young lady had a brother in the Freshman class,—lo, the pipe-line of information was laid !

One day, a little later, Mathewson of the Freshman class blustered into the corner room on the ground floor of old Appleton.

"Tucker," he fumed, "that cartoon's come ! It's in Ware's room in Winthrop—yes, sir. There's been a steady stream of Sophs going in and out all the morning, and every man Jack of 'em's grinning and hugging himself—confound him !—when he comes out."

"Hold on ! Where'd you get so chockful of information?" demanded Tucker, whirling round on his pivot-chair, "Get your breath, man, and then sail in."

"Oh, it's straight goods, all right. That beastly cartoon is up there just as I say, and I'd give my year's allowance to get my hands on it ! If you don't believe me, look out the window, will you ? There comes Chippie Pike on a bee line from Winthrop.—Well ?"

"I'm satisfied," groaned Tucker, "It's writ large on his face, confound his impudence ! The jig's up, Mathew."

"No, sir !" roared Mathewson. "I won't have it up ! I tell you we've got to save the class—be Joan of Arcs—er—that is—"

"Oh, that's all right. Don't hunt up anybody else. We couldn't improve on the old girl," rejoined Tucker drily.

The conversation was stopped here by the arrival of recitation hour. It is safe to say that neither young gentleman made any material advancement in the knowledge of Greek versification that day, though Mathewson distinguished himself by locating the Acropolis on the third floor of Winthrop Hall. His mind was busy with ways and means for getting possession of the obnoxious cartoon in Ware's room. The discomfiture of his class must be warded off by fair means or foul. It was not a time for nice discriminations.

When the recitation ended, he turned off by himself and sauntered by the rear of Winthrop, locating Ware's room by a rapid glance. He noted with grim satisfaction a circumstance that had escaped him heretofore, that an iron water pipe ran near the window. Ware, he knew, roomed alone. Now, if he would only take it into his head to be away that evening!

In the course of some quiet investigation during the afternoon, Mathewson ascertained that Ware belonged to a Sophomore Whist Club which met two evenings a week in a room in Appleton. The next meeting was on the night following. Delay seemed hazardous since at any time the cut might be posted away to the engravers. Yet there would appear to be nothing for it but to wait. That, in the eye of the law, the abstraction of property from another's premises would be regarded as "breaking and entering," did not escape Mathewson's observation, but his feelings were roused to such a pitch that nothing short of hanging would have deterred him from the attempt to save his class. He would, of course, say nothing to Tucker—better take the risk alone.

At nine o'clock the next evening Mathewson slipped gently over to Winthrop, congratulating himself that the moon was hidden behind dense clouds and that nearly all the windows in the End were unlighted. He stole around to the rear of the building and, after making sure that Ware's window, too, was dark, went up the iron pipe, hand over hand, with the ease of an athlete. The window on the third floor had been left open, as the weather was mild. There was nothing to impede Mathewson's entrance. Burglarwise, he had come supplied with a dark lantern, though the professional article is not usually improvised from a pasteboard box and a wax candle.

The amateur "grafter" slid noiselessly through the window and dropped to the floor within. Moving softly to the opposite side of the room that he might light his candle as far out of window-range as possible, he pulled out of his pocket the lantern and matches. It was just at this instant that the door of the sleeping room swung open and a figure barely outlined in the darkness glided forth.

Mathewson held his breath in the horror of the situation. His heart suspended its beats, then began raining sledgehammer blows against his ribs. In a flash he realized just what had happened. Ware had not gone to Whist Club,—headache, likely,—gone to bed early, heard noise,—defend his own or die,—great Heavens !

The figure advanced across the room. Mathewson knew that if it reached the mantle and struck a light the jig was up. There was no time to get to the window, and he boldly resolved upon the only alternative. With a light bound he was on the silhouetted figure and grappling with it.

Ware was a muscular fellow, as Mathewson well knew. As a matter of fact, the two were finely matched in point of endurance and athletic skill. The Freshman had been picked for all his class contests and for one of the 'Varsity teams as well. It looked like an even chance. Mathewson's fierce onslaught bore his opponent to the floor, but there the advantage ended. Then began one of the most evenly-matched contests of physical strength and skill that Bowdoin ever saw.

Mathewson's plan was to force Ware back into the bedroom and lock him in, thus affording himself opportunity to make good his escape. But the plan did not work. The man he had grappled with was as strong and determined as he and apparently as skilful a wrestler. Every effort on the part of either one to gain an advantage was checkmated by the other. If with a desperate lunge the Freshman bore his antagonist toward the sleeping-room, he was sure to find himself forced back as far and as lustily. Now they fought standing, locked to each other in an embrace of iron. Now they plunged rolling upon the floor. Their muscles stood out in ridges on their heaving bodies.

For obvious reasons Mathewson uttered no sound. He was grimly determined not to give himself away. In the interstices of the struggle he was forced to admire the other's pluck in gamely fighting to the finish, instead of calling loudly for help, as he might easily have done.

Twenty minutes passed without a sound except the dull thuds of their bodies on the floor, as with plunges and counter-plunges they tried each other's strength to the utmost. A half hour passed. Still they wrestled on grimly, the sweat streaming over their foreheads and into their eyes. The blood of both was "up." There was no thought of calling a truce.

At three quarters of an hour the fight was still on, but nearing a finish. Flesh and blood have their limitations even when muscles are at their finest. Each nerved himself for a final, desperate struggle in the darkness. For the first time in the terrific encounter, a twisting, wrenching side-throw on the part of each tore their weakened hold asunder, and both fell heavily to the floor, just as a bar of clear moonlight slanted into the room.

Then Mathewson saw, sitting opposite him on the floor, not Ware but his own particular friend, Tucker ! Both glared at each other with wrathful eyes.

"What—in—Hades—have—you—been—punching—me—for?" gasped Mathewson windedly.

"What—in—Tophet—did—you—pitch—into—me—for?" demanded Tucker hotly. Then the humor of the situation appealed to both, and they grinned. This relieved the tension and paved the way for explanations.

"I must have shinned up the water-pipe about three minutes before you did," Tucker panted, not yet in command of his breath, "I came after that beastly picture."

"Same here, 'Great minds', etc.," smiled Mathewson feebly.

"Well, I was on the trail of a match. Forgot to bring any, confound it ; When you sailed into me, I thought the judgment day had come, for sure."

"Same here."

"Thought you were Ware, blest if I didn't !"

"Oh, same here, same here !" groaned Mathewson, rubbing himself solicitously. But I say—we'd better be lighting out of here, or Ware'll be home, and I'll bet he'd do us both now. I'm played out."

"Same here," quoted Tucker mirthlessly.

As they got painfully to their feet the tricky moonlight deserted them, and the room was in darkness again.

"I'm not going now till I've got my grip on that picture," vowed Tucker. "Think I'm going to give it up after you've broken all my precious bones over it ? Got a match ?"

They groped about on the floor until the little improvised dark-lantern Mathewson had brought was found. Then by it dim light they ransacked the room. The desk in one corner came under fire and drawers were pulled out and pigeon-holes ruthlessly hunted through.

"Here she is !" whispered Mathewson excitedly, holding up a flat package he had unearthed in the lower drawer. Tearing apart the wrapping, he disclosed the pen-and-ink drawing for which they had both risked so much. It lay between two pasteboard protectors and leered up at them shamelessly.

In the instant of their triumph, they heard a step somewhere down the hall. It was coming toward them and they jumped guiltily.

"It's Ware, as I'm a sinner !" breathed Mathewson.

"The window—run for it !" hissed Tucker between his teeth. And within three seconds both sinners were sliding noiselessly down the water-pipe. Mathewson gripped the precious picture tightly under his arm. One soft thud close on the heels of the other, they dropped to the ground and scudded silently away. Safe in Mathewson's room, Tucker dropped in a heap on the couch and mopped his face.

"Great Scott, that was a close shave !" he ejaculated. "I shall have nervous prostration. I'm tottering on the verge."

"On the verge ! I'm *there*. I've landed on all four feet," mumbled Mathewson weakly. "I'm a physical wreck ; my own mother wouldn't know me."

"Well, you do look considerably like a ruin, but chirk up, old man, 'All's well that ends well.' We've got that scurrilous cut, any how. That is worth getting pummelled for, even by your best friend. Let's have another look at the thing, will you?"

With an effort he got to his feet again and crossed the room to peer over the other's shoulder. One look satisfied him.

"Heavens and earth, ain't it the 'most unkindest cut of all!' " he fumed, brandishing his clenched fists and scowling with rage.

"It's all o' that. Confound the Soph—hullo, what's this ?" Mathewson held up a slip of paper which had dropped from between the protectors of the picture. It was a Post Office money order, on the New York Post Office, for one hundred dollars. There was nothing to explain its presence to the two bewildered gazers, but the mere fact of its being there was enough. Cold shivers travelled rapidly up and down two weary spinal columns, and the sweat of horror beaded their faces.

The money order had been returned by the artist out of courtesy to the Bowdoin man. He had chosen to do the work gratuitously for his friend's college acquaintances, though this, of course, was not known to the two Freshmen. Ware had carelessly allowed the order to remain in the package, as, being class funds, there was no present demand for it.

"Oh, Lord !" groaned Mathewson, "We've done it now ! This is burglary with a vengeance."

"State's prison offence," mumbled Tucker.

Not feeling exactly like standing, they both sat down and continued staring at each other foolishly.

"Why in thunder didn't you light on the money order when you opened the thing in Ware's room ?" demanded Tucker at length in strong accents of reproach.

"Well, I call that cool !" Mathewson rejoined with heat, "Weren't you looking on all the time ? Besides, what time was there to 'light' on anything ? We had all we could do to light out ! But that doesn't count now. What I want to know is how in creation's name are we going to get this blamed thing back where it belongs ? I shan't sleep a wink till I get it off my hands. Ugh ! they smell of blood !"

Tucker laughed in spite of his own gloom.

"Well," he said, "We can't get rid of it to-night, that's certain. Ware's in his room. The fates send he won't miss the thing short off ! Don't you worry, old man, he won't. We'll hit on some way to get it back into his desk to-morrow."

But the seriousness of the affair weighed heavily on Mathewson. He realized that it was no light thing to enter a man's premises and carry off a hundred dollars. He failed to share in any cheerful views concerning the wretched matter.

"What's done at all has got to be done to-night," he said finally, "There'll be another procession of Sophs in to-morrow to gloat over that funny picture and it won't be there. Then where'll we be ? We've got to hit on that nice little plan of yours straightway. Go ahead,—out with it."

Both fellows sat in a brown study for some time. Then Tucker had an inspiration born of his desperate need.

"I have it !" he said jubilantly, "We'll hatch up a telegram from his folks,—sickness—suicide—cholera—anything good and urgent. We'll have it delivered before he's up in the morning which won't be before seven, likely. Ware's a dozy cad. You see that'll start the dear boy off on the early train and give him something besides guying the Freshies to think about."

"It'll do !" nodded Mathewson approvingly, "When you're drowning you catch at straws. I've got a lot of dispatches here from the mater. The luck's on our side. They're written in lead pencil by the operator down town and it's easy enough to rub 'em out." He hunted up half a dozen yellow envelopes and spread them out on the table.

"Seems to me your mother takes an expensive way to communicate with you," remarked Tucker.

"Oh nothing's too good for me !" laughed the other, but there was a tender quality in his tone that did not escape his friend.   "These are 'health telegrams.' The mater lives out West, where the weather's born and she gets the advance tips. All our hot and cold waves and big storms travel from west to east, you know,—that makes it dead easy for the mater. She keeps me informed a day ahead." He took up two of the little messages and read them aloud.

"Cold wave coming. Put on thick undershirt.   MOTHER."
"Expect rain to-morrow. Don't forget rubbers.   MOTHER."

"By Jove ! *that* one came to-day," he exclaimed. "Can't take that. It's got to go up on the bulletin board." And he pinned it carefully in a bit of bare wall space. The plastering looked worn and fretted as if other health messages had hung there in their time.

After diligent use of erasers, a blank and envelope sufficiently fresh in appearance for their uses, were found.

"Now for the wording of it, said Tucker. "Where does Ware hail from, anyhow ?"

They got a catalogue and settled that point speedily. "How's this ?" went on Tucker, after scribbling for a moment.

"Your mother not expected to live. Come home at once. FATHER."

"What's the matter with that ?"

"No, hang it !" cried the other, "don't say, 'mother not expected'—make it 'father.' We've got some decency left." Which went to further prove that Mathewson had a soft spot in his heart for mothers. Accordingly the two words were interchanged in the improvised dispatch and the two wicked ones gazed at it critically.

"Seems most too bad though to make the poor devil think his pater's going to die, doesn't it ?" said the more conscientious Mathewson.

"Didn't say he was going to die," Tucker retorted." 'Not expected to live'—forever, I meant, of course, but that makes eleven words, and this thing's got to go for a quarter. The unexpected joy he'll experience when he gets home and finds the old man alive and kicking will make it all up. That's the plan on which joy and sorrow, weal or woe, sickness or dea—"

"Oh, chuck it !" growled Mathewson. "How the deuce are we to get this nice little message delivered to Ware ?"

"Hire a messenger-boy down town. Kiddie Quinn's just the ticket. He'll do it for love of me—and a quarter. Keep mum about it, too."

Kiddie did it for a quarter and kept mum. But for some reason the message did not appear to produce the effect upon Ware that had been expected. He did not take the early train for home. At ten o'clock he was observed by both Mathewson and Tucker going about his daily business in a most matter-of-fact way. No one would have dreamed that he was threatened with the loss of a parent.

"Unnatural son !" exploded Mathewson under his breath, "Hasn't the duffer any sort of affection for his dying father ?"

"Perhaps the kid laid down on his job, who knows ?" Tucker suggested. The idea seemed worth investigating. They hunted up the kid.

"Look here, Cap'n," cried one of them with startling abruptness, "did you deliver that telegram ?"

"Yep."

"Sure ?"

"Cross me heart."

"And the gentleman opened it before your face and eyes?"

"Yep."

"Well, what did he do ? Hurry up !"

"Nothin'—just grinned."

"Didn't he say anything when he read it ?"

"Said he was an orphan."

"Oh !—oh, he did, did he ?" And two subdued Freshmen walked back up the hill without another word.

"We'll simply have to trust to luck that he won't miss the picture to-day," Mathewson said, when they were in his room once more. "We'll watch out and if we see Ware making for down town this evening, one of us will shin up the pipe again and put the package back in its place, minus the picture. That's all there is left to do."

"And we'll do it. Don't you worry, old man. Ware always trots down to the depot with the rest o' the chaps at train time, to see if there isn't 'somebody from up home,' aboard. That's our cue."

For two hours that evening they kept watch over the north end door of Winthrop, from near-by shrubbery. Train time came and went and still they waited. They were finally rewarded by seeing Ware issue forth with a friend and take the path across the campus toward Maine street. Waiting only for him to get well out of sight, they crept round in the darkness to the rear of the hall, and Mathewson was soon going nimbly up the water-pipe once more. Tucker did sentry duty below. Everything was dark and still and favorable.

Mathewson carefully replaced the flat packet where he had found it the night before, and had just started down the slippery pipe again when a noise at a window above disconcerted him for an instant. His hold weakened and he plunged heavily to the ground.

Tucker helped him back to Appleton and into his own room, then went for a doctor This gentleman set half a dozen of his ribs, put him into a plaster jacket and ordered him into bed. But broken ribs are of small account when a man has saved his class and rouses out of his groans to find himself a class hero. That should make up for a good many pains and beastly long hours of lying on one's back instead of running bases or swinging racquets out in the sun. Tucker, too, would have been regarded in the light of a hero, had it not been that all his ribs were intact !

The class felt profoundly grateful for its deliverance from the threatened ignominy and could not apparently do enough for its deliverer. Thus it happened that Mathewson's room became the gathering place for as many of the Freshman class as it would hold. Intent upon entertaining him they taxed the accommodations of the place to the utmost.

The room was well filled one morning about ten days after the accident to the class-god, when a shrill cry was heard from the campus outside. It was repeated from hall to hall and swelled to a chorus.

"Hark !" exclaimed one of the assembled Freshmen, "Methinks I hear the Bugle-call !"

There was a rush down stairs and a scurrying off to the room where the newly-arrived Bugles would be on sale, then a hot race back to Mathewson's bedside with the books. A shower of them fell upon the bed.

"There, old man, we'll give you first peek. You've earned it."

"By George, yes ! If it hadn't been for you there'd have been a beastly grind on us in there."

"Open it, open it, old man !"

Mathewson seized one of the books and opened it. Unkind trick of fate ! The leaves parted at exactly the page where reposed, in all its cutting irony,—in all its sardonic glee,—the "grind" on the Freshman class !

The plate had been engraved in New York and the sketch from which it was made sent afterwards to the Sophomore class, merely as a souvenir of their triumph.

The roomful of faces melted quietly away. The class hero sank heavily back on the pillows with a pain in his ribs.

IN THE PRESIDENT'S ROOM

Henry S. Webster, '67

IN THE PRESIDENT'S ROOM

TOWARD the close of a September day in the year 1864, a crowd of students was collected on the Bowdoin campus near the Thorndike oak. Each class was not only represented, but present almost in its entirety ; still, as the college at that time bore upon its rolls only about a hundred names, the reader is not to imagine the assembly as one of remarkable proportions. The several classes, without being grouped as separate bodies, were in a measure distinct, as if their members were drawn together by community of sentiment or interest. The center of the throng was composed mainly of Sophomores who, to the melody of tin horns, devil's fiddles and watchmen's rattles, from time to time added vocal effects scarcely less loud and discordant. Next to them stood the open-eyed Freshmen, eagerly appreciative of the novelty of the scene ; while most of the upper-class men were ranged along the outer edge or a little apart, and were endeavoring to preserve looks and attitudes of aloofness and indifference.

The object of attraction appeared to be a tall, spare man who was standing upon a rude plank-and-barrel rostrum, and, whenever the uproar would permit, launching his remarks in a violent manner at the bystanders. He was apparently some sixty years of age. His head was uncovered, showing his hair thin and streaked with gray. His face was smooth except for a stubbly two days' growth of beard, and was wrinkled and browned by exposure to the weather. Beside him upon the platform rested a dilapidated silk hat which, as well as his suit of rusty black, looked as if it might have been discarded some years before by its former owner. They were not, however, incongruous with the rest of his attire, since both his dickey above and his shirt below his black stock bore the same signs of poverty and neglect.

I had been engaged that afternoon on a delicate mission. A pailful of water, designed for the discipline of some offending Freshman, had been precipitated by mistake upon the head of our Latin professor, and I had been delegated by my classmates to explain to our venerable instructor just how the untoward event had happened. The interview was a protracted one, and the admonitions which I then received have probably had a marked effect in forming my character. Be that as it may, I was late in my arrival at the scene on the campus and in consequence heard only the conclusion of the speaker's harangue.

"Gentlemen," he was saying as I approached, "what do we mean when we say that a man is 'some pumpkins' ? We mean that he is full of ideas just as a pumpkin is full of seeds. What do we mean when we say that he is a 'brick' ? Why, a brick is part of a building. Let us now consider the attraction of gravitation, that mysterious force which binds together atoms and worlds, princes and parallelograms, cones, pyramids and the Sphinx. A traveler is lost on a Western prairie. He has wandered all day, far from home and with nothing to eat. Night comes on. The wolves begin to howl in the darkness. At last he reaches a log cabin, almost in ruins. No matter, it will afford him shelter for the night. Scarcely has he entered and composed himself to rest when a violent storm arises. Thunders roar. Lightnings flash. The snow heaps against the door. It grows bitterly cold. What shall he do ? He can't stay there and freeze to death. Let me illustrate. Two darkies, walking down Broadway, saw a quarter of a dollar on the sidewalk. One of the colored gentlemen said to his companion, 'Sambo, don't you freeze to dat quarter. I seed it first.' That is just the idea. He can't stay there and freeze. His soul—but what do we know about the soul ? Is it homogeneous or heterogeneous? Who can tell ? Who except me, Daniel Pratt, the Great American Traveler, and soon to be President of the United States ? Why not ? Was not imperial Rome once saved by the cackling of a goose ?"

The applause, by which the orator had been frequently interrupted, at this point became so vociferous and long continued that it was impossible for him to proceed. He at last desisted from his attempts to do so and descended from the platform. He had been speaking more than three-quarters of an hour, and the students, tired of listening to his rambling and incoherent remarks, had adopted the most efficacious method of bringing his address to its conclusion.

THE GREAT AMERICAN TRAVELER.

"Lives there the man so lean or fat,
Who never heard of Daniel Pratt?"

The chairman of the meeting had been taking things easy. After introducing the speaker, he had seated himself on the edge of the platform and lighted his long-stemmed pipe. There he had remained, quietly smoking, with his feet dangling over the side. He was a Junior and was often pointed out as the most popular man in college. As he scrambled to his feet, one of his classmates shouted, "Hi there ! Listen to the red-headed boy !" His rising or the impertinent remark was the signal for another outburst of applause ; but the tumult presently subsided and he spoke as follows :

"Fellow students—for I shall not imitate the gross flattery indulged in by the preceding speaker by addressing you as gentlemen—with what rapture have we listened to the eloquence of our distinguished friend. I stand not here to praise him, for he needs no encomium of mine. Where is the man who has not heard of Daniel Pratt ? Where is the child that is not taught to prattle that immortal name ? Where is the 'yagger,' even, so ignorant as to be unacquainted with it ? North and South, East and West his fame extends, and I shall not waste your valuable time in efforts to gild the refined gold of his character or paint the spotless lily of his reputation. I now have the honor to propose this remarkable man as our candidate for the office of President of the United States. All in favor of such nomination will please to say aye."

Every voice responded, "Aye !"

"Those opposed," resumed the chairman. "will also say aye."

Another chorus of ayes followed.

"The ayes have it," said the presiding officer. "It is a vote."

Then the Junior who had "roughed" the chairman on his red hair, in a jargon invented by his class in its Sophomore year called for "three-gee chee-geers for Pre-gesident Pra-gatt." They were given with a will ; and after it was again quiet, the chairman again begged the indulgence of his audience for a few minutes. There was a ceremony, he said, which commonly followed their candidate's orations. It might be considered commemorative of the passing of King Arthur, for it was known as the passing of the hat. At the present time it was of more than passing importance. Mr. Pratt was not a crafty and designing politician. He was a man of open countenance, but his countenance was no more open than his boots. Should they compel him to stand upon their platform in such a pair of boots as that ? Heaven forbid ! Let him not have to say that his visit to Bowdoin had been altogether bootless. Mr. Pratt's hat, which was already *passe*, would presently be passed. Let the results of their generosity, in the language of their esteemed Prex, "be adequate to the exigencies of the occasion." Let every man now search his pockets. A good many doubtless would find nothing there, but such would be expected to borrow of their chums. That was the course which he himself intended to adopt. One suggestion, not altogether impertinent. Mr. Pratt's clothes were somewhat the worse for wear, but they possessed their full complement of buttons. The hat would now be moved among the audience, and it was hoped that the audience would be moved to fill the hat. During the ceremony, Mr. Pratt would repeat one of his poetic gems. It was already familiar to them, well worn as a gem always should be, but one which they never tired of hearing, as they would admit on being informed that it was the one beginning with the lines, "Sound, sound the ponderous hugag ! Great Daniel Pratt appears !"

Daniel Pratt, who has now been introduced to the reader's notice, was well known to the college student of thirty or forty years ago. He was a half-demented but harmless vagrant whose time was spent in wandering from place to place and delivering his lectures, as he termed them, wherever he could find anyone willing to listen to him. He still retained some traces of good birth and breeding. It was his especial delight to visit college towns and address the students. Some of his college acquaintances had composed for him pieces of doggerel, often expressing sentiments uncomplimentary to himself, which he had committed to memory and was accustomed to recite at the conclusion of his lectures. The character of the latter may be fairly judged from the specimen given above, which is largely reproduced from memory. The conferring of a degree, or his nomination as a Presidential candidate, was a staple part of the fun which the students were accustomed to have with him when he honored them with his presence. He died some years ago at an almshouse in some part of New England.

On this particular occasion, the liberality of his audience corresponded with the appeal which had been made in his behalf. With his pockets well replenished with scrip—coin of all kinds was then in hiding—Daniel, at the head of a procession composed of the greater part of his auditors, was noisily escorted to a boot and shoe store far down Maine street. There the vagrant's ragged foot-wear was replaced by a serviceable pair of cowhides. After a substantial meal at the railroad restaurant, he was reconducted to the college grounds. It being now dark, his disposal for the night became a matter of serious consideration. The problem, however, was finally solved ; for at a timely hour he was taken to a dormitory room which, although destitute of a bed, contained, in addition to its furnishings of desk, table and chairs, a comfortable lounge which promised a luxurious night's repose for his weary limbs.

Now the room selected by the students for the entertainment of their guest was known as the President's Room. It was situated on the second floor of Appleton Hall at the northeast corner. It was occupied in the daytime by the head of the college as occasion required, his residence being at a considerable distance from the campus, near the lower end of Federal street. Some Sophomores had unlocked the door by means of a false key, and had carefully locked it again as soon as they had seen their visitor comfortably fixed for the night.

The tramp was tired out with his day's travel and exertion, he had partaken of a hearty meal, and as a combined result of fatigue and fullness he slept late into the next forenoon. He was awakened at last by the turning of the President's key in the lock. That functionary, on entering the room, was astonished at the sight of a human figure seated on his lounge. Nor did the appearance of the stranger reconcile him to the unexpected event. The President was an urbane man, but a shade of annoyance was perceptible in his rolling, sonorous voice as he spoke, albeit his perturbation of mind did not detract from the accustomed stateliness of his style.

"My dear sir," he said, "by what surreptitious means you gained access to this apartment I know not ; but I must take the liberty to inform you that it is designed for my personal convenience, and not as a harborage for vagabonds."

The vagrant looked intently at the President, and the eyes of the latter fell before his gaze. Heaven had vouchsafed to the poor lunatic a brief respite from the tangled web of thought in which his mind was ordinarily involved. An expression of manliness and of suffering had transformed his face, and his voice was tremulous with emotion as he replied to his interlocutor, who in the meantime had sunk into a chair and was leaning his head upon his hand.

"Vagabond ?" repeated the outcast. "Yes. I am a vagabond. You do right to call me by that name. I am a vagabond, a wanderer to and fro upon the face of the earth, penniless, friendless, homeless, O God ! Men shun me. Boys mock me and use me for their sport. All hope is gone, all aim in life wasted or thrown away. Perhaps I had as fair a start as you. When I was young, I was fond of reading, I had a good memory, I was apt at my lessons. My parents were proud of me, my teachers praised me, my playmates liked me and sought my company. How did I fall so low ? The old, old story ! Reckless associates, self-indulgence, disgrace, crime, then banishment from decent society, and at last poverty, misery and a distracted mind. Once in a while the darkness lifts : the sunshine of reason makes a rift in the clouds. O the anguish, the terrible, terrible despair of those moments ! When insanity begins again to benumb my faculties, how I welcome its approach ! There at least is forgetfulness— forgetfulness of the past and of the present. Such is the story, of my life. With you, Mr. President, how different ! You have made the most of your powers, both of body and of mind. You have been always wise, always prudent, always helpful to your fellow-men, always solicitous for the good of humanity. The young men whom it has been your duty and privilege to instruct have found in you a guide, a friend, a father, one in whom they could confide and to whom they could look for counsel. So now, when we are both nearing the end of life, you are contented, self-satisfied, tranquil in mind, a stranger to remorse, while I am—what I am !"

The vagrant stopped. The light faded from his eyes. He had relapsed into his former self. Approaching the President, whose head had now sunk upon his arm, he touched him familiarly on the shoulder and said in his old sharp voice, "Cheer up, old man ! I harbor no grudges. When I am President, would you like to be minister or consul ? London ? St.

Petersburg ? Constantinople ? You have not long to wait. The hour of my glory is about to dawn.

> "Let Shakespeare go behind the door,
> Let Milton show his head no more,
> Bid Pope and Byron leave the room
> And give the American Traveler room."

Before the end of his speech he had left the apartment and his new boots could be heard clamping down the stairs.

For a long time the President sat with his head resting on his arms. What thoughts surged through his brain. Wasted opportunities ? They crowded in myriads upon his mental vision. He recalled the bright promise of his youth, the hopes and prophecies of his friends and classmates. He remembered his visit to the Old World and the plans, aspirations and resolves which the sight of its treasures had awakened in his soul. He pictured himself again in Rome and conversing in Latin with the Holy Father, with the proud consciousness of equalling that dignitary in the correctness, fluency and elegance of his speech. Through what avenue had the poison entered his soul, the distrust in his own reason, the doubt whether it is worth while to contend for absolute truth and right, the indolence of thought which leads one to submit to the tyranny of custom, to renounce his ideals, to become the slave of use and precedent ? He had assumed the presidency, of Bowdoin in the vigor of his young manhood. His inaugural had entranced his hearers and had elicited praise from the coldest and most severe of critics. But it had been his high-water mark. Never again did he reach so high a level. Consciousness of ability was not wanting, but a fatal paralysis seemed to have benumbed his will. How, too, had he performed the duties devolving on him as head of the college? Had it not been in a perfunctory way, without a due appreciation of his responsibilities, if not with a wanton disregard of the preciousness and needs of the young souls entrusted to his charge? Had he given them the help, the sympathy, the encouragement which it was their right to expect ? Had he exemplified to them the ripe and cultured scholar in his beneficent influence upon the spirit and institutions of his country and his age ? Had he so drawn them to himself, so won their affection and esteem, that he would be to them through their lives never failing source of inspiration, courage and enthusiasm ? Alas! he was now an old man. No longer was it in his power to redeem the past or to atone for its errors. The characters which he had inscribed on the pages of his life must remain as they were written. He could only hope that Time, the all-destroyer, might blot them from remembrance, and that the recollection of them might not haunt him in the grave whither he was hastening. To whom of us, in hours of solitary reflection, do not thoughts equally bitter and despairing come !

How far the President's future career was changed or his character ennobled by that hour's meditation may not be told. The effect of spiritual experiences cannot be traced and noted with the same accuracy as the influence of the magnetic current or the results of chemical reaction. I only know that there was an especial fervor in his voice and an unwonted simplicity in his speech as he said to us in chapel that evening:

"If I were to give a young man the best counsel which it is in my power to utter, distilling into a few words all my past lessons and experience, I would say to him, Be true, be earnest, be self-reliant ; have faith in God, have faith also in yourself ; avoid the sins of sloth, idleness and indifference ; keep every fiber of your being responsive to the claims of duty, to the needs of humanity, to the promptings of what is best and noblest in your soul ; then, as you draw near the evening of your days, you will not stand at the bar of your conscience with your original gifts wrapped in the napkin of an easeful and inglorious life ; but, glorying in their more than ten-fold increase, you may with assurance await those words of approval and reward, 'Well done, good and faithful servant, I will make thee ruler over many things : enter thou into the joy of thy Lord.' "

THE STORY OF A
BOWDOIN STORY-TELLER

WILMOT B. MITCHELL, '90

THE STORY OF A BOWDOIN STORY-TELLER

"**I**T was a sad day for the Children of Israel when there arose a king in Egypt that knew not Joseph. It will be a sad day for Bowdoin College when there arises a generation of students that know not Elijah Kellogg." Thus it was, I recall, that one Sunday afternoon in my Senior year, President Hyde introduced to the students of Bowdoin a little, bent, bronzed old man who spoke to us with simplicity and eloquence of spiritual blindness. "A man of small body and large soul," said one of the fellows afterwards,—an impression which, I think, Mr. Kellogg made upon us all. We shall see this whole-souled man upon our campus no more, but he will speak to Bowdoin students for years to come. For although he held no college office, it goes without question that no one was more loved by Bowdoin men than he. From the day he came to Brunswick, sixty-four years ago last autumn, and presented himself, as he says, "a sedate and diffident youth, between the two maple trees that relieved the monotony of this arid and barren college yard, and, like friendship and misfortune, flung their shadow over the steps of Massachusetts Hall, and sued for admission to Bowdoin College," even to the day when the students gathered around his bier, the boys have felt that he was their friend, a man after their own heart.

It is of interest to go back, in imagination, to that autumn of '36 and see the young college with this young man at its doors. To outward view, the college then was not the college of to-day. There was not the grateful shade of elm and maple ; there was no King Chapel with its stately spires; no granite hall memorial of war and sacrifice ; no Searles Science Building witnessing that "Nature's laws are God's thoughts ;" no Walker Art Building teaching that beauty is truth and truth beauty. On the "college yard" not more than one-fourth the size of the present campus there were only five buildings,—old Massachusetts, of course, Winthrop, Maine, a wooden chapel and the President's house. But though with small material equipment, the college had a corps of instructors of sound learning and strong personality. There was the "impassive, inflexible Allen," soon to be succeeded by the affable and brilliant Woods. There, too, were the "gentle Newman," the "magnificent and massive Cleaveland," the "indomitable and uncompromising Smythe," the precise and polished Packard, the "sensitive and saintly Upham," the accomplished and gracious Goodwin. Into these surroundings and under these benign influences came young Kellogg of Portland.

Small of stature but strong, sharp-eyed, brown and wiry, we can well imagine him on that October day when, "with humility," as he says, he "requested an inhabitant of the village to point out the President of the college," and he "gazed upon that great man with anxiety and solicitude inspired by the belief that" his "fate and that of his companions lay in the great man's clutches." Though the son of a city minister, he had not spent his twenty-three years shut up in a parsonage. He knew how to swing the scythe and to handle the "narrow axe," knowledge that was to stand him in good stead in after years. This he had gained on his uncle's farm in Gorham where his mother had sent him that he might be away from the alluring voices of the sea. For from early boyhood he had loved the water. When but a youngster, the story goes, he went to sail in Back Cove with a sugar box for a boat and his shirt for a sail. As a boy he was never so happy as when having stolen to Fore Street, he could listen to the yarns which the old sailors spun. On one occasion this pastime brought him to grief. One Sabbath morning his father missed him from church, and when about noon the boy returned from the wharves, his father demanded an explanation of his absence from divine service. The youngster asserted that he had attended the Methodist church. His father, doubting his word, asked him to give the text. This the boy readily did ; and then, being requested, began to give an outline of the sermon. But alas ! young Elijah had been brought up on doctrine strictly Congregational and knew not the tenets of John Wesley. When he was about two-thirds of the way through and imagined he was doing bravely, the stern preacher gave him a ringing box on the ear and demanded that he stop his lying ; no Methodist minister would ever preach such doctrine as that.

Though his uncle's farm, upon which he liked to work, was some distance inland, there was ever resounding in his ears the irresistible roar of the ocean. To this he at length yielded ; but after a year or two of life upon the sea, which to his last hour he loved much, persuaded by his mother he fitted in his father's study and at Gorham Academy, and sought and gained admission to the college.

Young Kellogg came from good stock. In him English and Scotch-Irish met and mingled. His father, Elijah, at fourteen was a drummer boy in the Continental Army at Bunker Hill, passed through the terrible winter with Washington's army at Valley Forge, later graduated from Dartmouth College, was a successful missionary to the Indians, a trustee of our college, and an influential preacher in Portland. His mother, Eunice, was a woman of strong and resolute will, a true-born granddaughter of Hugh and Elizabeth McClellan, those early settlers of Gorham, who "risked their scalps for land" ; who indeed, as Mr. Kellogg has shown us in "Good Old Times," braved the perils of the sea and the savages to found a home in the new country. For a lad with such strength behind him, half of the victory is already won. He has chosen his grandfathers well.

Here at Bowdoin young Kellogg soon became a popular member of the Peucinian society, in fact, a favorite of the whole college ; not because he had much money to spend, for he was to a great extent dependent upon his own resources. A few years ago he said somewhat jokingly, "I worked my way through college with a narrow axe, and when I was hard up for money I used to set the college fence afire and burn it up, and the Treasurer would hire me to build another one. Let the young man who has to help himself thank God, keep his powder dry, and take to his bosom the old motto : *Per angusta ad augusta.*' " Popularity, at Bowdoin then as now depended upon something more to be treasured than money. "In Kellogg's social life," writes one of his college mates, "he was always boiling over with good humor ; very fluent in talk, and exceedingly interesting as a conversationalist. Indeed as a whole, Kellogg was literally *sui generis.*" "He was universally popular," writes another, a classmate of his in both academy and college, "but he had his own chosen favorites, and one characteristic of him was his strong personal affection towards them. His soul burned with love for those whom he loved. This was the secret of his power for good, for his influence upon others was always good." And still another, "I remember him as companionable, a good story-teller, vivacious and even playful. No one would have guessed that he was the son of a grave minister and missionary."

His college life, I judge, was not always as the Faculty or his parson father would have had it. Doubtless from early boyhood he was a pretty wide-awake youngster, hardly willing to sit in his father's study and read Bunyan's "Holy War" or Pike's "Persuasives to Early Piety," two books which I noticed the other day in his father's library. "He was in a pickle most of the time" is the way his niece, justly proud of her uncle and well-informed in family tradition, put it. Turn such a lad active, daring, resourceful, inventive, full of fun to his finger tips, into the college as it was then, with but little baseball, football or rowing to aid, as he mid once, "the germs of mischief to ooze out in copious drops of perspiration," and he is likely to occasion more or less parental solicitude and require a good deal of Faculty surveillance. If young Kellogg really played one-third of the pranks which apocryphal college tradition ascribes to him, even his resources must have been severely taxed. Let a Bowdoin student to-day climb as high a church or chapel spire as he can, Elijah Kellogg, he finds, went several rods higher. For every gill of molasses a Sophomore to-day pours into a Freshman's bed, Elijah Kellogg poured gallons. For every one Freshman whom he sends to the President to "make up chapel," Kellogg sent dozens. Many of these traditions, we discover as soon as we try to verify them, are only Canterbury tales, but there are then enough left to save his reputation as a practical joker.

During his Sophomore year, one morning as the students went to prayers, they saw "Old Gul's" (short for President Guilielmus Allen's) hat, a big open-work affair, on top of the chapel steeple. They did not seize upon Kellogg and bear him on their shoulders triumphantly into chapel, as did 'Ninety when Chandler put the tall hat bearing the insignia of Phi Chi on top of the lightning rod ; "there was no doubt," however, writes one of his classmates. "that Kellogg put it there, for no one else had the daring or power to perform such a feat, but I do not remember that he was ever called to account for it."

At another time when he climbed the belfry with the intention of silencing the bell,—an intention which in these days would have seemed laudable, for it called the students out at six o'clock in the morning,—as he thrust his head into the bell-tower, President Allen's hired man was there to seize him by the hair. What penalty was meted out to him Mr. Kellogg did not mention when in after years he told the story with twinkling eyes. But possibly he had not got entirely over his chagrin at getting caught, when a large gander, bonneted in a Brunswick woman's green calash, went flying through an open window of the President's house, much to the horror of the company assembled there at an evening reception.

A story often told concerning Mr. Kellogg runs as follows : A sign had been stolen, "swiped" the twentieth century student would say, and the men in Kellogg's dormitory were suspected. Now we must know that in those early days students were not allowed to do their own sweet will in the dormitories but were carefully watched by tutors or "tutes." According to the regulations a tutor was not to enter a student's room when he was at devotions. In this instance, the story goes, when the sign was almost entirely consumed in Kellogg's fireplace, a "tute" approached his room. Receiving no response to his knock, he listened and heard some one reading the Scriptures. After a moment or two he caught these words : "And he answered and said unto them, an evil and adulterous generation seeketh after a sign ; and there shall no sign be given to it."

Although so full of fun, Kellogg had underneath it all a pretty serious purpose. He was never lazy. He was always ready to work his way. Much of the time in college he boarded with Mrs. Susan Dunning on the corner of Maine and Noble streets just in front of where Professor Robinson now lives ; and he paid for his board by cutting wood. He was proud of his ability to use an axe ; he never tired of telling that the size of his chips and the way he made them fly showed conclusively, the wood-cutters thought, that he was not a "colleger."

It was while working for this good woman that he had the great satisfaction of seeing President Allen laugh. The well-sweep was broken and Kellogg had agreed to repair it. As the snow was too deep to take the cattle out, he took a sled and going to a wood lot cut a big, heavy pole such as was needed for one of those old well-sweeps. "I put it on the sled and tried to haul it," he said, "but the long end dragging in the deep snow made that impossible ; so instead of hauling it, I took hold of the end and started pushing it home. It was hard work, and to make matters worse whom should I meet but the dignified President Allen. 'Well, Kellogg,' he said, 'I have heard of putting the cart before the horse but I never saw it done before.' Then he burst into a hearty laugh, and that's the only time I ever saw him even smile in all the years I knew him."

In his studies he by no means stood at the foot of his class. Although he doubtless liked a college prank better than the mysteries of Calculus, he was appointed to take part in the Junior and Senior Exhibition in his junior year, an appointment made on the basis of rank. He enjoyed the classics exceedingly and was even at this time a good writer. "He was strenuous and persistent in whatever he undertook," writes a college mate. "I remember when he was composing a poem or preparing an essay, he gave his whole soul to it ; his demeanor showed that he was absorbed in it and absent-minded to everything else, until that one thing was done."

During his Junior year he was one of the editors of his society paper, and it was about that work, indeed, that he intended to write a story for this very volume. "When I was editor," he said, "contributions came in slowly, so I had to do most of the work myself. Well, how do you think I managed it ? Why, in this way. President Allen had conceived the idea that he could write hymns; so he proceeded to write nearly a whole volume of them. You can find them now in the college library. And four of the Faculty thought they could sing and withal could sing the President's hymns, which they tried to do much to the delectation of the students. So when I was without contributions I used to fill up my paper with parodies of those hymns." And then the old man, with a boyish twinkle in his eyes, only a month before his death, repeated from memory twenty or thirty lines of one of those parodies.

Mr. Kellogg's close connection with the college did not end with his graduation. For the next three years he was at Andover, to be sure, but even while there he made a place for himself very near to the heart of all school and college boys ; for it was at Andover that he wrote those matchless declamations, "Spartacus to the Gladiators" and "Regulus to the Carthaginians." Even more than Anthon,—the editor of that famous edition of the classics which might well be called centaur-like, for it was half man and half "horse,"—Mr. Kellogg won the gratitude of every school and college boy. What school boy has not "met upon the arena every shape of man or beast and never lowered his arm ?" Surely scores of our graduates have deserved the name of "Reg,"—which has attached itself inseparably to a member of '87,—if it is to be given for liking to declaim "Regulus to the Carthaginians,"—for beginning in a low, subdued tone and standing "calm and unmoved as the marble wall," and ending with gutteral tones and in a fine frenzy on "Cut as he would have carved you. Burn deep as his curse."

How he happened to write "Spartacus" he used to like to tell to college boys. In the rhetorical exercises at the seminary, each student was required to speak something he had written. Afterward he was criticised by the class and then by the professor. The class criticisms were sometimes pretty pungent and those by the professor, though just, were always searching. Consequently the students came to dread the speaking. "At last I made up my mind," said Mr. Kellogg, "that I would try to get something so unusual and so interesting that it would hold their attention too closely for them to think about criticisms. Well, I wrote 'Spartacus.' When I began, it worked just as I had expected. They were taken by surprise. You could have heard a pin drop while I was speaking and they didn't recover till after I had finished. Then when Professor Park turned to the students and inquired: 'What criticisms have you to offer, young gentlemen ?' there wasn't one of them had a word to say ; for they were all thinking of the piece and hadn't noticed anything else. 'Gentlemen,' said the professor, 'we are not here for theological disquisitions nor for learned arguments, but these exercises are purely rhetorical, and, gentlemen, that is rhetoric.' Then turning to me he remarked : 'I could criticise you, Kellogg, but I don't know whether it would do you good or harm ; on the whole, therefore, I think I will say nothing.' So," said the old man laughingly, "I got out of it pretty easy that time."

From Andover to keep a promise made in his undergraduate days that if the people of Harpswell would build a church, he would be their minister, he came back to where he saw much of the students. Since then, with the exception of the ten winters he was in Boston, he has been almost under the eaves of the college.

For some years the college had the custom of sending men whom it "rusticated" to stay with Mr. Kellogg ; and doubtless his strong, manly character brought more than one boy to his better self. That his treatment of these boys was not exactly that of Squeers, this instance will show. One young fellow whom the college sent him was especially rebellious at first. Through cheap story papers he had become cheek by jowl with Old Sleuth and his boon companions, and he sought to emulate them by carrying a revolver and a dirk knife. Mr. Kellogg told him that as he would not find any Indians or many wild beasts down there, he had better surrender his weapons. This the young man did after much reluctance. During the first day Mr. Kellogg left him to himself, as he was inclined to sulk. In the evening he began to talk to the boy indifferently at first, afterwards kindly. All the time—lover-like—he kept edging up nearer to him on the big sofa and finally in his genuine, whole-souled way, put his hand affectionately on the lad's shoulder. To such treatment the young fellow was not accustomed. It was so different from his over-stern father's that it threw him entirely off his guard. He could not withstand the man's kindly interest and genuine manner. His rebellious spirit was broken. The boy dreaded his father's rebuke, and the next day, unknown to him, Mr. Kellogg wrote to his mother telling all about her son and urging that the father write to him kindly and not sternly. A few days after this the young fellow was surprised and delighted to receive from home a letter of forgiveness and encouragement.

On July fourth, there was to be a celebration in Portland. The boy wished but did not expect to go. "Well," said Mr. Kellogg one day after they had been speaking of the matter, "I am afraid you can't go. I have no authority to let you. But, then, I really want to attend that celebration myself and I can't be expected to leave you at home alone." When the day of celebration came the student and the preacher could have been seen tramping the streets of Portland, both, I have no doubt, having a right royal good time.

In 1852, when the college celebrated its semi-centennial, Mr. Kellogg was asked to write the ode. "I didn't know anything about it beforehand," said his niece, "but I was staying with Uncle Elijah then, and he asked me to attend the celebration with him. At supper, the evening before, he said to his housekeeper, 'Well, Mary, pour me a Birch Island cup of tea to-night.' Birch Island tea, he always said, would hold up an egg. After supper I heard him in his study overhead walking back and forth and talking to himself, but I did not know what he was doing. As we rode up to Brunswick the next morning he seemed much preoccupied and kept mumbling over some poetry. He left me at my cousin's and went off, as I afterwards learned, to the office of Mr. Griffin, the printer. There he repeated to him the ode, and just before it was time to sing it, the freshly printed slips were brought in and distributed." That Birch Island tea did not drug the muse the following lines will show :

"From waves that break to break again,
    From winds that die to gather might,
How pleasant on the stormy main
    Appears the sailor's native height.

*   *   *   *   *   *   *   *   *

But sweeter memories cluster here
    Than ever stirred a seaman's breast,
Than e'er provoked his grateful tear,
    Or wooed the mariner to rest.

'Twas here our life of life began—
    The spirit felt its dormant power ;

'Twas here the child became the man—
    The opening bud became a flower.

On these old trees each nestling leaf,
    The murmur of yon flowing stream,
Has power to stir a buried grief,
    Or to recall some youthful dream.

Each path that skirts the tangled wood.
    Or winds amidst its secret maze,
Worn by the feet of those we loved,
    Brings back the form of other days.

Of those whose smile was heaven to thee,
    Whose voice a richer music made

Than brooks that murmur to the sea,
  Or birds that warble in the shade.

Around these ancient altar fires
  We cluster with a joyous heart,
While ardent youth and hoary sires
  Alike sustain a grateful part."

Between 1865 and 1880 came his books ; and these bound him still closer to the college ; for in his "Whispering Pine Series" he has given us a good look into the lives of the students in the early days and has caught in the amber of his story many Bowdoin customs.

He pictures vividly to us the early Commencement, when nearly the whole District of Maine seemed to keep holiday. From far and near came people in carryalls and stages, on horseback, in packets and pleasure boats, to join in the college merrymaking. Hundreds of carriages bordered the yard, and barns and sheds were filled with horses ; hostlers were running to and fro sweating and swearing ; and every house was crammed with people. To Commencement came not only the beauty, wit and wisdom of the District but also those who cared little for art or learning. With dignified officials, sober matrons, and gay belles and beaux came also horse-jockeys, wrestlers, snake-charmers, gamblers, and venders of every sort. The college yard was dotted with booths where were sold gingerbread, pies, egg-nog, long-line cigars, beers small, and, alas ! too often for good order, beers large. While Seniors in the church were discoursing on "Immortality," jockeys outside were driving sharp trades and over-convivial visitors engaging in free fights.

In his "Sophomores of Radcliffe" Mr. Kellogg tells us of the Society of Olympian Jove, a society whose customs perhaps sprang partly from the author's imagination and partly from his experience. His description of great Jove seated upon his majestic throne, under a triumphal arch, reminds us of the council chamber in Gomorrah when the "ponderous gewgag" was brought forth ; or of a coronation in the present reign of King Mike when canes are "sprung," and cakes are cut under clasped hands. In those days the initiate was made to rush through the pines and ford the dark Acheron, and was carefully taught the signals of distress ; signals which James Trafton, with work unprepared, the morning after his initiation, much to the merriment of the class, proceeded to give to his irritated professor by squinting at him through his hand.

Perhaps the most interesting of the Bowdoin customs which Mr. Kellogg describes is the "Obsequies of Calculus." This custom was in vogue many years, and a headstone can yet be seen upon the campus marking the spot where the sacred ashes were consigned to dust. At the end of Junior year when Calculus was finished, the Junior class gathered in the mathematical room and there deposited their copies of Calculus in a coffin. The coffin was then borne sorrowfully to the chapel, where amid bitter wailing and copious lachrymation a touching eulogy was delivered. The orator was wont to discourse of the "gigantic intellect of the deceased, his amazing powers of abstraction, his accuracy of expression, his undeviating rectitude of conduct," his strict observance of the motto that "The shortest distance between two points is a straight line." Then came the elegy in Latin, after which, amid the grief-convulsed mourners, the coffin was placed upon a vehicle called by the vulgar a dump cart, and the noble steed Isosceles, which "fed upon binomial theorems, parabolas and differentials, and every bone of whose body and every hair of whose skin was illustrative of either acute or obtuse angles," drew the sacred load to its last resting place. The funeral procession, consisting of the college band, Bowdoin Artillery, the eulogist and the elogist, and the Freshman, Sophomore and Junior classes, moved slowly down Park Row through the principal streets of the village to the rear of the college yard. Here the books were "placed upon the funeral pyre and burned with sweet odors, the solemn strains of the funeral dirge mingling with the crackling of flames.

> "Old Calculus has screwed us hard,
>   Has screwed us hard and sore ;
>
> I would he had a worthy bard
>   To sing his praises more.
>
> Peace to thine ashes, Calculus,
>   Peace to thy much-tried shade ;
> Thy weary task is over now,
>   Thy wandering ghost is laid."

"The ashes were collected, placed in an urn, and enclosed in the coffin. A salute was then fired by the Bowdoin Artillery. The epitaph, like that upon the grave of the three hundred who fell at Thermopylae, was brief but full of meaning, having on the tablet at the head,

CALCULUS

on that at the foot
$$\frac{dx}{dy} = 0.\text{''}$$

But the Whispering Pine books were written for other purposes than simply to depict the life of the college or to let us into the *escapades* of the students. The dictum that "All art must amuse" did not go far enough for Mr. Kellogg. With all his fun and "frolic temper" he was too much of a Puritan to make amusement the chief end of his writing. His books, I suppose, must belong to the hated purpose stories, if to such belong stories written with the avowed purpose of making boys more robust and genuine and manly, of giving them redder blood and broader chests and larger biceps, and at the same time making them hate gloss and chicanery and love straightforward, courageous, Christian dealing. So imbued was the author with this purpose that he wrote his books, as he expressed it, while upon his knees. Often at first he felt that he should be preaching rather than writing stories ; and it was not until letters came to him from all over the country that he realized he was reaching more boys with his pen than with his voice. But though written with a purpose, it is noticeable that his books are not of the wishy-washy type. His boys are not Miss Nancies and plaster saints. They do not die young and go to heaven ; they live and make pretty companionable kind of men. Mr. Kellogg was too much of a story-teller and too strong a believer in truth to distort life for ethical purposes.

One does not have to delve deep to find the lessons which he would teach. Choose your chums well, is his advice to college boys. College is not simply a place where learning is bought and sold, where you pay so much money and get so much Greek or so much philosophy. It is more than that. Not all college lessons are in your books, neither are they all taught in the class-rooms. You will learn them on the college paths, in your sports, in your dormitories ; and generally it is your chums that teach them to you. The set of fellows with whom you cast your lot may make or mar you. College ties are strong. The boys with whom you eat and sleep ; those with whom you solve the difficult problems and pick out the tangles in Greek and Latin, with whom you stroll of an evening to the falls or a Wednesday afternoon to the shore, to whom you tell your future plans, your love affairs, and your religious doubts, whose sympathies mingle with yours "like the interlacing of green, summer foliage," those fellows are going to mould your ideals and determine your character.

Again, he believed that boys must not be afraid to lock horns with an obstacle. A difficult job may be their greatest blessing. Richardson coddled at home felt himself a weakling by the side of Morton whom difficulties had made self-reliant. "Hardship is a wholesome stimulant to strong natures, quickening slumbering energies, compelling effort, and by its salutary discipline reducing refractory elements." The boy who is always dodging difficulties will make a gingerbread man. Only by grappling can we gain power to achieve. Only by having tough junks to split can we learn to "strike right in the middle of the knot."

The value and dignity of labor is the ever recurring burden of these stories. Mr. Kellogg believed with Carlyle that all work is divine, that to labor is to pray. Especially did he wish to get out of boys' minds the false notion that only mental work is honorable. He thought that often it is as honorable to sweat the body as to sweat the brain. As honorable and as necessary ; for he believed that it is only by keeping the lungs full of fresh air, and the pores open by perspiration, and the limbs strong by activity, that a man can keep his vision from being distorted. "The essence of hoe handle, if persistently taken two hours a day," would, he believed, cure many diseases of the mind and heart. The devils of fretfulness and faultfinding are not always to be cast out simply by prayer and fasting. Often it requires labor in the fresh open air,—a good pull against the tide, a long ride on horseback, or an hour's chopping with the narrow axe. Many a disheartened preacher who now mopes in his study and who "takes all his texts out of Jeremiah," would get "Sunday's harness-marks erased from the brain," and preach glad tidings of great joy, if he would only start the perspiration by healthful outdoor exercise. Mr. Kellogg thought a boy should learn to work with his hands as well as with his brain ; to look at things from a farmer's point of view as well as from a scholar's. All learning, he knew well, is not in school and college. He appreciated the value of book-learning, but democrat as he was and well acquainted with common people, he knew that an illiterate Jerry William or an Uncle Tim Longley can teach scores of valuable lessons to many a schoolman. The boy who is too lazy, does not know, or does not want to know, how to do some of the practical duties of life, who thinks it disgraceful to work with his hands, can have no part or lot in his kingdom. His ideal college boy is Henry Morton, who is a keen debater, a good writer, a lover of the classics and a lover of nature but at the same time a man who can hew straight to the line, cut the corners of many a farmer, and take the heart of a tree from more than one woodsman.

This, I take it, is the prime lesson that he wished the hearty, robust lads that live in his books to teach to us, and it is the doctrine that Mr. Kellogg lived as well as preached. When in Boston at the Seaman's Bethel, he was often found in his blue overalls down on the wharves at work with the sailors ; and for the fifty years he has preached in Harpswell he has lived in a house whose timbers he cut and hauled himself. There on his farm he has himself cared for his cattle, sowed his seed and harvested his crops. Book and pen, boat, scythe and hoe, all have been his ready servants in doing God's work. One Sabbath some years ago at the close of his sermon he said : "Widow Jones's grass I see needs mowing. I shall be there with my scythe tomorrow at half past four. I shall be glad to see all of you there who wish to come and help me."

Almost any day's record taken from Mr. Kellogg's journal, which I have recently had the privilege of reading, shows how beautifully prayer and deed were intermingled in his life ; how hand, as well as heart and brain, was made to do its part.

"Friday, September 29, 1887. Rose early, prayed and gave thanks. Hauled in the forenoon all the rocks required. Mr. Getchell finished at noon. In the afternoon I took him to Brunswick, paid him, got my lime and sand and got home by dark. I have knelt down beside the wall that is

Elijah Kellogg.

now finished and humbly thanked God for doing this kindness to me, for He has done it. Blessed be God for the mercies of this day."

"Tuesday, October 25, 1887. Rose early. Prayed at the hearthstone and the threshold. John came. We sawed, split and hauled the wood. The old house windows surprised John. We then prepared for horses, and at noon John went home. Though pressed with work, I felt prompted to go to the burnt tree and went to that and to the old maple and thanked God and prayed for little Frank. Made my fires and the company began to come. They poured in with full hands and warm hearts to the number of eighty or more. Surely God's dealing with me in most unthought-of ways. Glory to God for the mercies of the twenty-fifth of October."

Seven years ago when Mr. Kellogg's *Alma Mater* celebrated her one hundredth birthday, from sea and shore her children gathered again around her knees. She was proud to welcome back her sons who had achieved success in art and letters, in medicine, theology, education and statesmanship. As one after another of these successful men arose to speak he was applauded generously; but when this little farmer-preacher stood up to address them, this crowd of Bowdoin men broke forth tumultuously. Then it was easy to see how large a place Elijah Kellogg held in their hearts.

In a style almost conversational, as a father talking to his sons, he told the simple story of his life. Effective it was indeed, but perhaps not so eloquent as when in 1890, looking back over a stretch of half a century, he said : "I stand here to-day like an old tree among the younger growth, from whose trunk the bark and limbs have fallen, and whose roots are dying in the soil. Then I could stand where the roads divide that lead to Mere Point and Maquoit, and hear the roar of the Atlantic in one ear and that of the falls of the Androscoggin in the other. To-day I have not heard a word except the two words 'Bowdoin College.' But there is no decrepitude of the spirit. Moons may wax and wane, flowers may bloom and wither, but the associations that link a student to his intellectual birthplace are eternal."

In these many lights have Bowdoin men seen Elijah Kellogg. They have known him as a jovial, vivacious, free-hearted boy. They have known him as a young preacher beloved by his church and as an author of robust and breezy books. In later years they have seen him drive into the village, sometimes with his old-fashioned wagon piled full of bags of potatoes, sometimes with his rack loaded with hay and drawn generally by oxen, but now and then by two cows or by a cow and ox yoked together. They have known him as he has farmed and fished. They have often walked down to his church on Sunday afternoons to hear him preach. They have known him as a man so generous that he was often himself hard pressed ; so pure in heart that he lived "as seeing Him who is invisible." They have known of his ministrations as he has christened the children, married the young men and women, soothed the sick, consoled the dying, and comforted the mourning of one generation after another of ship-builders, fishermen, and farmers in his country parish. They have chatted with him in the Alpha Delta Phi hall, and they have heard him at Sunday chapel services, at Y. M. C. A. meetings and Commencement dinners. And they have come to see that this quaint, unconventional, retiring, simple, eloquent man was no ordinary preacher. They have found that somehow he could understand them. They could tell him their jokes and their serious plans, and he could see through their eyes and hear through their ears. They have found that he was interested in them not simply as a professional duty but because he couldn't help it. They have found that he loved boys, that he was happy in their companionship, delighted to talk about their work and their sports and to tell tales of his own college days. They have found that he, more perhaps than any other man they have ever known, was all the time at heart a boy himself. And I think that for Bowdoin students to have known a man like Elijah Kellogg, who through the rubs and chances of a long life kept his spirit young and his heart free from bitterness and guile, has helped their faith in God, in themselves, and in each other more than many books.

THE EDUCATION OF
JACOB SHAW

FRANKLIN C. ROBINSON, '73

THE EDUCATION OF JACOB SHAW

W HEN Jacob Shaw went to Bowdoin he was just about as green, and inexperienced in life and unformed in his character as the majority of Freshmen are ; that is, he was not green or inexperienced or unformed in character at all. It is only a college fiction that Freshmen are thus constituted. That fiction assumes that all young men who go to college have spent their previous years in almost solitary confinement, in order that they may get the full benefit of the college course, and especially that they may receive with due appreciation and openness of mind the firm but proper guidance which upper-classmen are prepared to give them. In fact, they have been exposed for the sixteen or eighteen most plastic years of their lives to conspicuous and subconscious influences which may, and generally do, affect them far more than anything to which college life exposes them.

College life is oftener the field upon which previously learned tactics are executed than the place where these are acquired. The reason why this is not more generally recognized is because subconscious influences are more powerful for character formation than any others, and outward action may not reveal at once real character. This is not saying that one may not be influenced for good or evil by a college course, for very many are, but even then pre-college influences have been important factors in the case.

There didn't seem to be anything about the pre-college influences which had acted upon Jacob Shaw to prevent his making the highest kind of a success of his college career. His father was a well-to-do lawyer in a moderately sized village of Northern New England, not reckoned wealthy, though he probably had more property than he paid taxes on ; but that is not an uncommon thing in any community. Jacob had always had his necessary expenses paid, and a fair amount of pocket money allowed, but his father wanted him to learn the value of money and so repressed any ideas of extravagance which might appear to be in his son's mind. His father had the deserved reputation of getting what he wanted, of being "a hard man to beat," etc., and Jacob was, of course, exposed to certain family discussions over things which came out as his father wanted them to regardless perhaps of strict ethical principles, but a boy couldn't be supposed to be affected by little things of that kind which he didn't understand. His father was not a religious man, but his mother was, pardon the solecism. I mean she had a sufficient stock of goodness on hand to provide for herself surely, and probably to pull him through any difficulty which might hereafter confront him. She was prominent in church affairs, gave liberally to all good objects, and took a humble pride in her interest in the poor, and her familiarity with certain wealthy families who came every summer to occupy cottages on the shore of a neighboring lake. She was sorry that her social duties took up so much of her time that she had to forego many visits to poor people which she would otherwise have made ; that is, she frequently said she was sorry and no one of her family disputed her.

If any two words more than others had been dinned into Jacob's ears they were "diligence" and "care." Sending him to college was a part of that diligence and care on the part of his father, to make him worthy to succeed in and to his business. There were no other children in the family so his outlook in this direction was the simple and natural one.

His parents supposed they had every reason to believe that he would go on at college just as he had at home, and of course if he did not it was the fault of the college. They were sure of that, and when Mrs. Shaw said it to her husband at their first meal after she came back from locating him, and seeing that his room was properly furnished, he nodded a most emphatic approval.

At about the same hour their son was sitting in his comfortable room in South Maine thinking how nice it was to have things one wanted, and how he would enjoy getting them himself for he confessed that he was getting a little tired of the home restraint, and rather longed to put into practice the precepts there learned. He was well dressed, knew the usages of good society, was accomplished somewhat in music and dancing, in short was one of those fellows sure to be vigorously fished by the various college societies. All this added a little to his natural complacency and self-satisfaction, but after he had accepted what he thought was the best offer, he was a little indignant at the lower value placed upon his acquaintance.

He was sorry on the whole to learn that hazing was entirely a thing of the past there. He thought he should enjoy being "put through" a little. It was on the whole attractive to listen to the stories told by the upper-classmen of what had been done to them. He could see by their talk how it had gradually passed away, for Seniors had apparently suffered more than Juniors, and Sophomores least of all. Happening to glance over a triennial catalogue of the college, and noticing the increasing number of stars opposite the names, showing members deceased, his first thought was that these had been killed by hazing, showing that this increase in severity extended gradually back to early times.

He was susprised after this to receive a visit one night from a howling crowd of masked men, who made him get up and make a speech to them, and then crawl over his bedroom door, which was not an easy nor decorous thing to do as he was, even with the kind assistance of some of his visitors. But his wrath blazed up brightly when some one from the back of the room suggested that he sing the hymn his father loved so well, beginning "I dearly love my farmer friends for they mortgage their farms to me." But it did no good to get mad and they soon left him with the advice to be "a good Freshie." He didn't feel that he had been treated very badly, but was provoked that he hadn't passed through the affair as boldly as all those fellows did, who had told him of their own experience. He expected that there would be a great excitement in college at this revival of hazing but there was not. He concluded then that the great secrecy with which it was done prevented it from being known to the faculty. Afterwards he doubted some whether this explanation was the true one. One thing was most astonishing, and that was how in the excitement of the time, he was unable to remember the next day all that happened to him that night, but it gradually came back to him with increasing minuteness of detail, though it was not till Senior year that he remembered the whole of it. Such is sometimes the effect of shock upon the brain.

He was a fair scholar and took high rank. He not only knew how to recite well but was careful of all other things which are supposed to bear on the subject of rank. When his professors got to talking on their "specialties," not "hobbies" of course, he was full of attention and wholly absorbed in what they were saying, so much so that his appearance could hardly fail to attract their notice, and he believed that such fleeting appearances were afterwards developed and fixed in the form of figures in the rank books, but of course they were not.

His Freshman and Sophomore years were on the whole, disappointing, and at their end he had half a mind to leave college and begin his law studies. He felt at times that he wasn't fully appreciated, and still he couldn't tell just where and how. When he came to think it over he concluded to stay and finish his course. The thing which really troubled him was not so much the lack of consideration given to him, as the increased influence of certain others in his class, who at first seemed of no account at all. They didn't dress as well as he did, were not as polished, and were not fished for the leading societies as he was. But somehow they were passing him in rank, and besides had a certain blunt way of talking, and straight-forward way of acting which irritated him. Most of all they got positions which he wanted on prize speaking lists, etc. Not that he cared to take part in such things for his own sake ; he would have got excused probably if he had been put on, but it would have made his mother feel better to see his name on the program, for she was troubled at his decreasing rank in his studies. He hardly knew how to deal with such fellows. He knew how his father dealt with those who stood in his way, but he couldn't just see how such methods could be applied in college. How such fellows could lead him in rank he couldn't understand at all. They occasionally took "deads" in the recitation room, a thing he never did. He flattered himself on his self-possession and ready command of English on all those occasions when he was "pulled" unexpectedly, and felt sure that he had even snatched "ten-strikes" as "brands from the burning" several times. A glance at the professor's rank book would have told another story probably, but of course he couldn't know that.

He also reasoned that Junior and Senior years would reinstate him fully in that prominent position in the class from which he had fallen.

These were the years when his society qualities would shine, the years of assemblies and society receptions, and of course this less cultivated element would be obliged to give way to fellows of his experience in such things. He had given up any idea of gaining high rank in his class. "There are other and full as important things as scholarship to be obtained from a college course, things that will help me more in after life." This is what he wrote to his mother upon his return to Bowdoin after his Sophomore vacation. It was written in explanation of his change of feeling, for after numerous talks with her he had expressed a determination to try and regain his old position in his class in rank. But it was one thing to talk with his mother at home and quite another to write to her from his college room, where the fact of his position as a Junior weighed heavily upon him. To his mother he was still her boy, but really he was a Junior, and he was just a little impatient that she didn't see the important difference.

"I shall give the studies all the time they ought to have," he went on to say, "have no fear about that, but we are taught here to look at things in a broader way, to give each element of life its proper weight, to correlate educational values in a way you probably could not fully understand. Some of our most important lessons are not learned from books." That settled it for his mother. She had taught school when a girl, and remembered similar expressions heard at educational meetings. She didn't know just what they meant but was proud of her son for using them.

Certain assemblies were planned for that winter at the Town Hall and he was put on the committee of arrangements. He insisted on going quite extensively into decoration for the rooms in which they were to be held, thus bringing into prominence his knowledge of how such things should be done. But he was a little chagrined that he had forgotten to notify the patronesses and this would have been entirely overlooked had not some other member of the committee asked him about it. This neglect was due chiefly to his contempt for women and girls in general. They were necessary of course for homes and social relations. He enjoyed seeing them at parties, or on the street, in their best clothes, and he was quite a critic of their style, etc. He knew how to offer all the little conventional attentions to them, but the things which make for their comfort did not trouble him much. Of course in due time he expected to marry one, but that was a very simple matter ; he would select carefully the one he wanted. The girls who attended the assemblies were partly town girls, and partly girls from the neighboring cities. He had not invited any girl for the first night. He knew that he would have no difficulty in getting all the dances he wanted, and he knew that there would be several girls as well as fellows there in the same condition. He had never met any of the town girls. He had seen some of them in church and had heard the rather familiar comment upon them made by the students in the galleries. He thus expected to find them anxious for student attentions, and ready to flirt. Now this matter of flirtation had not previously troubled him, but was, as he now conceived, a necessary part of that "broader culture" which he had written about, and he made up his mind that he must have the experience of it, and here was the chance to begin.

He was not a little surprised at the decided repulse his first efforts in that line met. He selected one of the most attractive and stylish of the town girls, secured some dances with her and made rapid progress in his acquaintance, but he soon learned that the slightest attempt of his to cross the boundary line between pleasant acquaintance and impropriety was decidedly checked, and after that there were no vacant dances on her order for him.

He then turned his attention in other directions but for some time with a like result. There were however a certain number of girls there of a much younger set, and some of these were seemingly much pleased with his appreciation of their charms, and flattered at his preference of them to the older girls. These "older girls" had reached the advanced age of nineteen or twenty perhaps, and were of course so near to being old maids that they could hardly hope to compete in attractiveness with girls of from fourteen to sixteen. But there was not quite the satisfaction he expected from flirting with the latter. They didn't know any better and that took away at least half the fun for him. Flirting seems to be an indulgence which owes its chief zest to mutual recognition of what they are doing by those who practice it.

He wound up the evening by escorting home one of these young girls, and felt well satisfied with his progress, when she lingered with him a few minutes before going in, and made no distinct protest when he left

THE SEARLES SCIENCE BUILDING.

her with certain pronounced squeezings of her little hand. He did not know that she went into the house with such extra color in her face that she did not care to go into the sitting-room where she knew her mother was waiting for her, but went directly to her own room.

Before the next assembly he had called upon Ellen Wallis and engaged her for the rest of the course. By the time these assemblies were over he flattered himself that he had been getting just the kind of experience he wanted, even though Ellen seemed to be taking his attentions rather too seriously. He thought at first he would "run her," to quote his elegant expression to some of "the fellows," during that season and then get another girl for Senior year. But she was pretty and attractive and seemed so fond of him that he rather enjoyed going with her, and especially the evenings he spent at her home. Her parents were good people of moderate means, and evidently flattered that their daughter had captured the son of such a prominent man as Squire Shaw of Boltville. He enjoyed talking to them, and if he did this in something of a learned and patronizing manner they were certainly not offended, but listened with the most perfect absorption in what he was saying, and Mr. Wallis expressed what seemed to be the family opinion when he said that "he guessed some of the college professors didn't find it an easy job to teach him ;" and really they didn't, though not for the reason Mr. Wallis thought.

Thus almost in spite of himself the acquaintance grew more and more intimate. Of course he was careful not to really make love to her, or become engaged, but he could see that the fruit was ready to be picked any time he might put out his hand. Once or twice he nearly forgot himself, but recovered in time. And yet Ellen Wallis was not a silly girl by any means. On the contrary she was sensible and modest, but somehow had started in on her young womanhood with false notions. Indeed her modesty was something of a disappointment to Jacob. His first meeting with her gave some promise, not to say hope, of familiarity which had not been fulfilled. Thus while he was as ready as ever to talk with the boys about the indiscretions of the town girls, he more than questioned with himself whether this talk had any real basis of fact.

His Senior year began with things in this condition, and despite several efforts to break off the intimacy, it ended with them very much the same. She was a pretty girl and whenever it seemed as though he had left her some other young man was sure to begin to pay attention to her. This would call him back to her side, and he would be received by the family with such manifestation of joy that even if Ellen herself was a little cold in her welcome at first, her coldness soon gave place to more than the original warmth.

His college course was closing in other respects as could have been predicted. His rank in his studies had gone steadily down until he would graduate somewhere in the lower half of his class. But he had the same smooth and polished appearance albeit there was that in his looks which suggested that in his search for "broader experience" he had spent some evenings, at least, outside his college room or the Wallis home. But the character of these last experiences could not but impress him even in a way he had not thought possible. There was the Last Chapel exercise on Ivy Day from which, after the impressive prayer from the President, his class had marched slowly out singing "Auld Lang Syne." Before the slow marching brought him to the door the thought of what he ought to have remembered of his college course, and what he actually did remember came to him with great force, and when the last cheer at the door was over he caught himself wiping away the tears which he could not control.

He passed that evening with Ellen and her family and all were much moved and edified at his solemn talk about his wasted opportunities. It is true they didn't believe but what he had done everything to make his college course a success, and knew it had been, but they liked to hear his humble talk, it gave almost the air of a prayer-meeting to their house and went far to quiet their consciences concerning recent neglect of attendance upon such services. Next morning at the breakfast table Mrs. Wallis referred to the evening's discourse and expressed her belief that Mr. Shaw would go into the ministry. "And how would our Ellen like to be a minister's wife ?" she said with a sly look at her daughter. Ellen pretended not to understand what her mother meant.

"I don't see any connection between Mr. Shaw's being a minister and my being a minister's wife" she said a little sharply.

"The connection is plain enough to every one else," said her mother slightly irritated, "and if it isn't to you it ought to be."

"I won't be talked to in that way" said Ellen as she arose from the table and passed angrily out of the room.

The truth was that she herself was troubled and nervous. She had become strongly attached to Jacob, and, if she didn't actually love him she thought she did. She had. questioned in her own heart whether he was treating her right, but she didn't want anyone else to suggest the idea to her.

Class Day was to close with the usual Dance upon the Green. The beautiful campus had been decorated with Chinese lanterns and flags, and the evening was one of those rare ones which June sometimes provides for such an occasion in order to show what she can do, regardless of the fact that it will prove a kind of *ignis fatuus* to lure other classes on to their destruction.

Jacob was chairman of the committee of arrangements, and to his persistency was due the decision of the class to try it once more in spite of several years of failure. He seemed to believe that he had been able to produce the good weather also, and was full of joy at the promised success. It went far to compensate him for the failure of so many of his plans. Of course he took Ellen to the dance, but they didn't remain all the time on the floor. It was so beautiful to stroll around the campus paths. It was like a scene from fairyland to look back at the dancers around the Oak, apparently gliding in and out among the trees. It seemed to Jacob also that he was looking upon the last passing glories of his college course. It typified that course to him. He had made it a time of selfish enjoyment, of personal gratification, and soon it would be wholly a thing of the past, would fade away like this scene on the campus, of which the morrow would find nothing but the unsightly debris scattered over the ground.

This thought carried him out of himself for a moment, or brought to the surface of his being that better self which had not been wholly destroyed. "And shall I crown all my other unfaithfulness by being false to Ellen also ? Is not this an opportunity for me to recover my lost ground? to retrieve myself ? and if not now what hope for me ?" With the sudden impulse born of this resolution he seized her hand and told her in passionate terms of his great desire that she would not let him go away from college without the hope that he might sometime return and make her his wife. He protested his own unworthiness, and begged that she would not send him away to worse failure in the future, for he was sure that there was no hope for him unless he had the strength of her love to help him.

It is needless to say that he did not have to wait long for a favorable reply from Ellen, and after some precious minutes which lengthened into nearly an hour they returned to the dance, which no longer seemed to him to typify the rapidly passing surface pleasures he had enjoyed but the glorious opening of a brilliant future.

His mother came to Brunswick for Commencement Day, but there were so many things for her to see that there was not time to explain to her the new relations he had entered into. She was also impatient to take him home again. She laid the blame of his non-success in a literary line to the college and the town, and wanted nothing to do with either of them further. They met one or two couples strolling about the campus, and upon his telling her that they were students and town girls who had become engaged, she told him how glad she was that he had not been so foolish. Of course he would explain later, but evidently it would not be opportune to say anything about Ellen to her then.

Ellen readily excused him for devoting his whole time that day to his mother. She was so supremely happy that no cloud could come between her and the sun of her love without being instantly dissipated. They had a tender parting when he finally left for home, and he promised an early return to make a few days' visit when publicity would be given to their engagement.

When a young man ends the college life and goes back to his native town, it seems to him that more than twice four years have passed since he left it. He may have spent every vacation at home and made many visits during term time, but still he has not kept in touch with it as he did before. His interests have been elsewhere and though he may have known of every important change there, he has not actually taken them in. Only when he finally comes back does he realize what changes the years have made. It seemed to Jacob as he began to go about and renew old associations in Boltville, that it was an entirely new place.

"So it seems that old Shanly is dead" he said at the dinner table one day.

"Why, Jacob, you knew that he died nearly four years ago," said his mother.

"I suppose I did, but I had forgotten it." And so one after another of the things that had happened in the town while he was in college came to his attention now as though for the first time.

He seemed almost offended at the important changes. He seemed to think that everything ought to have remained just as it was until after he had finished his education.

Possibly the carrying out of certain resolves he had made to mingle more with the town's people than he used to helped make the changes in town more noticeable to him. For he was full of his new love and hope and anxious to get established in business as rapidly as possible in order to warrant getting married.

He wrote often to Ellen telling her of his devotion to law books and how he was becoming acquainted with his "future clients."

"They are not such disagreeable people after all," he wrote. "Of course they are ignorant and do lots of things because of it, but they are thrifty and most of them have a little money laid up, and I am sure there is a good opening for me to get a living here even while the 'old man' is active, and of course when he gives up I shall have the whole." He told her many of his funny adventures. It is true they were actually not so very funny, but things didn't have to be absorbingly interesting in themselves in order to be appreciated by the lovers.

The widow Shanly and her son Billy served to fill up many of those necessary spaces in his letters between the reiterated expressions of his love and devotion. "She is sort of a religious crank" he explained, "and lives with her half idiotic son on an old farm with tumbledown buildings out on the road where I go to the pond for fishing. It is a short cut across their pasture to the pond and one day I was in such a hurry that I left the bars down, and when I came back I saw that some of their cattle had got out and gone into a patch of sweet corn and had nearly ruined it. It was great fun to see the old woman trying to drive them out. They would run this way and that, and she after them with a broom in her hand and all the time yelling for Billy in a thin, squeaky voice. I nearly died laughing to see her antics. I think it didn't make her feel any better to see me laughing at her." There was little wonder that Mrs. Shanly was excited, for it was on this piece of corn that she was depending to get money to pay the interest on a mortgage held by Jacob's father.

Weeks went by without the promised visit to his *fiancee*, but there was no change in the character of his letters, and though Ellen gently chided him for his failure to carry out his first plans, still she felt more solicitude for his health because of overwork than for her own pleasure. Her replies to her lover's letters were such as would be expected. Her sense of triumph and satisfaction was so complete that, beyond ardent expressions of her desire to see him, she said little of his continued delay. After his account of his experience with Mrs. Shanly and the cattle, she said in one of her letters, "I read your interesting description of Mrs. Shanly and her funny actions, to mother, and she was much amused at it, though of course the telling of such a thing is never quite so interesting as the seeing it. Then, too, mother remembered that one of her girl friends married a Shanly, though of course this wasn't the one, and that seemed to prevent her from enjoying the story as much as I did. I shan't read to her any more of your adventures until she teases me *real hard*, and that will pay her for almost disapproving what you did. But it was so comical, wasn't it ? I have read it over many times since, and each time enjoy it better." This latter statement was not strictly true, but she felt after what she had said about her mother, that she must emphasize her own oneness with him in sympathy and appreciation.

Meanwhile Mrs. Shaw began to suspect that her son had some attachment or other to his college town not of a literary nature. She noticed the frequent letters he got from Brunswick and, though Ellen had cultivated a certain masculine style of penmanship, it did not wholly allay the suspicion that the address was written by a feminine hand. Not that Ellen made any effort at concealment, she never thought of such a thing. It happened to be a fad among her girl friends at that time to write in that way. She was even slightly troubled that many of his letters were posted at some neighboring town, and failed to take the hint when he suggested, jocosely, that she follow his example. It was such fun, he said, when one was out riding and passed a post office, to jump out and mail a letter. It made people think one had a large business correspondence. A suspicion of what was going on was no sooner entertained by Mrs. Shaw than attempts were made to verify or disprove it. Such attempts of course soon brought out the truth. At first she was wild with anger and grief. She thought she would go to him and upbraid him as an undutiful son and make him give up the prospect of such an unworthy or unfitting, which meant the same thing to her, alliance. "To think of it," she said to her husband, "that our boy should have been led away by such a designing creature." Thus the college fell still lower in her estimation. Her idea seemed to be that the office of a college was, like that of a sausage machine, to stuff the skins of young men full of properly minced and seasoned material and make them into "strings," each individual "link" of which was to be cut off at Commencement time, and given, smooth and plump and unctuous, into the hands of expectant parents.

But Squire Shaw was full of worldly experience. He was no less angry at the discovery, but he felt that the better way to accomplish their wishes was to ignore their knowledge of Jacob's engagement, as far as he was concerned. "The best way to fight fire on a meadow is to back fire it," he craftily said. "If it's a girl he wants, let's get one here for him. An air-tight stove is more effective to warm a man on a cold night than all the stars in the sky, for he can get closer to it. Who is there you can invite to make a visit to you this Winter ?" Mrs. Shaw saw the drift of his remarks but did not wholly approve of the plan. She was close in money matters and rather indolent, and a young lady visitor meant parties and much trouble and expense. But in the end she bowed to the greater wisdom of her spouse and after some trouble fixed on a young lady of good family and some property whose acquaintance she had made through one of the Summer colony which spent few weeks each year on the shore of the lake.

To Alice Sprague she wrote a letter strongly urging her to come and spend some weeks with her. "You have never seen Boltville in Winter. It will make your next Summer visit all the more delightful when you can compare it with a Winter one." She said nothing about her grown-up son being at home, indeed Alice did not know she had a son. She had spent only one Summer at the lake, and Jacob was not at home and if he had been she might not have met him. She herself had just graduated from college and was full of enthusiasm for college settlement and other good works of that kind, and hence had been much interested in Mrs. Shaw's account of the benevolent work she did in the town and the great need of doing more of it. Like many city people she had a general idea that most country folk were to be greatly pitied, because of their primitive condition and lack of comforts of life. She could see how by the help of the Summer visitors they managed to eke out a picturesque existence in the Summer, but "what could such people do in the Winter ?" This visit might show her and she would at least get material for "talks" on the subject at the ladies' club, so she accepted the kind invitation and before long was on the ground.

She was much more stylish than Ellen Wallis, and could talk better, and Jacob could not but make the suggested comparison, which resulted not to Ellen's advantage. He didn't realize at all that he himself was the cause in great part of Ellen's lack of more educational advantages. He had put foolish notions into her young head, talked to her and her parents learnedly about the greater need there was that "women should cultivate domesticity instead of aping men in literary pursuits," so that she had given up the ideas she once had of going to college herself, and now he mentally blamed her that she did not compare favorably with this bright and cultivated girl.

To complete the scheme, when it was evident that the "air-tight" was working as Mr. Shaw had predicted, Mrs. Shaw caused it to be known in Brunswick that her son Jacob was engaged, or likely soon to be, to a certain cultivated and attractive girl then visiting in Boltville. This had the desired result, a letter of gentle inquiry from Ellen, a complaint of her lack of faith from him, and soon a breaking of the engagement.

The result was one more "college widow," one more young man freed from embarrassment, and one more father and mother congratulating themselves on their shrewdness in promoting their son's best interests.

Now he was free to use the result of his "experience" in another case. But alas ! like many another experiment, the conditions were not similar and the results not correspondent at first. The wooing of Alice Sprague was a very different matter. She was responsive to all other sensations, but not to that of love. She took long rides with him alone, a thing she would never have done with a young man at her own home. But "it was so delightful to disregard for the time such conventionalities and be just like the other country girls." This is what she wrote to her college chum.

She went skating ; she made calls ; she even insisted that she be allowed to visit the Shanlys and did so, though Mrs. Shaw did not accompany her but had the coachman take her there and wait for her. She took copious notes of all she saw that was novel and felt as though she would spring a genuine sensation when she returned to her home. All the time she persisted in treating Jacob as a boy, much to his inward wrath. Jacob was desperately in love with her, and she must have seen it, but somehow he never could get up his courage to actually make love to her, though his mother contrived all sorts of opportunities for them to be alone in suitable situations. Just before she went home she seemed a trifle more responsive as he thought, and as she promised to come the next Summer, he felt that he was sure to win in the end.

He wrote to her and she answered his letters, telling him how much she enjoyed her visit and with what interest her description of life in the country in Winter had been received at the clubs where she had given it. "I really am getting more and more interested in it myself, and am almost sure that if other country towns are like Boltville, I should be quite contented to live all the time in one." This admission seemed so significant to Jacob that his ardor was kindled afresh, and he looked forward with almost feverish impatience to her coming the next Summer. It tended also to confirm his earlier notions about girls, notions which had received some slight shock from the quickness with which Ellen had given him his freedom, and Alice's general treatment of him.

But her Summer coming was on the whole an illustration of the old saying about anticipation and realization. She was glad to see him but quite unaccountable in her behavior to him. Sometimes she was cold and unresponsive and at others quite the reverse. She would not go with him as freely as she did in the Winter, but his mother told him that that was favorable rather than otherwise. His greatest disappointment was that she would not go rowing with him in the new boat he had bought, and fitted with cushions, and made in every way as attractive as possible. Something always seemed to stand in the way when he would try to arrange a time. "Don't try to plan ahead for such a thing," she would say, "I am enjoying the present so much that I can't bear to look even a day into the future. Just come over when you feel like going and if I can arrange it I will go." But somehow she never could arrange to go, at least for any long trip. She had at times been able to get in and go for a short row, but never to the other side of the lake where he wanted to take her. As the time drew near for the party to break up she seemed at times almost rude to him, and was especially so two or three days before, when he had made her a call.

On the evening before she was to go home she had wandered down to the shore of the lake and was taking a last farewell look at its evening beauties. Where on earth are there such beauties and such influences as come from the scene before her ? It was not the boundless ocean which speaks of endless striving and endeavor, which wakens ambition to go on and on in never ending labor, even to eternity. It was a definitely limited expanse of water shut in by the hills, with a further shore just far enough off to have its exact contour hidden, leaving suitable scope for the imagination to speculate as to just what was there, but making it sure that no startling discovery could possibly be made by visiting it. Such a place is of all others the one to bring thoughts of earthly love and contentment. Alice, too, had been long enough out of college to get back again in great measure to the realities of life, to see its limitations, and be more willing to take up its plain duties feeling sure that great privileges would come also with these. She was slightly aroused from her revery by the grating of a boat's keel upon the shore near, and turning her head saw that Jacob Shaw was its occupant.

"I have been watching you for some little time," he said, "and thought I would see how near I could get without attracting your notice. I believe you would have sat there all night without moving if my boat had not touched the shore. Come, now, get in and let's take a last little row."

He said this with such an almost hopeless tone that she assented without a word of objection, and soon they were gently moving along in the shadows close by the shore. "Stop rowing," she soon said, "this is too beautiful to disturb. The glassy surface of the water and the stillness protest in the strongest possible way at even the slight disturbance we make." He rested on his oars and both gazed for a while in silence and apparently in full sympathy with the scene.

"But yet," he finally said, "this is an unnatural condition and cannot and ought not to last long. The true and best condition of life is one of effort, mutual effort. Notice how the little waves we make go in pairs out into the moonlight in ever widening circles, one just behind and close to another, and see how much brighter and more beautiful the path they make than the previous glassy surface they have broken in upon."

"Quite a poetic idea," she replied, as if for the first time aroused from a lethargy and coming to her old self, "but I don't just like that idea of tagging along behind each other. It is too much like the Irish couples I see going to early mass in the city."

"O Alice, do be serious on this, the last evening you will be here," he quickly added in a tone as though hurt by her words.

"Pardon me, I should not have spoken so, I suppose. I do not wish to hurt your feelings. But come, we must go ashore, for I make an early start in the morning. It was imprudent in me to have gotten into the boat at all."

"Not till I have told you of my great love, and how necessary you are to my happiness. I came this evening determined to do so and must not, cannot, keep back the words which come to my lips. Only say you are not wholly indifferent to me and give me some hope that I may in the future win your love if I have not now." He spoke with great earnestness, dropping the oars and clasping his hands to emphasize his appeal.

She looked, as indeed she felt, greatly disturbed. "I am sorry for this," she finally said, "but I know I am partly responsible. I should not have given you the opportunity, but now that it has been said I will speak frankly. What you ask can never be. You can see clearly that I do not love you now and I am sure that I never could grow to do so. I am not blind, I have seen for some time that you thought you loved me, but I did not believe your feeling was so strong as your words show. I feel sure, however, that it is a temporary condition with you and will pass away as perhaps it has done before in your life. Come, we must go ashore." She spoke with such firmness and self-composure that he saw that further words were useless, and as if dazed prepared to comply with her wishes, but when he came to look for his oars he found that, as if typical of his experience, they had both floated out into the darkness beyond his reach, and he was compelled to make the best progress he could by using an old piece of board for a paddle.

The boat had hardly touched the shore when Alice jumped out and without a word ran up the steps of the cottage and into the house with mingled feelings of regret and satisfaction.

Jacob fastened his boat and started to walk home. Perhaps he remembered that evening a little more than a year ago when the brilliantly decorated campus spoke to him so eloquently of his bright prospects, while now the dark shadows from the sinking moon, and the obscure path before him suggested his baffled endeavors and uncertain future. He passed through the Shanlys' pasture and down by their house. Just as he was passing it he stopped suddenly. "What did she mean by saying I had possibly passed through such a condition before ? Could she in any way have heard of Ellen Wallis ? If she had, you told her," and he shook his fist angrily in the direction of the house. Of course the inherent absurdity of that idea came at once to his mind and he continued his progress home.

Sometime in the middle of the next forenoon his mother found him in the office busy apparently in the study of a law book. "Why, Jacob," she said, "you ought not to stick so close to these dry books. I know you said good-bye to Alice last night, but I supposed of course you would want to go to the train and see her off this morning. Remember what you once wrote me from college, one gets some of the most important parts of his education from other sources than books." He turned impatiently in his chair and made no reply, but he agreed with her, just the same.

A SMOKE TALK IN No. 7

CLARENCE B. BURLEIGH, '87

A SMOKE TALK IN NO. 7

L ON Remick was standing before the mirror in the bedroom of his apartments at No. 7, preparing himself for the closing German in Lemont hall. His roommate, Cal Burke, who "hated functions," lounged in the doorway and watched the operation with languid interest. He was evidently in a nagging spirit that evening, and his somewhat personal comments did not tend to impart an atmosphere of serenity to the occasion.

"Well, you do look scrumptious, old man," he said. 'How purple and fine linen do become you—and the girls, what one of them could resist you ? My blessings go with you, my boy, and be sure you bring home all your favors. I'm planning to work out our society letters with them and hang them over this doorway."

"You may have all I get, and welcome, if you'll only help me on with this confounded collar. I'm late now," responded Lon impatiently.

Cal took up the collar and looked at it with a quizzical smile. It was in the fleeting and somewhat exaggerated style of the time, with points that began to turn back from under the ears, and tips that rested well down upon the shoulder blades.

"Great Cæsar's ghost ! where did you get that ?" he demanded.

"Why, that's the latest thing. Haven't you seen them yet?"

"Certainly, my boy. There's nothing new about them. My great-grandfather wouldn't wear anything else. The last one I particularly noticed adorned the end man in a minstrel show. Alas for the duplicity that would prey upon bucolic innocence! I plainly see that the good name of this room makes it my solemn duty to go out and kill someone—and who sold it to you ?"

"Oh, come off, old man," laughed Remick. "Be serious for once in your life, if you can. Now tell me, honest injun, what do you think of it ?" and he frankly lifted a somewhat perplexed face to his room-mate, who,

171

having buttoned the collar in place, had stepped back a few paces, and was viewing it with a simulated dignity of criticism that was belied by twinkling eyes and twitching mouth corners.

Remick's face flushed. "You don't like it," he said uneasily. "Why don't you say it ? You think it looks like the—"

"Easy, old man," interrupted Burke. "I haven't objected to it in the least. I am dazzled but not overcome. Verily I say to you, my boy, that in my humble opinion Solomon in all his glory never had an outfit like that. Is there anything more I can do for you ?"

"No, thanks. I'll excuse you now," said Remick, a little stiffly. "I see you are in one of your humorous moods tonight."

"Never more serious in my life," said Burke with mock solemnity, as he retired to the study room so quietly that Remick, who was once more viewing himself in the mirror, failed to note his departure.

"I swear, I'm a good mind not to wear it—Why—er—hullo, Pegs !"

Remick turned to meet the smiling face of "Pegs" Derrill, who stood in the doorway his room-mate had just vacated. His presence on this particular occasion was not altogether welcome, and made Remick feel decidedly uncomfortable.

Pegs looked him over slowly with critical gravity until his eye rested upon the collar, then stuffing his handkerchief into his mouth to stifle a giggle, turned abruptly back into the study room.

"Confound his impudence," muttered Remick between his teeth. "I'll make him eat dog some day to pay for that." He turned to complete his toilet ; but not in peace. Pegs was the first of a procession which filed into the study, one by one, paused by the bedroom door to bestow an appreciative smile upon Remick's new collar, and then grouped themselves in lounging attitudes about the open fire in an interchange of college opinions and anecdotes.

No word was spoken to Remick ; but he was by no means insensible to the pantomime of which he was the victim. The big collar was securely in place ; but the boy who a little later bore it in frigid dignity among the grinning group in the study was decidedly "off his moorings." He drew himself up proudly, faced his tormentors with a flushed countenance, and addressed them with chilling formality.

"Really, gentlemen, so unimportant a person as myself is scarcely worthy of all this attention," he said. "I certainly regret the trouble I have evidently put you to. If you will kindly complete your inspection, and pass your criticisms, I will bid you good night."

"What's the matter with Lon ?" demanded Burke.

"He's all right," was the chorused response, accompanied with a pedal emphasis that shook the blower from the standard grate, and made the bric-a-brac rattle upon the mantel and desk tops.

"Thanks," said Remick with sarcastic brevity. "Come !" he added, in a louder tone, in answer to a knock from the hallway. The door opened to admit the bulky form and good-natured face of Cutty Norton, the college catcher.

"Anything private ?" he asked as his eye rested upon the group.

"No," said Burke, "only an End mass meeting. Lon is going to represent us at the German tonight—and we wanted to make sure that he was in good form. Now look him over, with your usual good taste, and see if he isn't a credit to his class and delegation."

"Our sacred honor couldn't be in better keeping," smiled Cutty. "By the way, Lon, I just came from Stetson's store and left the proprietor reading the riot act to that French clerk of his. It seems that you had inquired for something new in collars. The boy knew there were none in stock ; but he remembered having seen a box of that description among the attic archives—and so he dug it out and sold you one. You see the present style is a renaissance ; all the go thirty years ago. A little accentuated—that's all. Stetson is awfully cut up over it ; says if you'll return the collar he'll refund your money."

A roar of laughter greeted this announcement.

"Very well done, indeed," sneered Remick coldly, as he drew on his gloves. "I presume this is the climax. Bah ! this is certainly edifying. However, I am glad if I have been able to contribute in ever so humble a way to your entertainment, gentlemen."

"I really don't know what you're talking about," said Cutty blankly, as he looked about him in evident amazement. "What I have told you is a fact."

The big catcher was no actor, and it was apparent to all that he spoke the truth.

Without a word Remick returned to the bedroom and tore off the offending collar. When he had arrayed himself in one less pronounced, he came back into the study and laid a box of cigars upon the center table. Then turning his back upon the smiling group, whose members forebore further comment, he passed out into the hallway, slamming the door behind him with an emphasis that voiced his chagrin more eloquently than words.

"Phew ! Lon's just a trifle hot," laughed Cal when he was gone. "Do you know, fellows, I never once suspected but what that collar was strictly a la mode. It generally takes about two or three months, you know, for a new style to make its way from Boston to Brunswick."

"I couldn't imagine what I'd run into," said Cutty. "I didn't know you'd been stringing him."

"It was quite impromptu. That collar was irresistible. I gave Pegs the tip and he passed the word to the boys in the End ; but did you get on to the look in Lon's face when he saw that Cutty was giving it to him straight ? It was a little rough on the old boy, but I owe him one for the way he let me down last week."

"How was that ?" asked Cutty, scenting a story.

"Yes, let's have it, old man," came from several other members of the group.

"Well, before I get to that, permit me"—and Cal gravely passed around the box of cigars. "I won't vouch for the quality of these," he said. "Lon bought them of a Jew peddler the other day; gave him nearly twenty-five dollars worth of second-hand clothing for them. I haven't seen my mackintosh, either, since the deal ; but he swears by all that's good and holy that it wasn't included in it."

"Speaking of Jew peddlers," drawled Pod Bennett as he blew a ring of smoke from his freshly lighted cigar and lazily watched it curl towards the ceiling, "you've had some recent experience with that fraternity, haven't you, Pegs ?"

"How did you know about that ?"

"Oh, the fellows are all on to it. You might as well make a clean breast of it here in the bosom of the family."

"What is it, old man ?" "let's have it !" "fire away"—came simultaneously from different members of the group.

"Why, there isn't much to it," said Pegs slowly. "One of them sold me a rug the other day ; said it was a handsome Smyrna, and a bargain at twenty-five dollars. I let him have all the old clothing I'd accumulated during the course for it—and you know I had a choice and varied collection. While he was still doing the End I had occasion to go down town, and saw one of those very rugs in Stetson's window marked a dollar and ninety-five cents."

"Probably a cheap imitation of your valuable original," said Dan Pickett soothingly.

"It would have been comforting if I could have believed so ; but a close examination convinced me that it was of the same vintage."

" 'Vintage' is good," laughed Rex Brown approvingly.

"Silence, trifler," ordered "Judge" Ransom with mock solemnity. "Let the brother state his experience. Confession expandeth the soul."

"Well, I was a little warm," continued Pegs, ignoring the interruption, "and I came back to the End determined to have those clothes back or take satisfaction out of the fellow's hide; but I was too late."

"Had the bird flown ?" asked Shorty Dixon.

"No, but the clothes had. I set out to thump the rascal once for luck, but what do you suppose he did ?"

"Settled in cash," ventured Punk Davis.

"Rats !" was Peg's sententious comment. "He backed up in a corner of the room and stood me off with a knife. He protested that he had told me nothing but 'der blain druth and that my rug was 'vell vorth efery tollar it gost me, so hellup him hemill.' "

"Why, didn't you get some of the fellows together and rush him ?" asked Cal.

"Why, I didn't consider the game worth the candle. I presume he was bluffing. Still I thought it was best not to take any chances. A man must expect to pay something, you know, for a college education."

"And didn't you get back at him at all ?" sighed Cutty regretfully.

175

"Yes, in a way. I managed, with the help of the fellows, to get about a tub of water onto him when he left the End. Of course it didn't bring back the clothes, but still I slept better for it."

"There are many things in a college course that are not dreamed of in the curriculum," said the Judge wisely.

"True for you, Sir Oracle," assented Rex, "but why all this digression? If I remember correctly, Cal was booked to tell us why he had it in for Lon tonight."

"Oh, there isn't much to that," said Cal. "I had a visit last week from a great-aunt of mine. She was on her way to Boston, and had planned to leave her son, a boy of about fourteen years of age, with me during the week of her visit there. The old lady is a Puritan of the ancient type ; but she has always credited me with habits of sobriety and a trustworthy character."

"She probably knew you best when you were younger," interposed Pod.

Broad grins greeted this sally ; but Cal was in nowise disconcerted.

"Of course I gave her a warm welcome," he continued, with a deprecatory shrug of the shoulders, "and tried to make her feel at home. I could see, however, that she was impressed with the idea that Satan finds a large amount of work to do in a college community. She frankly told me that she had been somewhat loath to leave her young hopeful amid the snares and pitfalls of such a place. I was protesting that he would be perfectly safe in my care ; that I would watch over him as the apple of my eye, when I heard Lon calling me from the upper floor. I opened the door into the hallway. 'What's wanted ?' I asked.

" 'Is that jug there ?'

" 'What jug ?'

" 'Why, you know, that punch.'

"You better believe I was hot. 'What are you talking about ?' I shouted angrily, 'You know very well there's never been any punch here.' "

"What did he say to that ?" asked Shorty.

"The rascal ! He laughed a skeptical laugh and said, 'Is it possible you've drank it all ? I thought you agreed to save it for our next poker game.' "

"You ought to have gone gunning for him," grinned Punk. "What did the old lady, say ?"

"Well, she didn't say much, but she looked volumes. In vain I protested that it was all a joke. The foundations of her faith were started. She said she hoped I was still a good boy, but I saw very plainly that she had her serious doubts about it. When she left for Boston, an hour or so later, she took her son with her."

"Well, that was a roast, for a fact," said Punk ; "but I guess you've squared the account. Wake up there, Pod !" he added in louder tones to Bennett, who was dozing on the sofa. "What's the matter with you ? Seems to me you don't appreciate good society."

"Oh, my appreciation's all right," said Pod, rousing himself to a sitting posture ; "but those riotous Sophomores kept me awake about half the night. Didn't you know about that ?"

"No, what was it ?"

"Why, it seems they had a pig yarded somewhere, and about midnight they towed him over to Memorial hall and put him into the Greek recitation room. I could hear him squealing all the way across the campus. It's a wonder they didn't wake up the whole college."

"A childish prank forsooth, and what said the Bird this morning ?"

"Oh, he got back on the boys all right. 'I see, gentlemen,' he remarked blandly, when they were called to order, 'that a new member has joined you, and I trust he will be able to make as good a showing as some of his classmates.' They didn't lose much time in turning him out after that."

"Who, the Bird ?"

"No, child, the pig. Somehow the Sophs haven't seemed disposed to say much about the matter since."

"Discussion isn't always valuable," said Cal wisely. "Do you remember the time we smoked out Freshie Fenlason ?"

"Well, I am sure that was a success," said Pegs.

"Yes, in a way, but I've often wondered who was the sickest that night—we or the Freshman."

"I am convinced, fellows," announced the Judge with decision, "that there are many forms of amusement that yield a larger and more satisfactory return on the investment. By the way, Cal, here we are well into the spring term of Junior year, and, if my memory serves me right, that whiskers committee of which you were chairman in our callow Sophomore days has never yet made its report."

"Be careful of your adjectives, my friend. 'Callow' belongs exclusively to Freshmen. Didn't you ever hear how that matter came out?"

"Never. I knew that you and Pod and Stout Wilson were appointed a committee of three with authority to remove all hirsute appendages from the cheeks of Freshman Bemis. He left college after that last ducking we gave him, and you have never had anything to say about your part of the program."   "Was there really a sequel ?" asked Cutty.

"There was, my boy ; but 'tell it not in Gath ; publish it not in the streets of Askelon.' "

"We're mum ; let's have it," said Rex.

"Well, we watched for a good opportunity to carry out our mission, and a rainy night, soon after, seemed to furnish it, especially as we learned that Bemis had gone for a call on a lady friend after supper. We were provided with scissors, ropes, black cambric masks, a dark lantern, about all the paraphernalia, in fact, that up-to-date highwaymen are supposed to carry. We kept well out of sight on the east side of South Winthrop, where Bemis roomed, and waited patiently for him to put in an appearance. Finally Pegs, who was doing sentry duty, reported that he was coming. Just as he reached the doorway, we closed in on him. By the shades of old Phi Chi ! I never dreamed the fellow could put up such a fight. I had my handkerchief in his mouth, and as it was about all I could do to keep it there, the laboring oar fell to Pod and Stout. I won't go into details of the scrap. All of us were pretty well winded, but still retained some clothing when we finally got him tied up."

"What did you do with him then ?" asked Dan, who, like the rest, was following the narrative with deep interest.

THE INTERIOR OF THE CHAPEL.

"We lugged him down into the pines and flashed a lantern on him, and who do you suppose he turned out to be?"

"Why, Bemis, of course," said Shorty.

"Bemis ? Not a bit of it. He was Arthburton of the Junior class."

A whistle of surprise came from the group.

"Well, you were in for it for a fact," said the Judge. "What did you do?" asked Punk.

"Well, I cut the ropes and took my handkerchief out of his mouth for the first thing."

"To give the oaths a chance, I suppose," ventured Rex.

"Not at all ; that's the surprising thing about it, wasn't it, Pod?"

"You could have knocked me down with a feather," answered Pod. "I never saw a fellow take a thing so coolly in my life."

"And what did he remark ?" asked Cutty.

"Why, he just laughed and said very quietly, 'Got the wrong pig by the ear this time, didn't you ?' "

"What answer did you make ?"

"Oh, I took up the burden of the song right there," said Cal. "You should have heard my humble and eloquent apology."

"It was a gem," assented Pod.

"How did he take it ?" asked Dan.

"In a most unexpected way," said Cal. "We were banking on our disguises to conceal our identity ; but they didn't amount to shucks. When I had done my best to explain things, he remarked with a dry chuckle, 'Don't say another word, Burke, I'm just as much ashamed of it as you are. If you don't give it away, I'm sure I shall not'—and this is the first time I ever have ; but, of course," he added, "this will go no further."

"It shall rest secure, old man, in the honor of the smoke circle," said the Judge.

"So say we all of us," was the comment of the group.

"By the way, Punk," said Cal, "what sinister motive had you in beguiling that little yellow dog into the club this noon?"

"Didn't you see the whole of that ?"

"No, I was just leaving as you were coming through the pines."

"Well, it was all for Dave Herrick's benefit ?"

"Haven't you got through nagging him yet ?"

"I've sworn off many times," said Punk regretfully, "but while the spirit is willing the flesh is weak. I hope when Dave is finally settled over some thriving church he will never be called upon to deal with backsliders like me."

"Well, that's all interesting, but indefinite," said Shorty impatiently. "Now perhaps you will condescend to tell us what possible bearing a dog can have upon Brother Herrick, and his theological aspirations."

"It's a trial of faith for him," smiled Punk. "Didn't you know what a strong aversion he has to the canine race ? I assure you it's a passion with him. Now, yesterday I enticed a friendly dog into the club, and made him happy with a juicy bone behind Dave's chair. Everything went along nicely until Herrick happened to discover him. Then there was trouble."

"What did our embryo minister do then ?" asked Cutty.

"He rose from the table with stately dignity and stalked from the room, as mad as a wet hen. 'Pon my word, he didn't eat another mouthful after he spied that dog. Just think of that for Christian charity !"

"That's worse than the mice," said Pegs.

"What of them ?" grinned Dan.

"Why, you know they got to holding carnival in Punk's coal closet on the crackers and cheese he keeps there for banquet purposes."

"Free lunch for members of the smoke circle, you mean," interposed Punk.

"Genuine luxury for the rest of us when we come to count the cost," said the Judge, "for, of course, we couldn't with self respect think of a return in kind."

"That's it," assented Rex. "Now the last time Punk dined with me I fed him on cold turkey."

"And I always suspected that it cost you less than my more humble but wholly, honest fare," laughed Punk.

"Beware of personalities !" said Cal. "It is never wise to be reckless with the truth. What about the mice, Pegs ?"

"Well, you see, Punk got tired of them after a while, and made Nipper Smith's heart glad by buying a mousetrap of him. The first night he had it set he caught three, and what do you suppose he did with them.

"Turned them over to Pinkie as a new food product."

"No, he went into Herrick's room and dropped one in each of the side pockets of his reefer. The third one he put in the pocket of his study jacket. When Dave started for the club that morning, he felt for his gloves. They were fur trimmed, and he was so busy talking that he didn't notice anything wrong until he held out the mouse in the palm of his hand. I wish you could have seen his eyes stick out, and heard the yell he gave. Talk about jumping Frenchmen ! They simply wouldn't have been in it. We were about half way through the pines when he dropped on to the second one, and he made another jump, not quite so high as the first, but still sufficiently so to have landed him a winner in the field day contests. 'Blast those boys !' he said. It was the nearest I ever heard Dave come to swearing. 'I believe they've filled every pocket in my coat with dead mice.' Then he made a very careful search of the garment before he was fully satisfied that he had seen the last of them. I strolled into his room after dinner to see him don that rainbow jacket of his, and settle into that big easy chair before the grate. It's funny how a man can enjoy hibernating that way ; but there's no accounting for tastes."

"No, I don't think, Pegs, that you are constituted just right to fully apreciate a dig" smiled Cal, "but go on. How did Dave perform when he found that third mouse ?"
perform when he found that third mouse ?"

"He was busy boning out his Psychology when he finally felt it, and the jump he gave landed him about half way across the floor. He looked at me with sudden suspicion. 'Did you put that mouse there ?' he demanded.

" 'Certainly not,' I answered with injured dignity. 'What have I ever done that you should insult me with such a suspicion ?'

" 'I sincerely beg your pardon, Derrill,' he said. 'This is the third one I've found in my pockets today, and the joke is getting a trifle monotonous.' 'I didn't notice anything monotonous in your movements just now,' I answered. 'I'm going to make an end of it,' he said with decision, and thereupon he made a most careful search of his room. Not a place big enough to hide a grasshopper was overlooked."

"And you ?" interposed Punk.

"Me ? Oh, I waited 'round till he was doing the bedroom, then fished the last mouse he had discovered from the corner of the grate where he had thrown it, dropped it into his reefer pocket, and came home."

The group laughed its approval of the narrative.

"Dave discovered that mouse the next morning," added Punk, "and now he lays the whole thing to Pegs. It is fortunate, however, for me, for it has done much to reinstate me in his good graces."

Cutty rose and stretched himself with a yawn.

"Where are you going, early bird ?" asked Dan.

"My fire is out, and I am under the painful necessity of appropriating a section of the attic floor."

"I'll hold the light for you if you'll cut up some for me while you're about it."

"Thanks, my lord ! Your self-sacrificing spirit touches me deeply."

"You might make a bee of it, Cutty," said the Judge gravely. "The rest of us will take hold with you, and do the heavy looking on."

"In the words of the late lamented Artemus Ward, 'This is too much, too much.' On the whole I think we had better work the thing on shares— each one his own share. Cal can come in on the average repairs. Good night, old man."

"Good night," chorused the others as they followed Cutty into the hall.

"So long, fellows," answered Cal as the door closed upon his departing guests.

"A little nonsense now and then, is relished by the wisest men," murmured Burke as alone with himself he turned to the window and stood, absorbed in his own reflections, looking out upon the campus. The mellow light of the new moon lent a magic charm to the scene. Never had it appeared more beautiful to Cal than at this moment when nature awakened from its Winter's sleep by the warm touch of Spring was budding forth in the fullness and perfection of life. The incense of opening buds and blossoms was in the softened air, and even the strident notes of the crickets had a music and an inspiration. He was aroused from his reverie by the distant singing of a party of students roistering homeward from a supper at "The Midnight."

"Should auld acquaintance be forgot,
And never brought to mind ?
Should auld acquaintance be forgot,
And days of auld lang syne."

The clear young voices came very distinctly upon the evening air, and a shadow crossed the listener's face. Alas ! how soon this happy life with its pleasant associations and inspiring opportunities must pass away !

With a sigh Burke turned to his desk and was soon absorbed in the morrow's lessons. His room-mate, returning from the German at two o'clock in the morning, flushed and happy in the consciousness of a social success, found him still busy with his tasks.

"Hard at it, old man ?" he called cheerily.

Burke rose a little wearily, and rested a hand lightly upon his room-mate's shoulder. "Welcome home, my boy," he said. "I see this has been your night."

Interchanges of sentiment never found expression in words between these two. They would have looked upon them as weak and effeminate ; but each knew and understood the other.

"Yes, it was a success," said Remick.

"And you won't mind my little pleasantry of the early evening ?" continued the other.

Remick smiled happily, and there was a world of affectionate good-fellowship in the warm clasp he gave the outstretched hand of his friend, as he answered heartily, "Don't mention it, old man."

HOW TRIANGLE WON

THOMAS LITTLEFIELD MARBLE, '98

HOW TRIANGLE WON

A GROUP of undergraduates stood before the Chapel bulletin-board reading the annual announcement that the celebrated race horse, Triangle, 2.14½, owned by Bowdoin's well known professor of Mathematics, would start in the free-for-all at the coming Topsham Fair, and that those students who so desired might obtain complimentary tickets for the event at the Library.

"They say the old horse is in the pink of condition," remarked one of the group.

"It's true," replied Ted Copley, a Sophomore of sporting proclivities. "I saw him step the last quarter of a workout mile yesterday at a 'ten clip. I was more interested than usual because we have entered a horse from the Farm this year which father has promised to let me drive—just for Sophomoric glory, you know—and I should hate like the deuce to be beaten by a razor-backed skate like Triangle."

" 'Razor-backed' is good," laughed a tall Junior. "The old horse is well named—he looks like a triangle."

"Yes, he is a trifle angular," declared another, "but it isn't surprising, for he feeds on logarithms, I understand."

Tony Davenport, a Freshman for whose edification the above conversation had taken place, turned from the bulletin-board with a smile of derision.

"You fellows must think I'm easy," said he.

"Oh, this is no jolly," exclaimed Ted Copley, with an air of injured innocence.

"Look here, Ted," interrupted Tony, "you know just as well as I do that there isn't a horse in the State by the name of Triangle with a mark of 'fourteen and a half."

"Ho, ho, Fresh !" Ted ejaculated. "We know a great deal, don't we ?" Then turning to the bystanders, "Gentlemen, this is Mr. Tony Davenport of the Mazeppa Stock Farm ; you will find Mr. Davenport an authority on all kinds of horses from quadrupeds to interlinears."

Tony joined in the laugh which this speech occasioned, then, leaving the group, strolled leisurely toward the End—leisurely, I repeat, despite the fact that a bag of water hurled by some vigilant Sophomore from a dormitory window fell at his feet with a thud and a splash. But the first few weeks of college life had inured Tony to the tribulations of Freshman year, and, though oftentimes inwardly raging, he submitted to the thousand and one annoyances that Freshman flesh is heir to with a calm exterior and a tantalizing smile.

Several days later there appeared in the local columns of the Orient the following item :

"It is rumored that the owner of Triangle will be unable to drive his favorite at the Topsham Fair this season, and that Tony Davenport of the Freshman class will handle the ribbons in his stead. Young Mr. Davenport is a worthy scion of the well known horseman, Woodbury Davenport, proprietor of the Mazeppa Stock Farm, and this fact alone is sufficient guarantee of his ability as a reinsman."

Apparently no one was more amused at this paragraph than Tony, yet all the while he was longing for an opportunity to turn the tables on his friends, the Sophomores. It was the Orient item itself which at length suggested to him the means of accomplishing his wish ; but the means so suggested required the approval and co-operation of Tony's father.

" 'Hoc opus, hic labor est,' " quoted Tony, who still remembered his Virgil, "which being freely translated means, 'That's the devil of it.' "

Yet Mr. Davenport was so indulgent a father that Tony did not entirely despair of success.

About a week before the opening of the Topsham Fair, Mr. Davenport received from his son a letter couched in the most persuasive terms. The letter began by explaining the custom among Bowdoin Sophomores of issuing each fall a poster advertising the appearance at the Topsham Fair of the horse, Triangle, said to be owned by the professor of Mathematics. "Of course," wrote Tony, "no such horse exists, and the poster is printed simply in the hope that some gullible Freshman will ask at the Library or treasurer's office for tickets to the Fair grounds the day

Triangle trots,—tickets which the poster asserts may be obtained free of charge. This year, however, it is claimed that Triangle will be driven by no less a person than your dutiful son, as the enclosed clipping will bear witness. Now, father dear," (Tony was nothing if not diplomatic) "what I am coming at is this: the bay colt, which you intend to start in the big stake races next season, has never been registered, and is consequently without a name. Why can't you enter him under the name of Triangle in the free-for-all at Topsham, and let me drive him ? I know it is asking a good deal, but if the colt is fast enough to win the race—and I think he is—he will certainly be a good horse in his class another season. If he doesn't win, he is still eligible for the stake races, and no harm has been done. Should you care to enter any of the other horses, the purses at Topsham are large enough to make it worth while." Then came the climax. "The Copley Farm will send a string of horses, and Ted Copley, wearing the Sophomore colors, expects to drive Cristo. If I could beat him, I should be the happiest Freshman in Brunswick."

To make the story brief, Mr. Davenport proved responsive to his son's wishes. Consequently, the printed list of entries for the Sagadahoc County Fair that season contained the names of Triangle and Cristo, entered by the great rival training stables, the Mazeppa and the Copley Farms. At first the college looked upon the matter as part and parcel of the venerable "Triangle" joke, but the arrival of a handsome bay colt, in charge of grooms from the Mazeppa Farm, at the Topsham Fair grounds one morning set the little college world agog, and the truth was soon apparent. Unbeknown to their wily rivals, the Freshmen held a meeting to select class colors, which Tony was authorized to wear in the coming contest. Then, with unconcealed eagerness, all awaited the opening of the Fair.

The eventful day came at last, and never did the Manufacturer of Weather present a finer sample of his handiwork. In the ruddy glow of October, dear old Bowdoin seemed most literally to possess the "dignity of age without its infirmities." Above the tops of Brunswick's famous "groves of pine" rose the sun, clear and bright, to gladden the heart of many an anxious student ; for "adjourns" had been granted, and an adjourn without sunshine is salt without its savor. Whiter than ever gleamed the "foam on Androscoggin's falls," while on the heights above, sentinel-like, stood the old red stand-pipe, lending a dash of color to the somber hues of the distant landscape. So calm and peaceful was the day that it seemed a sacrilege to rouse sedate old Topsham from her proverbial sleep.

Early in the afternoon, large numbers of students flocked to the Fair grounds, where the Sophomores, more jubilant than the rest, were strikingly conspicuous. Here divers 'Varsity ball players essayed their skill in "hitting the nigger's head" ; there a group of upperclassmen could be seen, chatting merrily with a galaxy of the fair sex from the Shipping City,—everywhere, that boisterous *abandon* so characteristic of the Topsham Fair. The commanding voice of the marshal "calling up" the free-for-all sent each group with a common impulse to the grand stand.

The horses were out when Tony, cool and collected, received from old John Maguire, the driver of the Farm, the whip with which John had urged so many gallant racers to victory. The talent had picked Cristo and Triangle as probable winners, for if the future can be predicted from the past, it was extremely unlikely that either the Copley or the Mazeppa Farm would start a horse without fair chances of success. But the drivers of the favorites were inexperienced college youths, and in that fact lay the hopes of the less speedy contestants.

Tony regarded it as a good omen that he should draw the last position, for old John had cautioned him against setting the pace, and had advised him to trail the field if possible. Starting in this position made it far easier to follow John's instructions. With a parting nod to his father, who occupied a seat of honor in the judges' stand, Tony mounted the sulky and jogged Triangle slowly up the stretch. By this time Tony's self-possession had deserted him, he was trembling violently, and his heart fairly leaped with fright. He was dimly conscious that the horses were turning, and that Cristo was next the pole. Triangle, whose education had been thorough, swung into line with little guidance, and the race was on. Twice the harsh jangling of the starter's bell called the horses back, and with each delay Tony's nervousness increased. For the third time they turned at the flag, as the starter's voice came to them through the megaphone : "Turn slowly ! Take back to the pole horse ! Take back ! Go!"

The whir of pneumatic tires, the pounding of horses' hoofs on the hard day of the track, a rushing sound like the roar of a cataract, and the great field of horses swept by the grand stand. The pace was terrific. It seemed to Tony that some invisible yet relentless force was dragging him to destruction. His breath came in convulsive gasps, and he felt so faint and dizzy that it required a supreme effort of will to keep his seat. The reins, which till now he had grasped mechanically, slipped through his fingers the fraction of an inch ; there was a sudden slackening of tension, then a violent tug. The colt, finding the pressure of the bit for the moment relaxed, missed his stride and broke. But Tony's was a character which adversity strengthens, and instead of cursing the fate which had unnerved him in this crisis, he set about to repair the mischief he had wrought. A strong breeze blowing down the back stretch cleared his brain and steadied his nerve. A firm, even pull on the bit brought the colt to a square trot, and then in spite of old John's advice not to do any "grand stand teaming," but to limit his horizon to his horse's ears, Tony coolly surveyed the field. Close behind him an erratic gray gelding was duplicating Triangle's performance, while the other horses were some lengths in front, closely bunched.

With the mechanism of perfect machinery, Triangle moved forward, and at the turn had lessened quite perceptibly the distance between himself and the leaders. Meantime, Ted was contenting himself with second position, while the chestnut mare, Rowena, led the procession with apparent ease. At the half, Triangle slipped into third place, and the cheers of Tony's classmates soon gave way to the Sophomore yell, as Cristo, with a brilliant burst of speed, took the pole from Rowena. Once headed, the little mare lost heart, and at the three-quarters mark yielded her place to Triangle. Cristo was now a good two lengths in the lead, and Tony realized that the decisive moment had come. Slowly and without lessening the pressure of the bit, he transferred the reins to his left hand and reached for the whip. The colt responded nobly, and as they swung into the stretch, was close to Cristo's sulky wheel. Again the whip descended, and again the speed increased. Inch by inch Triangle crept upon his rival. Neck and neck they swept down the stretch with the wire scarce twenty yards ahead. Neither had the advantage now, and the least mistake would prove fatal. Ted knew that an increase of pace, however slight, would win the day. Cristo had always finished with a rush. Could he be relied on now ? Ted thought so. Thrice the whip lashed Cristo's flank, but the noble horse had reached his limit. Tony saw the striped nose tossed high in the air, and realized with savage joy that Ted had forced his horse to a break. The next instant, Triangle shot under the wire, the winner of the heat.

It was the crucial test. There coursed through Triangle's veins the blood of countless race horses with not a single "quitter" in the list. True to his illustrious ancestry, he proved unfaltering in the successive heats, and passed the wire for the last time amid the plaudits of a host of admirers.

As for Tony, no words can describe his excessive happiness, for the Sophomore champion had been defeated, and Triangle was no longer a fiction.

After the race the Freshmen chartered an electric, and rode back to Brunswick singing "Phi Chi." The Sophomores held them in Chapel the next morning, to be sure, but in view of their recent victory, even that humiliation seemed slight.

AT THE ALTAR OF TRADITION

GEORGE BRINTON CHANDLER, '90

AT THE ALTAR OF TRADITION

W E are all more or less Pharisees. We like to indulge in wise head-shakings over things forbidden, while outlaw memories still linger in the recesses of our affections and give the lie to our grave and ceremonious faces. The same bald-headed drove of parsons, doctors, and lawyers who always declaim virtuously against the latest hazing outrage, may be seen congregated in little knots about the campus each Commencement, swapping yarns (that have not lost incident and color with time) and making the welkin ring with bursts of unholy laughter. The time they shaved Watkins' head and proclaimed him "the only and original human billiard ball," or the night the Green boys were put through the shirt-tail drill, comes back to them from the fugitive past with all the flavor and zest of youth. And when at Commencement dinner the band strikes up old "Phi Chi," lo Ben Adhem's voice leads all the rest !

Hazing is passing away. It had to. The inexorable tribunal of public sentiment, which possesses the power to grant or withhold students and funds, has declared against it. So has Congress. It often crushed timid spirits. Occasionally it broke them. On the other hand it gave many bumptious youths their first genuine taste of the wholesome truth, that he who runs counter to established usages must be bruised. It is also a drastic application of the law of the survival of the fittest. It either exterminates or develops. Of the number of lights it has put out we have no means of telling ; neither can we know how many may have been trimmed and fed by it. But certain it is that the generations of Englishmen who fagged and were fagged, and the generations of young Americans who hazed and were hazed, have small need to apologize for the part they have borne in the strife and stress of a splendid century. Though the old custom be an evil, perhaps it has not been an unmixed one. But all this is apart from the question. We need not haggle about it now. Football and the more rugged

197

athletic sports have come to take its place and perform more rationally and efficiently the same saving part.

In Bowdoin College the two Greek letters, Φ X, usually accompanied by skull and crossbones, have long stood as the peculiar symbol of hazing. Phi Chi (pronounced with a long *i* according to the old method) formerly was used to designate a Sophomore secret society which lived and flourished throughout the 'sixties and 'seventies, and maintained an intermittent warfare with society in general and the Faculty in particular, until finally it came into collision with the principles of latter-day civilization and was wiped out of existence. But, like old John Brown of Ossawattomie, its soul goes marching on. Its purpose and intent was to maintain the functions and ideals of orthodox sophomority, and to harry and chastise obstreperous Freshmen. Within its limitations, it was tremendously efficient. The words "Phi Chi" have become historic. With their ominous and sepulchral accompaniment, they have carried terror to the hearts of many succeeding classes, and long after the society as an organization had ceased to exist they remained the audible rallying cry and visible badge of that rude justice whereby the sons of the Puritans held fast the landmarks of special privilege. They represent the worship of precedent and the rule of conservatism. In this, at least, they may not have been wholly bad.

As might be well expected, so significant and valiant an institution was not without its characteristic song—old "Phi Chi," from the pen of E. P. Mitchell, '71, now the brilliant New York editor. From the battle hymn of a defunct society, it has arisen in the fullness of time to the dignity of a college epic, and has even been borrowed by some of our sister colleges which never knew Phi Chi and know nothing of its traditions. It is sung to the martial strains of "Marching Through Georgia ;" and, like "Dixie" in the South, it is the haunting refrain of a lost cause. It is in the mouths of all Sophomores and upperclassmen. It may be heard of Summer evenings, sung by groups of students on the campus ; it is the battle song of intercollegiate contests ; and in the long Winter evenings, when tasks are burdensome and time hangs heavy, it is a perpetual solace and inspiration. No Commencement dinner, no assembling of the sons in distant cities, is formal and complete without its stirring measures.

AT THE ALTAR OF TRADITION

PHI CHI.

There's a baby born to Bowdoin, boys,
    Way back in 'Sixty-four,
Who's thundered for admission
    At many a Freshman's door ;
And, thanks to God and — — —,
    She'll thunder evermore,
For Phi Chi's in her ancient glory !

CHORUS.

Hurrah ! Hurrah ! Hurrah, for old Phi Chi !
    Harrah ! Hurrah ! And may she never die !
While pluck beats luck, and the Prex. is stuck,
    And the Profs. are high and dry,
We will follow her to glory.

Swing out the brave old banner, boys ;
    The resurrection's come.
Swing out the horn of plenty,
    And the old ancestral drum.
Bring out the pondrous hewgaw,
    That has made Gomorrah hum ;
For Phi Chi's in her ancient glory.

CHORUS.

There are pails and there are windows,
    And there's water in the well ;
As the Freshman will discover
    If he tries to cut a swell.
Cold water for his diet,
    Till existence is a hell,
For Phi Chi's in her ancient glory.

CHORUS.

Bring forth the grinning skeleton,
    And close the coffin lid ;
And screw the Freshman in it,
    Till his infant form is hid.
For he must learn that he must do
    Precisely as he's bid ;
For Phi Chi's in her ancient glory.

CHORUS.

199

This indefinable combination of song and symbol stood, too, as the especial mark of emancipation from the servitude of Freshmandom. No member of the first year's class used to be permitted to give utterance to the words "Phi Chi" in the presence of an upperclassman. He might not print the symbols by chalk, pencil, pen, or any other means or implement whatsoever. Neither might he permit it to remain upon any of his impedimenta or belongings, if printed there by another person. Neither might he sing, hum, or give other musical utterance to, any bar or measure of the song of Phi Chi, or the air upon which it is based. The penalty for such offense is to be spoken of darkly and in secret places. The Freshman was supposed to emerge from his cocoon at the completion of his final examinations for the year, when he blossomed forth with silk hat and cane, and marched across the campus in a body prior to taking his departure for Portland ; where from time immemorial has been held the annual Freshman dinner. Such was the old dispensation. All of this came to be as much a part of the traditions of Bowdoin College as Longfellow, Hawthorne, Elijah Kellogg, Parker Cleaveland, the "Thorndike Oak," the "Whispering Pines" ; or Professor "Cosine" Smith's horse, "Triangle," and the famous gig with elliptical wheels.

When, therefore, upon one crisp morning in the Fall of 1888 a white banner, bearing jauntily the figures of the year of the Freshman class alongside the privileged letters of Phi Chi, was found floating from the pinnacle of the north spire of King's Chapel, there was panic and consternation in the ranks of the class of 'Ninety. Ancient prerogatives had been challenged, and the organic law of the institution had been rudely violated. It was the most daringly revolutionary act of undergraduate history. 'Ninety was loaded with ridicule and contumely. The upperclassmen hooted and jeered at us ; the Freshmen became perceptibly insubordinate ; the Faculty indulged in covert smiles and half-phrased innuendoes ; and, as if to add a final straw to our burden of perplexity and humiliation, the yaggers became all at once significantly insolent and aggressive. A general "yagger war" came near being precipitated by an attack made by them upon a foraging party of Sophomores, which was returning with a "set up" that had been

IN THE FALL OF 1888.

commandeered from Bill Field's on the account of some opulent and obnoxious Freshman.

It was undoubtedly the critical period of 'Ninety's history. Who could have been the culprit ? How had the daring offense been committed? If found, how should the offender be adequately punished ? And, finally, how should the haunting emblem be removed from the Chapel spire ? We were not long in finding a solution to the first of our problems in the continued absence from chapel exercises and recitations of a quiet, unobtrusive Freshman, whom a few of the Sophomores recalled by the name of "Cilley." John Cilley was at that time a ruddy-cheeked lad, under medium height, but with square shoulders, erect bearing and compact, muscular build. The circumstance that he wore spectacles may have given to the unobserving a first impression of effeminacy. Upon his own initiative and unassisted he had climbed hand-over-hand a distance of one hundred and twenty feet, by means of the lightning rod, and had fastened to the pinnacle of the spire the colors of his class. His continued absence from regular college exercises had been due to a fall of twenty or thirty feet from the rod to what was then the old Museum. His hands, also, had been lacerated from contact with the rod and staples. The feat had been performed in the night. It was the daring act of a resolute spirit. John Cilley subsequently came to be respected in Bowdoin College, even more for his ability as an oarsman and general athlete and for his high qualities as a student and man than he was at this time admired for his brave and spectacular achievement. When, a few years after his graduation, he was called out to the great Beyond, the young manhood of his generation sustained a grave and irreparable loss.

The discovery of the offender by no means simplified our problem. To exact physical punishment from an injured man would be an act of palpable cowardice, and by no means to be sustained by the sentiment of the college. To pass the matter over in silence would be the bald abrogation of a time-honored privilege. As as conservative middle course it was, therefore, decreed that Cilley should be levied upon for a class "set-up." He was, as we had ascertained, amply able to stand the expense ; and our visit would not work any bodily injury upon him. Under the circumstances the solution had seemed statesmanlike and the punishment mild. But in some way the upperclassmen got wind of our contemplated visit to young Cilley's apartment. Either they misunderstood the punishment to be administered, or else they had come to the conclusion that in this instance tradition must be violated and a sweeping exception made. When, upon the appointed evening, our class appeared at the entrance of South Winthrop, we found the entire Junior and Senior classes lined up in the darkness of the stairways with pails full of water ready summarily to quench our thirst for justice. An altercation ensued and hot words were passed. We retired to the Chapel for a council of war. A noisy, but by no means uninfluential, minority was for securing base ball bats and forcing a passage at the point of the bludgeon. As we afterward discovered, one member of the class was armed with a revolver. At length cooler heads and wiser councils prevailed and we withdrew from a contest in which we were outnumbered more than two to one, and in which our only chance for success lay in physical violence and ultimate disgrace. The other classes made light of our surrender but indulged in some ridicule on the following day. As a matter of fact, it had been a moment of grave danger to the good name of the college as well as to the personal safety of some of the students. The punishment of Cilley was dropped and never came up again.

The problem that still confronted the class was the removal of the defiant emblem, for throughout all of our deliberations and controversies "Φ X '91" had been waving undisturbed over the heads of the college. Several unsuccessful attempts were made by the more athletic spirits of the class to duplicate Cilley's feat. I believe Dr. Turner of Augusta conceived the ingenious plan of reaching the rod from the belfry and thereby shortening the route. But this was found upon investigation to be impracticable. Along with the rest of my classmates, I presume I gave the matter no small amount of study and speculation. At length a plan occurred to me by which, if the staples could be relied upon, the ascent seemed easy, practicable, and comparatively safe. That is, it required no marked degree of dexterity or endurance. Any young man with a steady nerve, who could climb a rope ladder a few feet, and then transfer his weight to another similar ladder, might readily carry it into execution. Two duplicate tackles were made, one of which may be described as follows : First, a light, strong pole was secured, long enough so that a man standing on a level with one of the staples might reach the staple above with it. (I think I used rakestales). This may be termed the "handle." Attached to the flattened side of one end of this handle was a strong iron hook, of such proportions as to grasp readily and securely the portion of the staples by which the lightning rod is fastened to the wall. The shank of the hook had to be made long enough to admit of its being bound securely to the wooden handle. If I were to attempt the ascent again, I would entrust this part of the mechanism to the blacksmith who made my hooks ; for, in spite of every precaution, one of the hooks worked loose from the handle before the descent had been completed. On the lower end of the shank of the hook was an eye. To this eye was attached a rope ladder, which in my device was merely a succession of clumsy loops, although my experience showed that a little care and ingenuity in its construction might have greatly facilitated the insertion of the toe in the loop above—a by no means easy process in the night. In addition to this there was attached to the upper, or hook end, of the tackle, an extra loop whereby it might be hung upon the forearm, thus leaving both hands disengaged.

The mode of ascent will be apparent from this description of "handle" and "ladder." I had simply to stand upon the ground and attach ladder No. I to the nearest staple ; next, to climb this ladder until, by reaching upward with the handle, ladder No. 2 could be attached to the second staple. I then transferred my weight to this second ladder, unhooked the first one from its place on the staple and hung it upon the forearm, and proceeded as before. The only difficulty to be encountered was in rounding the abrupt turn from the wall of the Chapel to the roof, but investigation had convinced me, what experience proved, that the staples are advantageously located for turning this angle. The chief strain was upon the ankles, which were found to ache considerably before the descent had been completed. I do not recall that there was any serious strain upon the hands or arms. In fact, were it not for the altitude, no one would consider the process a difficult one. Of course, when the preservation of one's existence is at stake, he is not inclined to forget the old precautions not to look down, nor to let his attention play him tricks.

The night selected for the trial was bright moonlight. Ernest Briggs, one of my classmates who died later in his college course, and Henry ("Bob") Hastings, also of the class of 'Ninety, stood upon the ground ready to gather up the *reliquiae* in case of accident. Some unknown person watched the proceedings from one of the hall-windows of South Maine, but for reasons best known to himself he kept our secret. He retired when Briggs approached the building. Aside from the trifling accident of the loosened hook, both ascent and descent were uneventful. Upon the roof of the Museum and upon the ridgepole of the Chapel, there was abundant opportunity for securing periods of rest. A small pyramid of granite surmounts the pinnacle of the spire, and the apparently insecure manner in which it is attached to the main frustum is calculated to send an uncanny chill down one's back, when the piece is grasped. Strapped upon my shoulders were the banner, "Φ X '90," which was speedily substituted for the hated rag of insurrection ; and a Phi Chi hat, that infallible emblem of sophomority, which was hung upon the tip of the lightning rod by means of a long stick. The latter was blown down in the early morning and picked up by Tom Burr, a prowling Freshman. It was subsequently stolen from him. In writing me recently from Ann Arbor, Michigan, where he is now located, Dr. Burr charged me openly with the theft, and demanded the restitution of the relic. As I had originally extracted it from the wardrobe of Lincoln Bodge of the Junior class, it may serve to prove an old proverb about the migratory habits of stolen goods.

There was the usual demonstration in front of the Chapel the next morning, and Cilley and I were compelled to join hands over the bloody chasm from the shoulders of our respective classes. Two or three times since the Fall of 1888 have students successfully performed the exploit. Tradition still holds her genial tyranny over the halls of old Bowdoin, and the generations continue to pass beneath its triumphal arches. The years change, but not the heart of youth.

> "A boy's will is the wind's will
> And the thoughts of youth are long, long thoughts."

INDIAN PUDDING

JOHN ALEXANDER PIERCE, '01

INDIAN PUDDING

I N accordance with the less mollified remains of Puritanism half a century ago, although supposedly not abhorrent to God, the chapel service in the young hours of the morning was peculiarly abhorrent to man. The reins of authority being held pretty tight also in other respects, in themselves seemed to suggest to the restive spirit that any slackening of their tension would be accompanied by sensations of unalloyed delight. To the freedom of the present time then, rather than to a lack of spirit, should be attributed the "decrease in romance" in student life ; there are fewer blockades and gauntlets to be run.

Miscellaneous regulations used to suggest miscellaneous infringements, but the early chapel was evidently one of the most grevious compulsions, for on cold winter mornings the clapper of the Chapel bell was so often missing that the college had learned to keep on hand a supply of tongues so that voice could be summarily restored to the bell.

When one pictures to himself the night aspect of the void and dark interior of the bell tower, a hundred and twenty feet tall, in which an ascent had to be made by scaling with a short ladder from successive beams and window niches, it it not hard to see how a student, in accomplishing this arduous feat to prevent a single chapel service, must have imagined himself to have been fired with the strongest altruistic principles. It was on the occasion of one Hallowe'en that the bell was thus benevolently gagged under peculiarly trying conditions. In the first place elaborate maneuvres had to be carried out in the very face of special watchfulness on the part of the authorities. Buckets of ice and water had to be lowered into the Chapel and hoisted separately to the belfry. Then the bell had to be turned over without a stroke and propped in an inverted position to receive the contents of the buckets. But the extreme and very unusual cold, which indeed was necessary to the project, was the incident of the greatest hardship, and above all, these responsibilities were divided on only two pairs of shoulders. At times the bitter cold almost extinguished the ardor of one of the confederates, and although now and then he worked furiously, bubbling over with enthusiasm at the brilliancy of the project, he fell again as surely into the alternate state of apathy. The other, the author and prime mover, persevered grimly and quietly, paying no heed to his second except to give directions. He had chosen his roommate as his sole accomplice in conformity with his favorite maxim that "Three men can keep a secret when two of them are dead."

"There," said Number Two as he stopped drawing up the bell-rope, "by the eternal Devil I've dredged up the last bucket from the Pit," and after pouring the water it contained into the bell, he sat down astride the beam on which he had been standing and began to hitch along as if endeavoring to keep his blood in circulation. Occasionally he uttered despairing groans in reference to his friend's arrival with the ladder. At last when a head did appear above the beam and a voice said, "Stubs," he started up and could scarcely contain his enthusiasm.

"It's freezing solid," he cried. "Oh, why have you such a name as Jedediah to confound the ballad-writers?"

Jedediah, familiarly "Jed," made an examination for himself and being satisfied that the water and broken ice in the bell were forming a homogeneous mass, he began the descent.

About fifteen minutes later they were huddled by the fire in their room in Winthrop, and it was only after considerable thawing that those two energetic brains appeared to be once more alert to the welfare of humanity.

"Noble Jedediah," said Stubs, "our family physician always maintained that there was nothing like a counterirritant to divert a threatened malady. Now wouldn't it be well to establish the grounds of our alibi ?"

"Exactly what I was thinking of," replied Jed. "Now while I don't claim absolutely that I originate everything brilliant, I am always happy to suggest an expeditious course, and although the idea may not in every case be new to me, I am no more a sycophant than the modern poets are who sometimes derive inspiration from their predecessors."

"A little too much air escaped with that for me to grasp your meaning exactly," Stubs said in a tone of remonstrance. "I am afraid your windpipe is getting out of your control. Pull your necktie up and take a hitch or two in the slack."

"Notice that I applaud your scintillating wit. When you interrupted me I was going to suggest that we should adopt a plan that has been attributed to our worthy predecessor, Elijah Kellogg. Something of proven merit is meet for the exigency and for Hallowe'en."

"The festival is surely as worthy in its observances as Candlemas or the Pentecost, and I am agreeable so long as it may truly be a counter-irritant."

"Oh, it's explicitly that, and if you will effect a sort of gathering of the clans as quietly as possible, I will attend to the other details."

Stubs left the room immediately and Jed concerned himself in the bed-chamber with the filling of an oil stove and fumbling in a box of various tin and glass utensils.

Presently the outer door opened and half a dozen fellows, at once annoyed and expectant, like pigs aroused for a meal, made their entrance. They threw themselves into various restful postures to await developments. Stubs leaned back in a chair and put his feet on the table. What he intended for a genial grin was rendered rather forbidding by black flakes of tobacco leaf that hid all but an occasional tooth ; but his spectacles, pushed up on his head, gave him an air of venerable erudition, and altogether this demagogue appeared to be about to regale his disciples with a profitable harangue. He added fresh tobacco to his apparently sufficient quid and tucked it away in some cavernous recess where it could not quite garble his elocution.

"Oh, tenderly nurtured youths," he began, "how unfortunate for you that you cannot always bask in the light of your Jedediah, who is now engaged in the pursuit of alchemy, and of myself, who has ascertained why Demosthenes wished to learn the art of talking with something in the mouth —"

"Say, is this all there is to be of the show ?" someone interrupted.

"I can't bear much of this," said another.

"We didn't come in, you know, to hear you bleat," put in a third.

"Another year of such tutelage," continued Stubs imperturbably, "and a dawn might break on your dark souls. You would in the first place be in a more recipient attitude, having become acquainted with the various statutes of this precinct through their various penalties. For instance, *de pipa portandi*, for negligently carrying a cask of wine, would teach you not to drop your oil can when returning from the grocer's." Here he paused for breath and a voice from the bed-room interposed :

"Sound the tocsin !"

This injunction seemed to be pretty well understood, for the fellows in the study immediately set up a terrific hubbub, by stamping and shouting while Stubs beat out a sort of irregular rhythm on the table with an old clapper of the Chapel bell. Presently the confusion subsided and Jedediah came out of the bed-room and shouted three or four times :

"You lie ! It's my deal !"

He had hardly uttered this reiteration when a loud knock shook the door. Silence followed and no one stirred. The knocking was continued with impatience. Stubs made a sign to one of those nearest to open the door. The latter turned the lock and opened as if reluctantly, when seeing the lowering visage of Tutor Blank, he swung the door wide.

Jedediah, who was standing, made a hasty motion with one hand from the table toward his coat-tail pocket. The others rose respectfully.

The tutor glided forward and looked about with a crafty smile. "Aha," he croaked, "playing cards again in Number Seven."

"I beg your pardon," began Jedediah, "but —"

"No falsehoods, sir ! Don't make it any worse ; your case is bad enough as it is !"

"But, sir—"

"Don't lie to me, sir !" said the tutor through his teeth. "You've got the cards in your pocket."

As Jedediah was apparently ready to utter unlimited negatives, the tutor darted forward as if to assert his prerogative of the right of search. Jed started back and cried :

"Oh, please don't feel in my pocket, sir !"

Tutor Blank grinned and said "Aha !" but far from relinquishing his search, he pressed forward with renewed interest.

"Oh, but I beg you, sir, don't do it, I pray you—!" exclaimed Jed, but his request was cut short by the tutor's making a snatch at the coat-tail and darting a hand into the depths of the pocket. This purpose was no sooner realized, however, than Tutor Blank uttered a wild howl, followed by an exclamation of a more articulate and impressive nature. For a minute or two he danced around on the tips of his toes, a perfect picture of anguish. Then he began to scrape a steaming yellow paste from the fingers of that enterprising hand, and when he had succeeded in fairly catching his breath he bawled :

"What did you do that for ?"

"Indeed, I *begged* you not to put your hand in my pocket!" replied Jed.

"That's nothing to do with it," roared Tutor Blank. "What have you in that pocket ?"

"An Indian Pudding, sir !"

"What in,—what on earth,—what right have you to have a pudding in your pocket ?" Tutor Blank howled.

"I didn't know there was any regulation about having a pudding in one's pocket, sir," Jed answered. "and besides I begged you not to put your hand in it, for I was afraid the mush might be hot."

Tutor Blank turned on his heel and beat a retreat, slamming the door after him.

The door had scarcely closed when a rather disrespectful shout of laughter burst out, and the "gathering of the clans" rolled about in ecstatic convulsions.

A HISTORY AND THE REASONS FOR IT

Edward C. Plummer, '87

A HISTORY AND THE REASONS FOR IT

I T has long been my fixed belief that no one should indulge in that species of composition which a boundless charity permits the prejudiced to call poetry, unless he can show a good and sufficient reason for being so favored. Whether or not the lines appended to this article can justify their existence under this rule, must be determined from the following historic facts.

Imprimis : The present Faculty of Bowdoin College will cautiously admit, what some of their former associates have at divers times so emphatically stated, that the late 'sixties and early 'seventies were years which brought to this famous institution the most nerve-trying students that ever sought intellectual development in the quiet town of Brunswick.

And this admission is no reflection on the very high grade of mischievous ingenuity which enabled other men to severely ruffle the theoretically placid waters of student life. The 'eighties certainly produced scholars who developed quite exceptional talents in this peculiar line, while many a snowy-haired graduate will now and then let fall an anecdote which shows that half a century ago the wrinkle-creating prank had developed to most troublesome proportions. But, as the pyramid has one stone which rises above all others, though many others are at a great height, so the period named above must be recognized as entitled to the peculiar honor accorded it here, despite the numerous, and unquestionably sincere, efforts of worthy competitors to carry away the palm.

That student, whose ingenious mind discovered that a most satisfactory and hair-raising bonfire could be produced by simply digging down to the gas main, knocking a hole therein and igniting the gas, thereby causing the fire department to actually hurry to the campus and attempt to extinguish the pillar of fire which other thoughtful students had caused the public to believe was destroying the whole institution, is not forgotten when the aforesaid palm is awarded ; nor is that benign-faced professional gentleman (now so well known in New England) whose mathematical exactness enabled him to so fasten the Chapel doors that nearly the entire Faculty together with the great body of the students remained in that unwarmed hall for nearly an hour of a remarkably crisp winter's morning, overlooked. But these young men can only be credited with isolated strokes of genius—lightning flashes from an otherwise fairly clear sky ; they lacked that persistent devotion to unremitting mischief, the sustained brilliancy in constantly devising unique and triumphant assaults upon the much-enduring patience of the professors which leads the average lay mind to unhesitatingly predict the gallows for every such individual, while causing a genuine tidal wave of thankfulness to flood the hearts of all instructors when he is gone.

That such a genius haunted Bowdoin some thirty years ago, cannot possibly have been forgotten by any who were even distantly connected with the college at that time. But as it is one of the eccentricities of human nature that while the mere entrance upon the college grounds causes even the most sedate alumnus (provided he has no student son there to observe him) to again see the deeds of his youth in all the glory of their old-time colors, as many a room in these venerable dormitories could testify after every Commencement reunion of old friends gathered there, yet the chill of the greater world's atmosphere is such that actors in those old pranks object to the general publication of their boyhood exploits. Therefore, while so many graduates can at once identify "Jim," I refrain from giving a more complete name at this time, but, with a passing reference to his skill as a midnight driller of Freshmen, to the fact that he filled with masterly success the highly responsible position of "Archon" in Phi Chi, to his humorous bull-dog of which Smith's "Ned" in the 'eighties was the first really worthy successor, I proceed to the recital of one exploit, which I make no doubt is still puzzling the then President of Bowdoin College, as an absolutely conclusive argument that Jim is entitled to be remembered in verse.

In the spring of '70, Jim, doubtless feeling the impulse of the season, resolved that the variegated program of mischief for that year should be completed by the removal of the Chapel bell, and, with the assistance of a corps of worthy collaborators who, geniuses in themselves, recognized a still greater genius in him and therefore crowded about him, even as the great marshals gathered about Napoleon and by such combination made greater conquests possible, mapped out the campaign.

Pennell's ship-yard was made to supply the necessary tackle ; the enthusiasm of minds on so bold a project bent furnished the necessary energy ; and as a result of that exceedingly hard night's work the Morning, had it been in the secret and supplied with sufficiently powerful eyes, might have discovered that Chapel bell safely buried under three feet of sand amid the blueberry bushes some two miles from the college.

Naturally there was a search for the bell, and threats of dire punishments awaiting the offenders drifted over the student body ; but as all this but added a more delicate flavor to the delight which crowded the breasts of the guilty parties, and produced no other results, notice was given that unless that missing Chapel appendage was restored within twenty-four hours a general assessment would be made upon the entire Sophomore class for the purpose of replacing the loss.

When the Napoleonic band learned that innocent parties were to suffer for their acts, with that sense of strict honor which always characterizes the true college mischief-maker, they determined to discover the missing article, and the next day a mysterious letter, locating the bell, reached the Faculty. So the bell was found—but it lacked a tongue.

A new tongue was procured and duly placed beside the resurrected bell on the Chapel steps the morning that the President had selected to address the students there, preparatory to hoisting the bell to its old place in the tower.

But Jim, with his marshals, was there ; and as the kindly President talked to the gathered students of the folly of such unusual tricks, involving so much useless peril, and, warming to the theme, appealed to them to abandon such senseless pranks, the lines gradually closed about the speaker until, when the address was finished and the beloved President, pleased with the expectant faces which had remained so earnestly upturned to him during the talk, ordered the restoration proceedings to begin, it was discovered that the tongue of the bell had again disappeared !

Jim had actually possessed himself of that important piece of metal while the President was speaking. It had passed from hand to hand among the faithful until at last it had found repose under the hedge. Later it was taken to one of the marshals' rooms where it remained while Jim's apartments, as a matter of principle, were searched—as usual, without results.

This exploit of stealing the bell's tongue from beneath the very eyes of the President and at a time when the janitor and his assistants were carefully watching all proceedings, confirmed Jim's title to the high position which he had attained among those who best knew the scope of his remarkable type of genius.

It is for this reason that I have felt convinced that no prose, however stilted, not even an extract from a Junior's theme, could do him justice. Therefore the results of his college studies, as well as the circumstances under which I recently renewed an old acquaintanceship, are sufficiently indicated in the following

HISTORY.

A song of days when the youthful life
   Was bright with the Morning's glow ;
When the fields of Fancy with hopes were rife,
And the heart was hot, and Time's old knife
   Had none of its flowers laid low.

    *   *   *   *   *

He came from a home in a quiet town
   Where he was the pride of all ;
His brow inviting a scholar's crown,
While a serious air, like a classic gown,
   Seemed over his form to fall.

    *   *   *   *   *

He came with a mind aspiring high,
   With the pulse of a lofty soul,
Resolved in the college world to try
His swelling powers, and he fixed his eye
   On the highest sort of a goal.

With awe he looked on the halls and trees
   And the points of the granite spires ;
And bowed to professors with fearful ease,

Resolved those wonderful men to please
   And know no other desires.

A HISTORY AND THE REASONS FOR IT

And every day through the campus walks
    He strode with studious look,
His heart attuned to the Muses' talks,
His castles built on the good old rocks
    Of a student lamp and a book.

And many a night did the midnight air,
    As it crept from the sleeping pines,
Lift gently the locks of the tumbled hair
From the throbbing temples of him who there
    Was charging the Grecian lines.

No thought of the World, or its social gem,
    Could stain that studious mind ;
The meerschaum bowl with its amber stem,
The equine books, and things like them,
    He scorned as of evil kind.

His cheeks grew pale with the ceaseless toil—
    But never a thought of rest ;
Early and late he was proud to moil

And plant much seed in his mental soil—
    His reward : a rank of the best.

    *   *   *   *   *

But Time, the fellow who never tires,
    Who ever has much to do,
Who cools the heart with the hottest fires
And steals our hopes and our fond desires,
    Brings change to the student too.

    *   *   *   *   *

That room still glows with the midnight lamps,
    But the Muses are far away ;
On the student's table a bull dog camps,
And smoke wreaths circle, and Laughter stamps
    His smiles on a group at play.

His numerous prints of the corps ballet
    He shows to his friends with pride ;
He affects the air of a child *roué* ;
All serious thoughts are to him *passé*;
    And he walks with a reckless stride.

And many a night doth his well-known shout
    Bring fear to the timid heart,

TALES OF BOWDOIN

As he leads a gay collegiate rout,
And tumbles the new-come student out
    That he may perform his part.

He drills pale squads in their white robes neat,
    In the "wee sma' hours o' the nights,"
And whistles a tune for their dancing feet,
While the bull dog aids in the curious treat
    By making pretended bites.

No longer the class-room seems the field
    Where glory and fame are born ;
The evening stroll and the love revealed
To ancient nymph, and the troth they've sealed,
    Have caused him his books to scorn.

He looks on professors as bloodless men
    Devoid of aspiring souls,
Content to dwell in a bookish den,
And burrow in this scholastic glen
    Like intellectual moles.

      *   *   *   *   *

Again the change : With superior eye
    He views all noisy sports ;
He lets the tasks of the world draw nigh
And turns his thoughts on the things that try
    The wisdom of camps and courts.

The problems challenging statesmen's might
    He solves in an evening's talk ;
He scales theology's awful height,
And puts the tangle of creeds aright
    In the chat of a morning's walk.

Philosophy soon absorbs his mind—
    He dwells on the things unknown,
And rambles around 'mid the undefined
A key to the riddle of life to find,—
    While leaving his books alone.

At last his days in the college o'er,
    He bids farewell to the halls :
Professors thankful he'll come no more,
While sundry damsels, as oft before,
    Shed tears at his final calls.

      *   *   *   *   *

A HISTORY AND THE REASONS FOR IT

We meet again : In the calm retreat
    Of a beautiful church in town,
Where gather the groups of the *bon elite*
In pious splendor, he takes his seat,
    A pastor of much renown.

The tender voice and the kindly eye,
    The charm of a noble heart,
The life to its standard kept so nigh,

Hath made him dear where his duties lie,
    And well he performs his part.

But oft as the learned language flows
    From his lips to his listening flock,
I see the Past o'er the Present close—
It brushes away Time's whitening snows,
    And dulls mine ears to the talk.

And Fancy another scene reveals,
    Set deep in the days gone by—
A youth o'er the silent campus steals,
A bull dog trotting behind his heels,
    And then comes a well-known cry.

The breath of the swaying pines returns,
    The river gleams bright below,
As Memory's glancing sunshine burns
The mists away, and the heart discerns
    The pictures of long ago.

The songs and the laughs and the old-time calls,
    The room and the old-time friend,
The trees and the paths and the plain old halls,
The gray of the Chapel's windowed-walls,
    From the clouds of the past descend.

    *   *   *   *   *

A sigh—and my wife with elbow strong
    Dispels the dream, and I wake
To the solemn fact of the closing song
And the contribution-box coming along,
    My hard-earned cash to take.

223

THE OLD DELTA

ALBERT W. TOLMAN, '88

THE OLD DELTA

T HE graduate who visits Bowdoin after an absence of several years cannot help feeling that there have been many changes for the better. Well-kept grounds, renovated dormitories, new buildings and many other signs of progress greet him. And if he chances to drop into town on a Spring afternoon when he has heard that the ball team is to play some other college nine, and loiters up to the Delta where he had supposed the contest would take place, a great surprise is in store for him ; for here is no grandstand, no gathering of students. and townspeople. But if he follows the crowd flowing down the Harpswell road and turns into a well-worn path through the pines, he is soon within the spacious enclosure of Whittier Field. And after he has watched the game from the new stand, joined in the college yell, and felt his heart thrill with oldtime enthusiasm in the companionship of undergraduates unknown to him personally but filled with the same loyalty to the old college, he will no doubt come away, convinced that the athletes of the present are fully as good as their predecessors, and that athletics in general are on a much better footing than formerly.

Yet after the contest is over, and on his return he passes the old Delta, empty and deserted, he remembers the games he used to see there ; and his thoughts go back till they rest on some June morning, ten, fifteen, twenty years ago.

*   *   *   *   *   *   *

All the day before it has been raining, and in the morning the tops of the tall pines are still full of mist ; but as the forenoon advances the sun has come out bright and hot, mirroring itself in the muddy pools on the diamond. To-day decides the championship of the Maine college league ; and down from Waterville has flashed a telegram that the Colby team is coming.

The grounds must be gotten in shape for the afternoon, and the manager is full of business. Brooms, sawdust, lime, bases and foul-flags are running riot through his brain. There is little work done in the recitation rooms that forenoon. Lessons are gotten through in a perfunctory way. Everybody's thought centres on the game. Somehow the hours drag by, dinner is over, and the crowd begins to gather on the Delta.

The pitcher's box is filled with sawdust, the base-lines are fresh-limed, the bases are in position. "Whisker" is there, and other local celebrities. The windows of Adams Hall are filled with interested Medics, lured for a few minutes from the delights of dissecting. The grandstand blossoms gaily out with a mushroom growth of ladies' hats and parasols ; the whitewashed fences stretching away on either side are lined with non-paying spectators ; the roads fill with carriages ; every moment adds its share to the crowd of students and townsmen.

Up the street from the Tontine across the railroad track, with bat-bags, mask and leathern breastplate, come swinging a little group of perhaps a dozen men in gray suits and red stockings, with the letter "C" upon their breasts, involuntarily clustering close together for the feeling of strength that numbers give them, for are they not on alien ground ? A few minutes more, and the rival teams are taking each other's measure on the field where they are to cross bats for the supremacy of the State.

There is a little preliminary warming-up by each nine ; then the captains meet to discuss the conditions of the game with the umpire, who consults the oracles by snapping up a half dollar. At its fall one of the teams takes the field on the run. The same arbiter of destiny produces from a bulging pocket a brand-new paper box, from which he tears the ball, white and round, and tosses it to the pitcher. One of the other nine who has been carefully weighing bats steps out from the little group around the settee, and stands at the plate, facing the man in the box. The latter, after a few cabalistic passes, draws back his arm and then suddenly hurls it forward. A streak of white crosses the plate above the batsman's shoulder.

One ball !

The game is on, and everybody breathes freer.

The coachers unlimber and converse across the diamond, expressing frank and unsolicited disapproval of the opposing pitcher's strength of arm, or alluding mysteriously to the excellence of vision of the man at the bat. As the game proceeds, let us take a look at the field.

There is the pitcher, on whose arm depends the fortune of the day, the mainspring of the team, confined for the time in his little white-lined parallelogram. Behind and to his right and left are shortstop, basemen and fielders looming large against the dull-green wall of pine, their seven pairs of eyes focused intently on the silent figure standing with firm-gripped bat across its shoulder near the dusty square of stone. Behind the batsman is the catcher, hands extended and feet astride, a masked, gloved, breastplated Colossus. Around the upper end of the field in the form of an irregular crescent stretches the crowd, an inflammable mass of human tinder, ready to be kindled with enthusiasm or chilled to despair by the varying fortunes of the game.

But what need to describe details ? There are good plays and bad plays ; pyrotechnic catches and stops, and heartbreaking errors ; breathless moments of excitement and occasional spasms of disgust ; long hits that start a twinkling scurry of red or blue stockings around the bases and send precious runs across the plate, and short hits that nip hopes in the bud and cause runners to be most unexpectedly doubled up. Now there is an error at a critical time, almost inexcusable, (as it seems to the anxious crowd), and at the end of the inning the man who has made it conies in, sometimes sullen, sometimes defiant, but oftener with hanging head and eyes that have a suspicion of moisture, swallowing hard to keep down an unnatural growth in the throat. Now a line hit, lost in the underbrush near the fence, sets the right-fielder madly pawing about in the grass and scrub pines, while the runners are tearing around the bases with a most unfeeling disregard for his anxiety. Occasionally a stray ball picks off one of the "yagger" heads that are watching the pitcher's curves from just over the foul-board. Then comes a panicky season when everybody is throwing wild. One man gets the ball only to hurl it over the head of the next, who follows suit, going his predecessor a few feet better. Finally some calm-nerved, clear-headed player stops the carnage, the smoke clears away, and casualties in the shape of runs made or lost may be counted.

Then comes the customary wrangle ; was ever a ball game played without one ? The umpire becomes an unwilling nucleus around which an excited group of players centres ; on him are the vials of wrath poured out; he is the scapegoat, the pariah against whom is every man's hand. Spectators add themselves to the circle ; there is a waving of hands, a shaking of fists, a turmoil ; everybody is talking at once. Suddenly, a scattering ; and the game goes on.

The sixth inning is over and the score is very close. From now on it is see-saw, anybody's game ; one error, one good play, one happy swing of the bat may decide it. The joviality of the first part of the contest has vanished ; there is no more "jollying"; matters are in a too serious condition ; Bowdoin has a lead of one run and is anxious to retain her advantage ; Colby is fighting by inches to overtake her ; the nerves of both teams are taut as fiddle-strings. Even the leathern lungs of the coachers show signs of wear ; they are hoarse-throated and dry-mouthed, and their voices break occasionally ; their assurance has disappeared. Among the audience nobody is really enjoying the game ; the interest has become too painful.

The seventh inning passes, and neither side adds to its score ; the eighth is the same. Now for the finish. One more chance apiece.

The sun is well down in the West, and its rays strike full in the faces of the fielders and basemen. It is a good time for the batters. Bowdoin is up with the weak end of her list, but she makes a gallant try to increase her score. By the time two men are out she has runners on second and third. And now come the strong batters.

"Here's where we clinch the game !" shouts the captain.

The man up swings his bat quickly at the first pitch. There is a sharp report, and the sphere darts away on a line toward the vacant spot between centre and right. A roar of applause rises from the crowd, for a safe hit means two runs. But alas for their hopes ! As the ball passes over the head of the second baseman he leaps into the air, flings up an avaricious hand, and pulls it down. An utter death like silence follows close upon that

THE OLD DELTA.

incipient abortive cheer ; then a hearty handclapping, for such a play, wins applause even from an enemy.

And now it is Colby's turn, with the heaviest hitters on her list to come. It is one to tie and two to win. What will she do ?

The first man answers his share of the question by striking out ; and there is some enthusiasm. The next player chills the general Bowdoin spine and sets the few Colby supporters delirious by a long level drive between centre and left, that puts him on second base. The third man flies to shortstop. Only one more, but the worst man on the team, the hard-hitting, devil-may-care Colby captain.

Now let the Bowdoin pitcher do his best, for the laurel of victory or the cypress of defeat hangs on the next few seconds.

The first ball is called a strike, and there comes a cheer from the stand. Then follow two balls. Then amid prodigious enthusiasm the batter lunges spitefully at a quick drop and misses it. Another ball. The next will settle it.

The stillness of death is over the field. You could almost hear a needle fall from one of the tall pines ; no sound but the rattle of wheels down the Bath road, the heavy puffing of a locomotive at the station. Five hundred graven images are watching the next move in the drama.

The players stand motionless as statues ; the fielders erect; the basemen and shortstop bareheaded, dusty, stooping forward with feet spread, left hand on the knee, the right shading the eyes, with lips apart, tense muscles, and palpitating hearts.

Perhaps the pitcher's arm was tired, as well it might be after two hours of strenuous work ; perhaps the crisis unnerved him ; or it may be that the batsman instinctively fathomed the curve that was thrown. Whatever the cause, the result is disastrous from a Bowdoin standpoint.

As he sees coming toward him the ball that is to decide the season, the batsman gathers himself together, and throws all his strength of arm and shoulder into one tremendous swing. There is a report like that of a young cannon. High in the air soars the ball, beyond second base, beyond centre field, until it plunges into the pines, still a good ten feet from the ground.

That settles it. Before the runner has made the circuit of the bases, the stand is emptying and the crowd has begun to pass out through the fence. Bowdoin may win the championship—some other year. But for this season the chance disappeared with the ball that the auburn-haired Colby captain drove into the pines between centre and right.

To-night no photograph gallery will burn ; no purloined sidewalks or fences will send up their sparks from the central walk of the campus to vex the midnight stars ; nor will the dreams of Brunswick sleepers be broken by the unmusical jangling of the Chapel bell. The talk at the clubs at supper is subdued, everybody gets to bed early, and an uninterrupted gloom reigns from Winthrop to Appleton.

Let no one think it strange that I have chosen to chronicle defeat rather than victory. It is no disgrace to lose to a plucky foe, and it is well for a college to remember that no matter how high her standing, it is always dangerous to be over-confident, and she must guard her laurels well.

It is enough for the most enthusiastic Bowdoin man that there was far more of victory than defeat on the old Delta. Memory runs back to the teams that used to come to join battle there. Perhaps it was M. S. C., with brown, muscular arms bare to the shoulder, as fine a looking ball team as ever set foot on a Maine diamond ; M. S. C. with a six-foot-six centre-fielder, who dropped on one knee and raised appealing hands heavenward when on the point of making a catch, and who was credited with the power of throwing the ball from his position over the catcher's fence. Perhaps it was Bates, always ready for a stubborn fight. Perhaps it was a picked team from Massachusetts, filled with the idea that anything was good enough to play ball down in Maine, who went back, sadder and wiser men, after having made the circuit of the State colleges and getting unmercifully trounced in each.

There were giants in the Maine league in those days, or at least so they seemed to undergraduate eyes. Goodwin, Wagg and Parsons of Colby ; Underwood. Thayer and Sandford of Bates ; Small, Rogers and Ray of M. S. C. ; and Bowdoin men from whom it would be invidious for an alumnus to make selections, valorous wielders of the ash, mighty on the coaching lines as Achilles good-at-the war-cry.

What memories of Sophomore-Freshman wrangles, of Senior burlesques, of alumni games with the college team trying not to get so far ahead of the old fellows as to hurt their feelings ! Some graduates may remember when one tall batter performed the unduplicated feat of putting the ball over the great pine in centre field. Perhaps, too, some will recall the song of Honorable Michael Coyne, which a soloist whose voice has been heard on many a platform during the last two Presidential campaigns, sang to a too partial umpire, with the front row of the grandstand joining in the chorus, the crowd cheering and laughing, the coachers shouting from the sidelines, and the unwilling object of these attentions endeavoring to make his voice heard above the tumult.

One of the most curious and exciting incidents that ever took place on the Delta occurred during a game with Colby. The Bowdoin batter knocked a grounder to the infield, and a runner started home from third base. The ball was returned to the catcher, who stood about four feet from the plate. Just as it touched his hands the runner dove between his legs, upsetting him, and down he came on the shoulders of his antagonist, pinning him to the ground. The shock caused the Colby man to drop the ball, which rolled two or three feet away. It was a most peculiar situation. There was the runner with eyes bulging from his head, nailed to the ground by the catcher's weight, straining to touch the plate, only about a foot from the tips of his fingers. There was the catcher reaching for the ball just about a foot from *his* finger-tips, but not daring to rise, for that would let the runner make the coveted distance. Matters were in this state for about fifteen seconds, when a Bowdoin player darted from the bench, seized the Colby man by the shoulders and rolled him off, allowing the runner to score. Just at this time the entire grandstand emptied itself in a rush for the spot. The catcher seized a bat and stood on the defensive ; but every one soon calmed down and the game went on.

BOWDON UNDER FIRE

CHARLES A. CURTIS, '61

BOWDON UNDER FIRE

I CANNOT contribute something concerning the Bowdoin Battalion of the early Summer of 1861, without first accounting for myself and explaining how I came to be its military instructor.

I fitted for college with the large contingent from Lewiston Falls Academy which entered Bowdoin in 1857, but did not present myself for examination. In February of the following year I entered the Military College of Vermont and received full instruction in infantry and artillery tactics, in fencing, and in the art and science of war. From early childhood I had known of Bowdoin and had looked forward to one day being enumerated among its students and graduates. Accident, the nature of which it is unnecessary to mention, ordered otherwise. My journeys four times a year to and from fitting schools and the Vermont college, from 1855 to 1861, always took me through Brunswick and I rarely neglected to stop off and visit Bowdoin friends, so that my acquaintance there was never fully interrupted until the outbreak of the Civil War.

At the Lewiston Falls Academy my fellow students fancied me a quasi-military genius and regularly selected me for marshal of their academic processions, and in the Presidential campaign of 1856 they made me commandant of a club which perpetrated more mischief than it accomplished good for the party of Fremont and Dayton ; notably the alteration of a Republican flag to a Democratic, which filled the papers of the partisan press for a month or more and frightened the reckless perpetrators of the prank into a silence which lasted for years.

In marching this youthful Republican dub my tactics were of the most original character, and it was probably owing to this fact that the Lewiston Academy boys transferred to Bowdoin, voted to a man against the proposition to employ me as the military instructor of the Bowdoin Battalion. The veterans of the old "F. U." could not realize that their former commandant had improved his tactical knowledge.

I had returned to my native State in the Spring of 1861, during a month's vacation, and was employed in drilling volunteers for the Civil War. While engaged in this work in the Kennebec valley I was invited to visit Brunswick and meet a body of the Bowdoin students with a view to its organization as a battalion for military drill.

The invitation reached me near the close of my vacation, when I was getting ready to return to the Vermont college ; but the proposition proved so attractive that I wrote President Woods and asked if I might be allowed to attend Senior recitations and lectures if I accepted the students' offer. He kindly consented and one pleasant afternoon I stood before about one hundred and fifty students drawn up in line before King Chapel. Thus I took my first step toward becoming an alumnus by brevet of Bowdoin College.

The student battalion was, of course, ununiformed. It was composed of members of all classes, an unsized mass of green, but intelligent and enthusiastic young men, who seemed thoroughly in earnest and proved themselves promptly responsive to every command given them, as well as attentive to all lectures and explanations. In after years, when drilling recruits for the regular army and finding the task weary and irksome, my thoughts have frequently reverted to the Bowdoin Battalion, the members of which so rapidly and readily acquired a knowledge of the drill.

The military exercises, as before remarked, began on the campus before the Chapel, that section of the grounds being at that time unobstructed by trees or shrubbery. Few instances of insubordination occurred as the work progressed. In abandoning the inalienable right of American citizens to buck against despotic rule or to submit themselves to the absolute authority of a military commander, there were but occasional instances of objection—instances invariably made use of to impress the young soldiers with the necessity of maintaining discipline and obeying orders.

The one serious as well as amusing case of mischievous insubordination I will now relate. One afternoon, some weeks after the formal organization of the battalion into companies and the election of officers, when all the formations and marching movements had been quite thoroughly learned, a dray delivered before the south front Chapel door eight boxes containing twenty rifles each. This door opened into a room which had been assigned the corps as an armory. Ready and willing hands conveyed the boxes to the interior, where they were opened and their contents displayed to the eager youngsters. A first view of the arms showed me that they needed cleaning from oil and dirt, and I accordingly distributed one rifle with a screwdriver to each student, and then in their presence took one apart and assembled it, requiring them to do the same. When this was done I gave some further instruction concerning material to be used in cleaning, how to apply it, and how to keep arms and accoutrements in serviceable condition, and then ordered every one to take his rifle to his room and next day appear in line with it in proper shape.

That evening at the club with which I messed—a club occupying a house near the Tontine Hotel—a student asked me how to make a cartridge. This was in the days of the paper cartridge and "load in nine times." I told him to obtain a piece of wrapping paper and I would show him. He went out and soon returned with sheets of manila paper sufficient to supply all the members of the club, and by using granulated sugar for gunpowder I showed them how to make blank cartridges.

As I left the table and was passing through the hallway to the outer door, a student who afterwards became a gallant Colonel of volunteers, asked me to accompany him on a drive to Topsham and into the country.

I gladly accepted the invitation and when I had taken a seat beside my friend in a light buggy behind a fine bay trotter, all the boys of the club surrounded us and wished me an enjoyable excursion and begged my companion to show me several fine moonlight views of the Androscoggin. He assured them that that was his intention and told his room-mate not to look for his return until eleven.

The drive needs little description. Every Bowdoin boy has been over the ground many times, driving, riding and walking. My companion whiled away the time, as we spun rapidly into the country, by relating college experiences—most of them accounts of his prowess in stealing marches and playing tricks upon an inappreciative and arbitrary Faculty,—stories which, after the college manner, never deal with cases where the professor proves himself the better man, but which always magnify the student's brilliancy and art in concealing his motives or accomplishing results. On the return drive he dropped into sentiment and confided to me the fact that he was ardently in love with a young lady student of the boarding-school situated opposite the campus. He had been fond of her for a long time and had exchanged many letters and gifts with her. He drew from his pocket a delicate note emitting a slight odor of violets and by the brilliant moonlight read a few lines in which the writer said that if he would come over that evening at half-past ten and whistle "Ever of Thee" from the clump of lilacs beneath her window she would throw him a beautiful bouquet.

"And of course you are going to do it ?" I remarked.

"That is what I wish to do," he replied, "but I don't believe I can manage the tune." And directly he began to whistle something which bore no resemblance whatever to the air mentioned, or any other air.

"Let me start it for you," I said, and I sang air and words through and paused.

"That's mighty, fine," he observed. "Now I'll try it." But his second attempt showed no improvement over the first. He slowed the horse to a walk and I patiently whistled strain after strain and he appeared as patiently to be trying to imitate me, but succeeded only in impressing me with the conviction that music had no place in his soul.

"Really, I fear you will not obtain that 'beautiful bouquet' unless I go and whistle for you."

"Will you—will you—Mr. Curtis ?" he exclaimed. "You do not know what a favor you will do me if you will !"

"But will not the young woman see two in the bush and fail to respond ?"

"Not a bit of it. We can reach the lilacs without being seen, and once among them no one will know whether we are one, two, or a dozen. Oh, I'm all right ! I knew I was whistling wretchedly. Give me your hand on it that you'll never tell a soul of this confidence I've placed in you, or of what we do."

I gave him my hand and he made me wince with the fervor of his clasp. Next he looked at his watch in the moonlight and remarked that we must continue to go slow for a brief time longer in order not to reach the seminary before half-past ten.

My companion continued to unbosom himself of many delightful sentimentalities and each succeeding moonlit view of the Androscoggin valley suggested some excursion, picnic, walk or ride in which she of the lilac bush had been a participant ; but in time we reached the Tontine stables, put up the horse and took our way up through the Mall to the boarding-school.

Screened by maples and elms we reached the school unseen, crept through a hedge into a back yard, where from lines stretched between posts and trees waved the spotless lingerie of the sleeping maidens, and at last stood concealed in a dense clump of lilacs beneath an oriel window, from which the "beautiful bouquet" was to fall.

I found it difficult to make the preliminary pucker, for my lips and tongue were as parched as those of a stage-frightened actor, and it took me several minutes to produce an imperfect and sadly modulated imitation of "Ever of Thee." But the promptness with which the young lady raised the sash, thrust out a shapely and snowy arm and dropped a bunch of fragrant roses showed that my friend would not have gone unrewarded had he done his own whistling and in any style.

We returned to the street without delay and as we paused for an instant on the sidewalk, facing the long line of college buildings, suddenly, from every window and every doorway of every dormitory blazed volleys of musketry filling the air with the rattle of irregular discharge. I remained standing in fixed surprise, but my companion rushed, without a word of leave taking, across the road at the top of his speed, vaulted over the fence into the campus and ran swiftly for his room in Appleton Hall.

I did not run. I walked slowly in the tracks of my wily friend, busy with the unpleasant reflection that the evening's drama had been played for the purpose of keeping me out of the way ; and that I had been made an instrument in aid of what was now going on. I had showed the boys how to make cartridges and for the five hours since I left the supper table at the club, a hundred and fifty youngsters had been busy in making preparations for a grand fusilade,—yes, they had successfully kept me amused and successfully prevented me from interfering with their plans. The constant flash and unceasing rattle of the rifles showed that the boys had wasted no time in their preparations.

Three years and more at a well-disciplined military school had caused me to forget the natural impulse of youths with firearms in their hands, and I had never once suspected the animating cause of what I had considered a commendable desire to know how to make a cartridge. Now it seemed plainly evident that from the issue of arms they had planned this demonstration and that every man of the Bowdoin Battalion had purchased powder and percussion caps and worked industriously in the preparation of ammunition.

I took my way to the Chapel and sat down on the threshold of the armory and continued my reflections upon what I had omitted to do when instructing my command on the cleaning and care of arms. I did not think of attempting to stay the demonstration going on. I knew that would be practically impossible. I simply determined that at the next drill I would take measures to prevent a recurrence of this noisy, dangerous and insubordinate conduct. In the midst of these resolutions five figures approached hurriedly from one of the paths—figures I presently recognized to be those of the President, a Professor and three tutors, and learned they were in search of me. The President made an instant demand that I should stop the firing. I replied that I should have prevented it had I not been out of town when the students were preparing for it, and that I should have stopped it promptly upon my return had it been possible— that the firing was too general and scattered for one man or a dozen to stop it—that an attempt to do so would afford the participants in the mischief more satisfaction than they were now deriving from mere fire and noise. But the President insisted I should accompany him and try to stop it.

I accordingly joined the party and we moved toward Appleton, I walking beside the Professor, a gentleman who went to the front a little later and who became a Major General of distinguished ability in the war, and who had shown considerable interest in the Bowdoin Battalion, frequently attending its drills, listening to commands and observing the responsive movements. I found the Professor entertained the same opinion I did of the firing. He remarked in an undertone : "The young scamps will have to carry their fun to the end, as the President will presently learn."

As we approached Appleton we found the north end in a blaze of light ; flashes of exploding gunpowder streamed from its windows and doorway, wreaths of smoke rose above its roof and floated into the pines in its rear, and the noise was continuous and ear-splitting. We walked toward the door, but instantly the firing party concentrated there and filled the aperture from top to bottom with sheets of flame and the President and his companions flattened their backs against the brick wall and waited.

"Oh, Professor !" shouted an irreverent Sophomore from a window overhead. "First time under fire !—How do you like it ?"

The Professor looked amused and then turning to the President he said :

"Doctor, I think Mr. Curtis is right, the boys will have to fire their last cartridge before they stop. We had better adjourn."

The President said something in reply which I did not hear, and a moment later the party disappeared down a path toward town. Left alone I again approached the door, watched for a lull in the firing and dropping upon all fours dashed under the rifle muzzles into the hallway and to the room of one of my officers.

I made no comment upon the proceedings, not even suggesting a stay of them ; but sat down and patiently awaited their cessation. About half-past eleven the reports became gradually desultory, and at last ceased, and I went back to my room in Winthrop Hall and to bed. Once more, near two o'clock, there was a slight resumption of firing but lighter than before and lasting less than a quarter of an hour. I felt satisfied that the last cartridge had been fired.

The following morning while at a late breakfast a messenger from President Woods summoned me to his office. I found the eminent gentleman in great apparent distress, disturbed by the unusual event just described and lack of a night's sleep. He received me with his usual distinguished courtesy, first speaking in praise of the military drill and commending the rapidity with which it had been perfected. He said he had watched the process with interest and felt pleased with the promptness in attendance which had been secured—a promptness the good effect of which the whole college felt in the improved attendance at chapel and recitations ; but that last night's experience had convinced him that firearms should never be intrusted to the hands of the ordinary college boy and that under no circumstances should they have in their possession the means of discharging them.

I replied that I had been connected with a college where arms were constantly in the hands of its corps of cadets, and that no firing occurred there except by order, and that I could effect the same observance at Bowdoin.

The President differed from me. He said Bowdoin was not under military discipline, that its Faculty was unacquainted with military methods of enforcing discipline, and that over twenty years experience in governing the young had taught him the wisdom of removing special temptations from their way.

I pleaded hard for the military feature—promised that if he would turn the management of the matter over to me I would guarantee that a similar disturbance should never again take place.

He commended my self-confidence—acknowledged it was an excellent trait for a military man—and apologized for doubting if a boy could develop the necessary authority over boys to warrant the college government in permitting the students to longer continue in possession of dangerous weapons ; finally reluctantly consenting to permit firing at drills for practice and under orders ; but insisting that rifles and ammunition should be regularly locked in the armory at the close of each day's military exercises.

It will be difficult, no doubt, for me to reconcile my subsequent conduct with my military profession. At Norwich I had been taught to obey orders unquestioningly, and for nearly four years had been in the habit of doing so. But when my battalion fell in the following day with shining rifles and bayonets and polished accoutrements ; when I saw it march down Maine street to the Topsham bridge in perfect alignment and step ; in column of company or platoons ; in parallel lines or extended column ; performing a succession of evolutions without an error or break, and when after a double-quick return to the college I brought it into line before the Chapel, a resolution formed and became fixed that I must show the President that this gallant corps of American boys was susceptible of thorough military control. I reflected that failure would cost me little and success would mean not only much for me but for all these boys. However, I did not at once yield to temptation and to my desire to show that military control could be successfully exercised over the Bowdoin students ; I waited until the third day after my interview with President Woods.

Before dismissing the battalion on the third day I made a short speech. I did not tell of my interview with the head of the college, and the surviving members of the battalion who may chance to read this will now first learn of it. I simply dwelt upon the gravity of their recent conduct from a military point of view, and of the disappointment it had caused me. In acknowledging the fact that we were only playing soldier I strongly insisted we should play it up to the best model. In closing I said : "Every man who will promise me on his honor as a gentleman and a soldier that he will not again fire his rifle except under the command of recognized authority or in the execution of duty, or do any other act likely to bring discredit upon our organization, will, at the command 'March,' advance four paces to the front and halt."

I gave the order and the whole line advanced one, two, three, four steps in perfect time and stood fast and silent ! From that day until I left Bowdoin for the Army of the Potomac each student had charge of his rifle and equipments.

July 16th arrived and I had made arrangements to accompany a Maine regiment to Washington on the 17th. I called on President Woods to say good by and then confessed that I had disobeyed his orders in regard to keeping the arms in the armory. He showed no surprise, but surprised me by saying that he knew of the course I had taken, and that while he could not commend it or think it consistent with my otherwise excellent military conduct, he would frankly acknowledge that I had excellent control of my command and that he was fast becoming a convert to the advantages of military methods in managing the young.

For years in the army I continued to meet brave and gallant officers who had taken their primary military instruction in the Bowdoin

Battalion. The triennial catalogue contains the names of many men who filled well every grade from Lieutenant to Major General, who were first under fire at Bowdoin on the memorable night I have attempted to describe.

The same afternoon upon which I took leave of President Woods I called at the young ladies' boarding school to say adieu to some pleasant friends I had made there. As I paused in the hall to lay aside my hat I heard some one in an adjoining parlor playing "Ever of thee I'm fondly dreaming," while some one else was executing a whistling accompaniment which was certainly artistically performed. Looking in at the door I saw the maiden of the snowy arm, who once dropped a bouquet from an oriel window, looking up fondly into the eyes of my companion of the Topsham drive, and heard her say : "And he really never suspected you could whistle it ?"

AN INQUISITION OF 1835

JAMES PLAISTED WEBBER, '00

AN INQUISITION OF 1835

I T is the year 1835, fifteen years before Harriet Beecher Stowe began writing "Uncle Tom's Cabin" in the white house on "Back" Street, twenty-five years before Major Anderson pulled down the Stars and Stripes at Fort Sumpter.

Conservative Brunswick town still looks askance at anti-slavery movements and feels that it is a pity that such a man as Prof. Blithe should so compromise his dignity as to identify himself with the unpopular cause. It is well known that he is an active station agent of the underground railway. Time and again in the dusk of twilight a black face has appeared at the Professor's door and a second later been hurried within to depart,—none can tell ; only the runaway, if such he be, disappears.

Remonstrance and pleading are alike unavailing. The Professor never swerves. Carry on his transportation, he will. Popularity and unpopularity are of small account to Professor Blithe. The earnest soul says, "I try to carry out, as far as in me lies, the duties which I feel God has placed upon me."

Sympathy awaits him, nevertheless, in at least one place. That is amidst the young democracy of his classroom, among the enthusiastic lads who in their manhood will shed their blood for this very cause, even as with words they fight out the Professor's battles with the townspeople.

But townspeople are not the only ones to look with disfavor on Professor Blithe's conduct. The Board of Trustees has long since got wind of his doings and frequent discussion of the case ripens into a determination to make some change in the Chair of Mathematics. Upon what ground shall they take this action and what shall be the nature of the change ? The last question is left hanging in air, but the first is readily answered. No matter how fine a master of Mathematics a professor may be, (and Professor Blithe was peer to the best), there are, as everyone knows, in every college class some notable laggards and dullards. The

Board decides then to swoop down suddenly upon one of Professor Blithe's recitations. notice that at least one or two men do not seem proficient in their work, and then make the change, whatever it may be, on the ground that while undoubtedly Professor Blithe is himself a competent mathematician, his classes are not making quite the progress desired.

News of the plot, however, reaches one of the boys the day before the proposed investigation. After class he notifies every member of the scheme to entrap Professor Blithe and each turns away with a look of determination. If you call at the room of any of those fellows early that evening, you will find the door locked. If you pound and kick until you get a response it will only be that the occupant is too busy to see you and that you had better go to blazes. If you call an hour or two later, you probably will meet with the same cordial reception. At midnight the tallow-dips still twinkle in many a room in Winthrop and Maine. How much later they burn depends upon their owner's ability in Mathematics.

At early chapel, the following morning, there enter three austere individuals, doleful as a coroner's jury. Many of the students do not know who they are nor the cause of their visit to Bowdoin, but everyone taking Mathematics knows. Professor Blithe too is not long in interpreting the sinister glance cast upon him as he takes his place.

An hour later the examination begins. The Three Worthies sit on a little, raised, platform in the recitation room in old Massachusetts, while Professor Blithe standing near by with his face full of serenity opens the recitation.

"Wigand."

Wigand ! Everybody knew that he was the worst man in the class. Why wouldn't the Professor confine his recitation as nearly as possible to the brilliant men? Why wouldn't he at least make a good beginning, say with Dalton, or Dole, the prize men, or with some of the lesser lights ? But Professor Blithe would sooner turn the odds against, than favor himself. "Wigand," repeats the Professor, "You may demonstrate the first theorem." The aforesaid Wigand has not opened his head in recitation for two weeks, but he is beginning right ;—beginning right, yes, he is continuing right. Through all the mazes of a really complicated

MASSACHUSETTS HALL.

figure he goes to his "Q. E. D.," which he gives with great gusto. With a feeling of relief, the class settles back, expecting that the next man up will be one of the real scholars.

"Bower !" calls Professor Blithe. Bower is a hardworking, slow-thinking chap who always gets confused under unusual circumstances and requires two weeks every time he has a new instructor before he gains confidence enough to do himself justice. "Bower," says the Professor, "may give the converse." A deep flush spreads over Bower's face, as the blood rushes to his head, and an ominous tremor accompanies his first words. Then with a clenched fist and a "do-it-or-die" look in his eye, in a tone of self-confidence which must have amazed even himself he landed safely on his conclusion.

A feeling of enthusiasm now seized the class. Man after man made a brilliant recitation, ten-strikes they would be called in modern days.

Nothing of criticism or correction was offered until Twing, the last man to recite, was half way through the last theorem of the lesson. Then one of the Worthies, glancing at his neighbors, as if to say "Now or never," prepared to interrupt the speaker. "Young man !" he broke forth, "Young man, go back and prove that line a b=line c d. You did not make that sufficiently clear." Poor old muddle-headed Trustee! Twing had shown twice in the course of his demonstration that the two were *unequal*, and he politely said as much, to the confusion of the inquisitor.

A moment later the hour was over and with it closed a Mathematics recitation whose like, I imagine, has never been seen before or since at Bowdoin or any other college. The boys with enthusiastic congratulation went to their next recitation. The Three Worthies, after shaking hands stiffly with Professor Blithe, betook themselves to the old Tontine that they might leave Brunswick on the next stage for Portland. Professor Blithe wended his way homeward, where he fitted out a packet for Sambo Snowball, who had arrived from "Ole Virginny, Sah !" via Boston and Bath, that morning, and must be shipped Canada-ward immediately, and then from his study window he threw to the breezes that swayed the whispering pines the first Abolition flag floated in Cumberland County.

RANDOM RECOLLECTIONS OF 1871-5

CHRISTOPHER H. WELLS, '75

RANDOM RECOLLECTIONS OF 1871-5

A TALE of Bowdoin ! But where shall one begin to write, and having once begun where shall he end? The experiences of a four years' course in college, delightful as they are, crowd confusingly in one's memory after the lapse of a quarter of a century. One who would record them hardly sees where he may first touch upon them, and once they have begun to be expressed they continue crowding so earnestly and in such a multitude that they almost command the pen to continue its work indefinitely. Whatever may be written here, however, will necessarily be at random, and disconnected, and will pertain to the lighter rather than to the more serious side of college life. Somehow or other those things which we go to college to acquire and which we ought to remember pass quickly from our minds, while all the things that we were expected not to learn cling to our memory with most delightful tenacity.

A college course, therefore, is not, in the memory of the average student, a succession of recitations and studies, of roots and cosines, essays and discussions, but it is a vitascopic picture of many a delightful walk and trip, of jokes and capers and unmalicious pranks springing out of healthful and vigorous animal spirits. Poor Richard has said that "Kings and bears often worry their keepers." He should to these have added college boys as a source of worriment to those under whose charge they are. If a chastening influence makes men better, college presidents and professors, who are at all times subjected to the quiet criticism and ingenious opposition of students, must be about as near perfect as human beings well can be.

Doubtless Bowdoin has changed much since the class of '75 left it. Educational institutions change in spirit and policy in the course of years. The alumni of preceding years fear that these changes are not for the better, and though the process of evolution leads upward and the educational movement is ahead, yet there are some conditions of the olden times which we would like to see remaining.

A quarter of a century ago the boys at Bowdoin constituted a big family. There were the Greek letter societies, of course, and at the beginning of each year there was considerable activity in "fishing" for candidates, but after these had been selected and initiated, society life was not unduly conspicuous in our college experiences. The societies tried to get the popular men, or the best scholars, but in the general life of the college then there was but little evidence of clique or faction. The students participated in affairs of friendship or society without special reference to what Greek-letter organization they belonged to. There was an air of comradeship running through the college, a communal feeling that made for the best results, both for the students and the college itself. Under such conditions a college is a grand school of democracy. It brings out the best there is in the student and places merit and character above adventitious circumstances. The recollections of a college life under such conditions are broad and catholic and peculiarly pleasant and satisfying. The recent tendency in college life seems to be in the direction of a narrower field of association, of a more restricted spirit of loyalty to college. The secret society seems to be uppermost in college life, and the life of the student comes within the narrower circle of its influence. The breadth of college life, the strength of college friendships and the fullness of college memories cannot be the same under such environment as they were in days now long gone.

"Bowdoin in the Rebellion" has been written, but, strange to relate, there is no reference whatever to that most momentous occurrence, the Rebellion of '74. This is one of the most important events in the history of the college and it seems as though allusion to it may properly be made.

The class of '75 was made the subject of various experiments. The members were healthy looking boys with generous appetites and a large fund of animal spirits, and the Faculty probably thought that they would be good subjects to begin on. So it was decided that military drill should be introduced into the college course coincidently with our arrival. The preliminaries to such an experience were rapidly passed over, uniforms of the West Point pattern were made by Bob Robertson, the tailor, and we were soon in the full gorgeousness of military embellishment.

It was not so bad at first, marching around in military manoeuvres and handling the gun in the manual of arms. Moreover it was splendid exercise for the body, tending to make one erect and strong and of easy carriage. Our commandant was Major Joseph P. Sanger, U. S. A., an artillery officer, now in service in Cuba. He was a diminutive man physically, but mentally he was clear and strong and a finely equipped officer. The boys all liked him and he displayed great tact and kindness in his treatment of them. He carried himself splendidly, and when in full uniform one forgot that he was not a six-footer.

Pretty soon we became fairly proficient in the drill and took trips about the town. At one time we appeared at the agricultural fair at Topsham. A circular is now before the writer in relation to that event, for a controversy arose concerning it. Our artillerists fired a salute to Governor Perham from our twelve-pound battery. The rustic steeds, hitched, or standing free, about the trotting park, were not expecting such a sudden and deafening volume of sounds, and as soon as the first gun was fired there was a commotion observable in all portions of the grounds, a noticeable feature of which was the desire of the aforesaid steeds to jump over the fence and make for home. After four guns were fired, the order to cease firing was given, owing to the evident disturbance in equine conditions. A controversy arose among the fair officials as to who was responsible for the order to fire a salute, and circulars and newspaper articles were published on both sides. It may be said, however, that Major Sanger and the Bowdoin cadets came out of the affair with flying colors.

Another incident of that day comes back to the writer. Major Sanger, being in full dress, wore his spurs. He had the companies formed in line marching across the parade ground in battalion front, and was himself marching backward in order to keep his eyes on the young warriors in the ranks. Unfortunately, however, one of the major's spurs stuck into a miniature eminence which had probably once been the birthplace of an humble potato, and as he did so he fell backward on the ground. His humiliation and the amusement of the cadets may easily be imagined. The smile on the faces of the boys was so loud that it is a wonder the horses were not frightened a second time.

Still another incident of our military life comes up in memory. Some of the artillerists went over to Topsham one Fall to fire a salute on the occasion of a certain important public event, and after the salute had been fired the firers were taken by a Topsham man of very hospitable nature to his house. They were of course very thirsty after their active work in firing minute guns, and the gentleman took them down into his wine cellar. It was a very imposing place, with its tiers of barrels and its various bottles and jugs. We were not there to ask questions and when our host drew out a tin dipperful of a red liquid from a barrel, he handed it to one of the boys, undoubtedly expecting us all to slake our thirst out of that one dipperful. The first cadet, however, swallowed the whole dipperful, and our host was therefore obliged in courtesy to draw out an equal amount for each one. It all went with the same gusto, and no questions were asked as to its alcoholic potentiality. It was our first experience with the army canteen. Of course we had a very jolly time, and as we look back at it now, it seems to have been a very thoughtful act for our host to have his team sent around to carry us home.

But the seeds of mutiny were sown when the students began to realize that the drill was obligatory. Human nature seems especially averse to doing that which it is under compulsion to do. The various general orders and accumulating restrictions presented upon the chapel bulletin-board fanned the flames of sedition until finally the students, in May, 1874, rebelled, refusing to report for duty. They were called individually before the Faculty and on persisting in their policy of disobedience were sent home. Their arrivals at the ancestral domicile were followed a few days later by a circular from President Chamberlain, giving a statement of the case from the Faculty's point of view. Of course we were wrong, and we all went back and submitted to the rules of the college, but the backbone of the drill was broken, and it died a speedy and unregretted death as a Bowdoin institution.

We used to have some great gymnasium work in our day. Dudley A. Sargent, now at Harvard, had charge of the gymnastic work at Bowdoin, and a fine gymnast and athlete he was, too. Some of the public exhibitions given in those years at Brunswick, Portland and other places comprised really remarkable gymnastic feats. The double eschelle we considered a crowning act of muscular skill and daring. Sargent was a fine performer on the horizontal bar, and excelled in trapeze-balancing and other feats. Once, I remember, an entertainment of gymnastics contained a feature that was not anticipated by the performers. One number of the program was somersaults from a springboard. The board would give the leaper additional energy and he would sail into the air, turn leisurely over and come down on his feet. That is: this is what he was expected to do. On this occasion, however, there was a departure from these lines. Either some one arranged the spring- bar wrong side up, or else the gymnasts had an attack of stage fright, for one after another leaped, but could not turn, and came down on the mattress flat on his back. The spectators enjoyed this fully as much as they did the most startling features on the program.

Although Brunswick is far removed from the centre of circles in which the aquatic spirit most strongly prevails, yet in those years she turned out some good crews and has since rendered a good account of herself on the water. There used to be an old patched shell that had seen better days, and four of us landlubbers used to take it occasionally for a row down the river. There was nothing professional about our stroke and we never took any prizes or medals for efficiency as oarsmen, but we had great times just the same. Each man had his own ideas as to about how rowing should be done, and as to about how often it was desirable to add to the stroke-precision by catching a crab. The necessity of frequent bailing was so great, owing to the leaky condition of the boat, that it was a question on the whole as to whether the boat went any faster horizontally than it settled vertically. It was a case of the pan being mightier than the oar.

There is before the writer a little circular which is worded as follows :

TALES OF BOWDOIN

BOWDOIN COLLEGE, Oct. 18, '71.

SIR :—I am happy to extend to you an invitation to become a member of the Peucinian Society.   A. P. WISWELL, Secretary.

Initiation will take place Thursday eve, Oct. 19th, 1871.

The invitation is about all the writer remembers of that old society, which, once so useful to the student, had, even in our day, in company with its fellow society the Athenean, begun to go into decay. The initiation was brief and not entirely unimpressive. The candidates then learned the true meaning of the term *pinos loquentes*. Bro. Wiswell, the secretary, was assigned to the rear of the writer's chair, and he has always felt that the thinness of hair on the top of his cranium was due to the vigor with which the present Chief Justice of Maine caused the pine to speak for itself.

A great many college pranks come to mind, but the necessarily restricted limits of this article will permit mention of but few of them.

There used to be a town liquor agency in Brunswick on the main street, not far from Billy Coffin's oyster-house. In front of the building was a large sign, placed well up over the door. The younger students had often cast longing eyes at that sign, and it was believed that it would be something of an ornament to the college grounds if it could be confiscated : But the place was so public, and the policeman of that section seemed to devote so much of his time to that vicinity, that any designs on that sign seemed not to promise success. One night, however, things looked propitious for the attempt. George S—— and Frank V——, whom we called "Pete" for short, were in the party, and one or two others whose names I do not now recall. We placed barrels and planks against the building and succeeded in wrenching the sign loose and taking it down. Just then the alarm was given that some one was approaching. It was the cop, and haste was necessary. George grabbed the front end of the big sign and the rest of us arranged ourselves alongside at various points. The way that sign moved up-street, with the animated legs underneath, must have suggested to a nocturnal observer the thought of a many-legged creature of the centipede variety. Pete, however, who was on principle opposed to active physical exercise, lagged behind and the policeman captured him. The sign was safely deposited under Appleton Hall, and on Pete's not showing up in due season we all proceeded back down town to see what the matter was. As we walked down the Mall the dejected form of Pete came in view through the darkness. Now Pete in his happiest moments had a solemn look on his countenance that ill-comported with his naturally jolly nature, and when he actually was dejected his countenance expressed absolute, awful, unspeakable wretchedness. We could almost feel the misery emanate from his countenance as he drew near. "It's no use, boys," said he in sepulchral tones, "the jig is up. You've got to return that sign." It seems that the policeman decided to let Pete off on condition that he would agree that the sign should be returned. So to save Pete we had to take that long-desired sign back and place it again over the door, under the supervision of the officer, interspersing our efforts with remarks uncomplimentary to police officers in general and the Brunswick police in particular.

"Tute" Card, the hackman, was a familiar figure about town, and the students all knew him, some of them to their cost. Tute was a sly one. Occasionally he used to ask the boys to ride down town from the depot in his carriage, and would make no charge for it. This was deemed quite a favor. One day, however, he put up a job on some of the boys. He had a crony with him and the crony said to several of the students, "Don't you want to ride down to the post-office, boys ?" Four or five of us boys, accepting the implied invitation, got into the carriage, but when we alighted at our destination, Tute coolly asked us to pay 25 cents apiece, the regular rate. We demurred and said that we had been asked to ride. "I didn't ask you," said Tute, "and this fellow here who did ask you isn't running this hack, so you'll have to fork over." It was perfectly evident that it was a swindling job put up by the two, but we paid ; that is, we paid by proxy, for Al Whit. was the only fellow in the party that had any money, and he settled the bill for the crowd. So Al was in a position to fully appreciate the little game.

The writer's chum the first year was Bill H——, one of the best-hearted and jolliest-natured fellows that ever lived. We used to call him "Mystery," as he seemed to have "up his sleeve" such a great variety of information on subjects that the general college public was not thoroughly conversant with. Bill could give a more significant nod than any man the world has known, and his wink conveyed volumes and volumes of suggestion. We all felt that if Bill would tell all he knew about things, the world's store of thought and information would be greatly enriched.

If there was one thing that Bill loved it was a practical joke, and he could think up more kinds of jokes and more opportunities for perpetrating them than any man in college. One day he planned one on the occupants of the room overhead—McQ—— and S——. We had to let Mac into the secret. One evening Bill got into their room and tied a rope to the leg of the bed nearest the wall and window. He passed this rope back of the commode and out of the window, the other end being carried into our room. In the late hours of the night, when S—— was asleep and snoring, we gave a strong, steady pull on the end of the rope. There was an overturning of furniture and a crashing of crockery, and a bed was heard to roll across the floor. There ensued a period of distress and confusion upstairs, pretended on the part of Mac, but real on the part of S——. It was some time before S—— discovered the cause of the agitation of the furniture, and we could hear him grunt with surprise when he finally came across the rope.

One of Bill's possessions which he brought from home was a large red pincushion, plumply stuffed on top. One would think to look at it that it was a light and airy affair that would almost sail into space of its own volition, but in reality it was a very substantial article, for its foundation was a hard-burned brick, and about the heaviest brick ever made. It would weigh something, but not much, less than a ton. One day Frank U—— and other boys were passing ball and loafing on the campus. Looking up and seeing Bill leaning out of our window, Frank said, "Throw down something for us to catch." "Catch this !" said Bill, tossing out the red pincushion. It sailed through the air down three stories in a most etherial manner. Frank held up his hands in a lightsome way to catch the feathery object, but when it struck his hands his look of lazy interest changed into one of startled surprise, for the cushion banged through his hands and half-buried itself in the turf. It was a long time before Frank could recover from a sense of the narrowness of his escape.

One day in the fall a trip to Goose Island was taken by some of us boys, sailing from Maquoit in a leaky and weatherbeaten old craft which met a squall soon after starting. Under the expert care of Mont Aldous, a student in the scientific department, we reached our destination safely. Such expeditions usually go equipped with everything except water, and ours was no exception to the rule. A hunt over the island in the gathering darkness failed to reveal a spring, and so at a late hour our thirst compelled us to row across the bay to Harpswell in the small and leaky boat's-tender, five or six of us, and there we went up to a farm well and drank delicious draughts of water, enough to last us during the remainder of our visit in that locality. It was late and we concluded not to row back that night, the water being very rough, and so we all laid down under the lee of a stone wall on the wet grass and. slept sweetly as tired youth knows how to sleep, in the cool air of the October night. Strange to relate! there was never a cold or a sneeze that resulted from this experience.

In the neighboring town of Topsham there was a tax- collector who was a more amiable and agreeable man than tax-collectors in general are supposed to be. No student had any opportunity to have a grievance against him, but grievances are not necessary in order to stimulate the youthful mind to acts of deviltry. One day this tax-collector was quietly walking by on the sidewalk of the Harpswell road when an insinuating voice from somewhere in Winthrop Hall said most pleasantly : "Will you be so kind as to step over here, Mr. P—— ? I want to talk with you." And Mr. P—— came over, like the accommodating man he was, to hear whatever the person of honeyed words had to say. On arriving at the hall entrance, however, his ears were assailed with most outrageously abusive language, to his great surprise and indignation. He started to come in and discover the perpetrator of the outrage, but his discretion prevailed and he nursed his wrath and went away in a towering rage.

Many other incidents come back to the writer in memory—the handcar expedition after turkeys ; the purloining of a yellow flag that was placed in front of a house downtown to indicate smallpox ; the visits and lectures of the late Daniel Pratt, always a source of interest to the students; the beautiful playing of a strolling violinist who made regular trips to Brunswick, and whose little finger of the right hand was always encased in a soiled rag, though he did not play in "rag-time." The writer recalls, too, the pleasant experiences in the class-room ; the games and sports on the Delta when baseball and football were not played as they are today. The delightful strolls into the surrounding country come back to him, and he lives over again the hours of social enjoyment, the communing of souls in boyish confidences, the building of air-castles, and the dreaming of bright visions of the future. But these recollections, delightful as they are to the writer, can offer in their recounting but little of interest save to those who were a part of them in the student life of a quarter-century ago.

JOHN FERRIS, GRADUATE

Edgar O. Achorn. '81

JOHN FERRIS, GRADUATE

J OHN Ferris stood alone in front of Memorial Hall, wrapped in meditation. It was near the close of one of June's fairest days. The Class Day exercises were over ; the graduating class had smoked the pipe of peace, cheered the halls, and disbanded ; but knots of people were still loitering about as if reluctant to leave a spot of such matchless beauty.

In a vague way John Ferris was conscious of the perfect symmetry of the Art Building and Chapel as they came within the range of his vision. He heard, but faintly, the voices around him, the joyous laughter, and the words of the familiar song wafted from the windows of Maine Hall :

> "We'll hail from the walls of old Bowdoin,
> Those walls so jolly with fame."

It was twenty years since his class had celebrated its Commencement and bid farewell to college life, and now those twenty years rose in a vision before him.

> "O ye familiar scenes,—ye groves of pine
> That once were mine and are no longer mine,—
> Ye halls, in whose seclusion and repose
> Phantoms of fame like exhalations rose
> And vanished,"

he quoted half aloud. Twenty years ! He was no longer young; his youth—his bright youth—had gone forever. Phantoms of fame ! Where were the ambitions of those early days now ? Thwarted, abandoned, dead. Some he had buried years before ; the long grass and weeds had grown over their mounds, and their epitaphs were dim and indistinct. But others there were—his greater ambitions—marked by fresh mounds and freshly cut headstones. These had died hard, and when at times, as now, a flood of memories came back to him, their recollection gave him the keenest pain.

271

"A penny for your thoughts." John Ferris roused himself, turned, and recognized his old friend, Grace Pennell, approaching, with her hand extended in greeting. "We have been watching you for the last five minutes. Come, explain yourself ; why this melancholy in the midst of so much festivity ? Let me present you to Miss Overton of Knoxville—she is with me for Commencement." While Mrs. Pennell was speaking, John turned from shaking hands with her to acknowledge the introduction to Miss Overton. He was met by a pair of serious brown eyes that looked squarely into his own. The uplifted face was beautiful in outline, denoting at once intellectuality, pride, and tenderness. The rippling brown hair, the well poised head, the graceful figure, all appealed and with irresistible force to his sense of the beautiful in woman. To John Ferris it was a new sensation ; in all these years of struggle and endeavor since his college days it had never seemed to him that there was any place for woman. He had never given her much thought, and so far as he had it was to regard her as a fellow pilgrim,—one quite apart from his own plans and purposes. And now, as he looked into this woman's face, he felt an indefinable sensation of pleasure, of anticipation, of confidence, and of mutual sympathy. "I must confess that you surprised me when I was feeling just a trifle disconsolate, but your coming has quite driven it away," he said, at length replying to Mrs. Pennell, but with his eyes still fastened upon her friend. "But how can you be sad in such an enchanted spot ?" exclaimed Miss Overton. "Why, I'm in love with old Bowdoin— to me, a Southerner, this campus is ideal."

"That is rather a difficult question to answer, Miss Overton, in a word. I am a loyal son of Bowdoin—none more so—and I am alive to the festivity of the occasion,—the beauty of the surroundings,—I too appreciate it ; but underlying all to me, when I stop to reflect, there is a very sad side to this coming back to Commencement. Nowhere else does one stand so face to face with his past life, with his failures ; nowhere are comparisons so odious ; nowhere does it come home to one with equal force that his life is slipping away and that he has accomplished nothing. With you in the South, everything dates from the war—with us, from our college days. It is twenty years since I graduated, and I have nothing to show for it. It may seem strange to you, but I had just reached the determination not to return here again for another twenty years." He spoke earnestly and with a tinge of bitterness.

"Ah, but you enjoy meeting the men of your time, John,—I should say, of our time—" said Mrs. Pennell, "or else you are very much changed since I knew you as a student, for we of the town used to hear startling rumors of your genial habits."

"Yes, to be sure I shall dearly love to meet the old crowd again, and after a few sips of the historic punch I presume I shall be quite like my old self ; but thus far I haven't happened to meet one of my class. It is a little early in the week ; doubtless they will be here in force to-morrow."

At that moment Mrs. Pennell, excusing herself, responded to a call from a carriage near, and the two were left alone. "Do you think that all college men feel as you do, Mr. Ferris, about coming back ?" asked Miss Overton. "The majority do not, I fancy. Such as do would be found among the number of those who, like myself, have won no great victories in the world's arena. Those who have written their names high on the scroll of fame, doubtless return with a sense of exhilaration and triumph, bringing their shields. They have the satisfaction of knowing that their success gives an added lustre to the fame of Bowdoin. Do you see the four men sitting together under the Thorndike Oak ? They are Chief Justice Fuller, Tom Reed, General Howard and Senator Frye. These are the men who must return with satisfaction to themselves ; but we poor unfortunates who are given over to the petty drudgery of life, who have failed in the running and know it,—what do you think our sensations are when we come up to this judgment seat ?"

"Ah, but, Mr. Ferris, surely you do not regard those lives alone as successful that have had to do with great affairs—that have brought public distinction. It is enough, is it not, that each one act well his part, there, as Pope has well said, all the honor lies."

"It is a very pretty theory, Miss Overton. and man is so constituted that no matter what cards he may draw in the game of life, he almost never throws down his hand ; he plays it out, even if he doesn't take a trick ; but I contend that a commonplace existence is 'one demd horrid grind.' "

"I do not agree with you. Greater heroism is required to live faithful to the small things of life than to the great, or, to use your own simile, to play a poor hand well than one full of trumps, and I for one most admire the man endowed with qualities that make it possible for hint to live happily in modest circumstances—the man who dignifies the everyday affairs of life. We are not responsible for being here, and if we do our best in our respective places we should have no regrets. We cannot all be great—let us at least try to be happy, which is of more importance. Isn't that after all the true philosophy ?"

Miss Overton spoke with earnestness and with a measure of sympathy in her voice and manner which moved John Ferris deeply. He was unhappy, forlorn, dissatisfied with himself, and her words comforted him. He was eager to continue the conversation, but his next word was cut short by Mrs. Pennell, who, returning, apologized for the necessity of their speedy departure.

"But surely, Grace, I shall see Miss Overton again," said Ferris, loth to have her leave him. "I should esteem it a great privilege to be able to contribute something to the pleasure of her visit to Brunswick."

"We are at home to our friends at almost all hours Commencement week, as you know," replied Mrs. Pennell, "and I gladly accept you as an ally in making Miss Overton's stay with me a success."

Standing in the same spot, John Ferris watched Nancy Overton as long as she was in sight, and then he fell into a brown study again. How womanly and sincere she seemed—what an atmosphere of gladness surrounded her—what depths of feeling stirred in her brown eyes. She had given life a new meaning. It made him ashamed of his own mood. He must see more of her—he must do something to redeem himself.

And he did, for that evening as they sat on Mrs. Pennell's veranda, under the inspiration of Miss Overton's presence he recounted tales and incidents of his college days with such inimitable wit and pathos that the whole company was alternately moved from laughter to tears.

The following day he took her on that beautiful drive across the Brunswick plains to the sea—and Nancy Overton with a woman's intuition came to realize that the man at her side, although bruised and hurt by some of the bitter experiences and disappointments of life. still had that fine sense of honor, that keen sense of justice, and that love of the good, the true and the beautiful which characterize a thoroughbred gentleman.

It was the night of the President's reception. John Ferris, dressed with more than ordinary care and with a boyish eagerness quite foreign to him, betook himself to Memorial Hall. While he stopped to exchange a word of greeting with those he knew in the throng that soon filled the place, his eyes constantly sought the entrance ; he grew more and more impatient as the evening wore away and Mrs. Pennell and her friend failed to make their appearance. When all hope was at an end, he left the hall with a keen sense of disappointment. Lighting a cigar, he strolled across the campus, down the Longfellow path, and seated himself under the spreading pines. The full moon sailed in a cloudless sky, bathing each blade and leaf in a flood of silvery light. The pine boughs over head moved by the evening breeze mingled their music with the myriad voices of the night.

The mysterious spell of the place and hour gradually stole over him,—old things passed away, and John Ferris came into his birthright at last, for the "whispering pines of old Bowdoin" sang unto his very soul in passion's tenderest cadence the priceless heritage of a pure and unselfish love.

At his room a telegram awaited him, demanding his immediate return to Boston, and boarding the "Flying Yankee" he was gone.

During the next month John Ferris sought to apply himself with his usual diligence to the multifarious duties of his law practice, but with indifferent success. An ungovernable restlessness seized him, and in the midst of his work his mind repeatedly wandered back to the Bowdoin campus and the woman he had met there. He found himself reviewing every detail of her appearance, recalling every varying phase of her expressive face. He longed to see her again, to hear her voice, to feel the influence of her presence. Unable to settle down to business, he packed his bag and took passage for Europe, reflecting that a rest and a change might restore his equilibrium.

On August 30th, John Ferris registered at the Beau Rivage, Geneva. He had come down from Ober-Ammergau and was journeying by easy stages toward Paris. It was his birthday. An intense feeling of loneliness came over him as he sat at dinner on the balcony of the hotel and watched the changing hues of the sunset play upon the snowy summit of Mt. Blanc. His outing had in no wise effaced Nancy Overton from his thoughts. In fancy she filled the vacant chair opposite and he realized that his happiness would be complete were she there to share the beauty of the scene with him, when a voice that thrilled every fibre of his being said, "How beautiful." He sprang to his feet and faced about. Nancy Overton in company with Mrs. Pennell was just seating herself at the adjoining table. Their eyes met, and in her answering glance John Ferris read a glad response to all the overmastering emotion that found expression in his face and manner.

When Mrs. Pennell left them together two hours later, she said, "Now I will give you two an opportuntiy to finish the conversation I interrupted last June on the Bowdoin campus." They finished it, and John Ferris convinced Nancy Overton that if he might work for love of her nothing in life would ever seem to him commonplace again.

DIOGENES

Henry L. Chapman, '66

DIOGENES

N OT the philosopher of the tub ! Far from it, indeed ! It is possible that some quibbling persons might question whether the Diogenes of whom I write could fairly be called a philosopher at all. There is, however, a convenient vagueness about the term which admits of its being applied to him in common with a varied and picturesque procession of personages from Plato down to Mr. Dooley. It is certain, moreover, that he had a touch of the cynic in his disposition ; and there was a quaintness in his manner, coupled with a mystery touching his birth and previous condition, which might be regarded as incidental but happy additions to his outfit as a philosopher. So much will have to be granted. But it is impossible to locate him in a tub. He would doubtless have been a more engaging figure if that could have been done, at least occasionally. But he had to be taken as he was, just as we all have to be taken as we are. And, so taken, he is, in some respects, pleasanter as a reminiscence than he was as a contemporary.

It was in August, 1840, that this new visitant swam into the ken of Bowdoin students. The heated term was drawing near the end—and the Commencement, also. The breathing-space of four weeks, during which, in the good old times, the Seniors were excused from other duties in order that they might put their varied learning into intelligible shape for the Commencement platform, was passing, slowly and languorously. Ezra Abbott, the critical linguist, and Elijah Kellogg, the wit and genius, with "full nyne and twenty" classmates—a number which will always retain the distinction which Chaucer gave it when he thus summed up the company of pilgrims at the Tabard Inn—these were the dignified Seniors who, doubtless, like Chaucer's Sergeant of Law, *seemed* busier than they were. There was no question of "seeming," however, with Juniors and Sophomores and Freshmen ; they had still "to grunt and sweat under a weary life," since the recitations in Greek, Latin and Mathematics rolled on as pitilessly as the burning August sun.

Upon the scholastic scene, thus modestly set in the Bowdoin campus, entered a small, shrewd, smoothly-shaven and sedate stranger, who was destined to remain upon the scene, an interesting and unique figure, for more than a quarter of a century. He came unheralded, but not unattended. A colored man was his companion, who, by virtue of his hue and his evident dependence, might have passed for his shadow if the two had not soon parted company.

The ostensible errand of the new arrival was to exhibit some petty mechanical contrivance or puppet-show, and to pick up some small coins by way of return for the entertainment offered. He had reason, or, at least, courage, to hope that the young men of the college were so far imbued with the Baconian spirit that they did not seek in knowledge merely "a terrace for a wandering and variable mind to walk up and down with a fair prospect," but "a rich storehouse for the relief of man's estate." How far his hopes were realized, and his own estate relieved, cannot now be affirmed ; nor does it matter. More important issues hung upon his casual introduction to the college. Either some delicate perception of the students' needs, (as he saw them gathered about his trifling show), or some open promise of patronage on their part—or perhaps both—moved him to abandon his strolling and precarious life, and shortly to establish himself in a small shop on Maine Street, on which a rudely-printed sign announced that clothes were promptly mended and cleansed within.

His years of wandering over, here, at length, he was installed in a domicile of his own, and busied, like another Teufelsdröckh, with the Philosophy of Clothes. His patrons were chiefly, but not exclusively, from the college, and so assiduous was he in the mending and cleansing of their garments that he became unwisely forgetful of his own.

It was not long before his philosophical meditations and his mending and cleansing processes were interrupted, when a right of way through the village was demanded by the Portland and Kennebec Railroad, and the spot upon which his little shop stood had to be vacated. But it was not much more of a structure to move than a tub would have been ; and, with all his belongings in it undisturbed, it was hauled to a more secluded spot chosen by himself, and continued to be his residence and workshop so long as he needed either. As the only window to his house was a skylight

THE ABODE OF DIOGENES.

he had an equally good outlook wherever the house chanced to be located, and an outlook, it may be added, peculiarly congenial to the mind of a philosopher.

He was already on the shady sign of middle life, with a considerable knowledge of books and a strong liking for them, a half-cynical fondness for human society, an undisguised appetite for stimulants, and a general personal atmosphere which did not promise much for the clothes which he professed to cleanse. Gradually he allowed himself to be drawn from his seclusion to perform various menial duties about the college buildings, partly for the students, and partly for the Corporation. For twenty-five years, at least, he was familiar to the Bowdoin campus, and must be a tolerably distinct figure in the memories of the students of those years. A short, grave, sturdy little man—in rusty ill-fitting clothes, wearing always a silk hat, which, like himself, more than hinted of decay and decrepitude—he was to be seen at almost any hour going in and out of the college halls, or studying the newspapers in the reading-room through a magnifying-glass set in a rude unpainted frame, square and substantial. But he was to be seen at his weirdest and best in the dim twilight before the dawn, going from hall to hall with a burning candle, or, if it was windy, with a lantern—which perhaps gave him his name of Diogenes—to light the fires in the rooms of a few Sybaritic students, and in the recitation rooms, which must be warm for the early recitation before breakfast.

For this latter service he was employed by the college authorities, and hence arose the necessity for an annual house-cleaning, so to speak, of his person. Once in the year, with considerable pains and awkwardness doubtless, but with conscientious regularity, he went through the ordeal of a toilet, and adorned himself with such niceties of dress as he could command, and brought forth a less dilapidated hat than he was wont to wear—and, thus arrayed, he proceeded with unaffected dignity to call upon President Woods, to receive from him an order upon the college treasurer for his modest stipend. Any student that chanced to meet him on one of those annual official errands deemed himself fortunate, as indeed he was. He would get scant recognition, to be sure, and very likely none at all, from the little philosopher—who regarded the students as belonging wholly to his work-a-day world—but he would see the shuffling menial transformed, for the moment, into a self-respecting gentleman who had relations with the President of the college and the picture was one that would not fade from the memory. It might be that his pathway to the President's house was illumined by the recollection of more prosperous days in his earlier life, and, therefore, until his errand was done, he chose not to notice the young fellows of the college, who were associated altogether with the servile condition into which he had fallen.

There is reason to believe that he was a native of the Island of Guernsey, and that he passed some years in France, where he learned the trade of a glove-maker. From France he wandered to Nova Scotia. and from Nova Scotia to the United States, and to Brunswick. There is little doubt that he was brought up in the Catholic faith, and among the students it was a favorite hypothesis, which came to be accepted by them as fact, that he had been educated, or partially educated, for the priesthood. Subsequently, however, he became an Episcopalian, and, though he rarely attended upon the services of the church, he remained to the end a stout intellectual adherent of St. Paul. That his life might not be lacking in the element of romance it was believed that in his youth he was "jilted" in favor of his brother. It was not, in itself, an unreasonable conjecture, and, perhaps, the only thing needed to make it entirely credible, was some knowledge of his brother. Be that as it may, the story would help to account for the fact that he was, after a mild fashion, a misogynist, and that he drank to excess.

Whether these items of personal history that I have mentioned are true or not, they did not come to us from his own lips. He was, in a marked degree, reticent and uncommunicative. Proof against persuasion, and incapable of surprise, he never satisfied our curiosity with any confidences concerning his earlier life. Though we met him not once but daily, he yet seemed to us to be wrapped in a mystery not unlike that of Melchizedek, King of Salem. The more sensitive of the students, I think, respected his reticence, but not all ; and it was surely fine to see the silent contempt with which he repelled the boisterous, and sometimes vulgar, familiarities to which he was now and then exposed. But he had his favorites and his failings, and unfortunately, as is sometimes the case with better men than he, it was to his favorites that he was apt to display his failings. To them he would so far unbend as to quote scraps of unalluring verse, often with emendations of his own, and repeat a few haggard and time-worn jokes, and sit overlong by their open fires. His sense of humor was of a pinched and primitive order, and it sometimes found vent in utterances that were not altogether fit for refined ears, though this was not of frequent occurrence. His laugh was an odd vibration of mirth, suggesting a sort of compromise between a chuckle and a hiss, and it struggled forth as best it could from between his tongue and his upper teeth, which seemed to come together in order to help or to hinder the demonstration, and one could hardly tell which. As a laugh, therefore, it was interesting, but not infectious.

The picture of him rises before me now, as he used to sit at times before my own wide Franklin stove, in which, through one luxurious winter, I employed him to light the morning fires. His poor, frayed, threadbare coat is buttoned close to his chin ; his trousers conceal a part of their poverty, being tucked into capacious rubber boots ; and his unspeakable hat is pulled down upon his ears,—for, like the English House of Commons, it was his custom to sit with his hat on. The expression of his face is shrewd and not unpleasing ; his talk has in it a distinct touch of the gentleman, and he passes from speech to silence (and, perhaps, even to sleep), as naturally and gently as a child. He has a word or two, very likely, of college gossip ; he says something of religion, buttressing his remarks, probably, with a saying of St. Paul's ; he speaks for a few moments of books; and after a short silence a sort of twinkle comes into his eyes, and he recites, with an unmistakable relish, two stanzas from Southey's "Devil's Walk" :

> "From his brimstone bed at break of day,
>   A-walking the Devil is gone,
> To look at his snug little farm of the world,
>   And see how his stock went on.

"How then was the Devil dressed ?
    Oh ! he was in his Sunday's best :
His coat was red, and his breeches were blue,
    And there was a hole where the tail came through."

Something in this poetic portrait has a persistent charm for him, and it is a favorite quotation ; and now, having repeated it to me, he gives one of his little dubious, Jesuitical laughs, and gets up and shambles out.

He was a diligent reader, with some claims—making due allowance for the narrow limits of his leisure—to the title of bookworm. In the dingy and cheerless hovel which served as his domicile—and which may still be seen in the rear of the Brunswick House on Maine Street—he had gathered a library of several hundred volumes, packed away in boxes which occupied the center of the floor, directly under the skylight, which, as I have said, alone furnished light to the apartment when the door was shut. Inconvenient as were his library accommodations, so familiar was he with his treasures that he was rarely at a moment's loss to know in which of the half-score of boxes any particular volume was to be found. He was reported to make additions to his library through a system of "forced benevolences," of which the successive Freshman classes were the victims. The benevolences were an undoubted fact, but whether the money was always expended for books was not so certain. In the later years of his life his necessities forced him to dispose of some of his treasured books, and, more than once, the present writer was persuaded to act as auctioneer for the sale of them, the auction being invariably held in the open space between the Chapel and Maine Hall ; and the sufficient commission to the auctioneer was the sincere but scantily-worded gratitude of the shabby philosopher.

He was probably somewhat more than ninety years old at his death, which occurred on the thirtieth of April, 1868. The funeral service was conducted by President Harris, and he was buried, in conformity with his expressed wish, in the town of Weld, because that was the burial place of the family of his landlady who had always been kind to him, and in whose house he died.

When, at last, he had left the solitude of his poor hut for the scarcely deeper solitude of the grave, it was impossible by inquiry or advertisement, to find any kinsfolk to inherit his meagre belongings ; and, after two or three years of fruitless effort, his administrator transferred his books to the college library, where they are still to be found bearing the label, "From the Library of Thomas A. Curtis." The law and the library knew him only as Thomas A. Curtis, but his contemporaries among the students remember him more familiarly and kindly as "Diogenes."

THE RIVAL FULLBACKS

Henry A. Wing, '80

THE RIVAL FULLBACKS

IT was Bowdoin's last and most important football game of the season. Whittier Field had never held a crowd so large or so enthusiastic. The contest had excited the keenest interest, and had been heralded in the newspapers for weeks previous. And now men and women, staid professors and undergrads not quite so staid, had gathered to witness the struggle which should decide the championship of the State. The grandstand was a mass of waving flags and fluttering ribbons ; the sidelines were crowded, and all available space about the grounds was occupied by cheering, excited spectators.

For thirty minutes the teams had been struggling in the fiercest contest ever waged on a gridiron in Maine. Bowdoin clearly hid the advantage, yet was unsuccessful in making a goal. Three times had the sturdy home team worked the ball to the twenty-yard line of their opponents ; three times had Hal Blackford, who was playing fullback, attempted place kicks, with the ball held by the quarterback, and failed. Then fickle fortune had changed, and the ball was sent into Bowdoin territory, out of danger.

"In Heaven's name, where is Phil Edson ?" muttered the captain to himself ; and in many minds the same query was uppermost. Phil, the most skilful goal kicker in the State ; Phil, the pride and safety of the team ; who had practiced with them, won with them, and sworn by them all his college years, the popular man of the college, who had been depended upon to win the game if it should be a close one, by a place kick. That morning he was in the captain's room, full of vigor and eager for the fray ; now no one could venture a guess as to where he was, or what had occasioned his absence. At the last minute Hal Blackford had been substituted, and bewilderment was followed by a vague uneasiness when this change was made apparent to the spectators.

A fourth time Bowdoin gained the twenty-yard line of the opposing team. The spectators were wild with excitement. The sharp "Rah ! rah !

rah !" of Bowdoin was heard high above the slogan of the enemy. A minute was left for play ; the signal was given for another attempt to kick. The long pass to the quarter was not accurately made ; the opposing team broke through the Bowdoin line ; there was a sharp mix-up, and when it was over Hal was taken from the bottom of the heap bruised, insensible, and carried from the field seriously if not fatally injured, as the physician after a hasty examination gravely pronounced.

Time for the first half was called and the Bowdoin players clustered together, despondent and almost without hope. Coaches and captain consulted mechanically, knowing that almost certain defeat would follow the only course now open to them. Another substitute must be put into the game.

The hopes of the opposing team had correspondingly risen. They had two reliable men to put into their line, and they were cognizant of Bowdoin's weakness with her best fullback absent, her best substitute disabled, her courage severely strained. With the indomitable spirit which has helped win many a victory for Bowdoin on field and on water, her eleven now awaited the call which might marshal them to defeat. The sky had clouded ; the depressing chill of winter was in the air, and as the sun sank fast in the November sky, the sighing of the winds through the pines seemed to the Bowdoin sympathizers preliminary tunings of the dirge of disaster waiting the champions of the white.

A thrill of excitement rising to an hysterical outburst ; a cry, swelling and bursting into a tremendous volume of sound, rocks the grandstand, echoes through the pines, and "E-D-S-O-N ! Rah ! Rah ! Rah !" rises and falls upon the air, from hundreds of throats, the college team frantic with glee leading the chorus. From somewhere, no one knows exactly where, a tall, athletic youth has sprinted into view, and the regular fullback of the team, the most skilful player in the State, is tearing up the path.

"This is no time for explanation," was Phil's hurried word in answer to the confused queries which greeted him. "Give me a suit of football clothes, and mighty quick, too." At the call of the whistle, Bowdoin faced her opponents with new courage.

Never before nor since has there been such an exhibition of football upon Whittier Field. At the beginning of the half the opposing team attempted one or two trick plays, but on these they lost ground. From that time on there was straight, old-fashioned football. Bowdoin had advanced the ball from the beginning of the half, but it had been lost on fumbles and kicked back to the center of the field. The visitors fought like fiends to prevent Bowdoin from getting the ball into position to try for a goal from the field, or a kick from placement.

Twenty minutes had been played, when the superior muscle, training and grit of Bowdoin began to tell. Slowly the ball was worked toward the goal of the enemy. They had persisted in keeping the ball from the center of the field, making an attempted goal as difficult as it well could be. Three minutes were left for play, and the ball was held on the twenty-five yard line. A desperate chance only could accomplish the coveted score, for the teams were near the sideline at the left of the field.

The signal was given ; the ball was accurately passed to the quarterback, who as quickly placed it on the ground and Phil sent the sphere whirling through space. Its progress was watched with breathless interest by the spectators, who for the moment had no further care for the two teams, though Bowdoin's stonewall line had been broken, just as the pigskin rose into the air. The wind apparently carries the ball away from the goalpost ; it wavers a bit, and the big audience as one man catches its breath ; but on it sails, swift and sure.

"GOAL !" shouted the official.

Time was up, and Bowdoin had won, 5 to 0.

A mighty cheer shatters the silence of the preceding moment; the pæan of old "Phi Chi" arises irregularly upon the air ; the undergrads break through the lines, and Phil is hoisted upon their shoulders and borne in triumph from the field. There is a scene of rejoicing which lasts many minutes, a "Bowdoin war dance," as one of the defeated disgustedly dubs it, and the happy company troops from the field through the softly falling snow, "the white of a Bowdoin victory."

*   *   *   *   *   *   *

"Kid" Barker had deposited to the best advantage his 225 pounds of avoirdupois on the captain's couch ; "Giant" Gray, the featherweight of the college, had taken up his customary position before the fire ; two or three others of the captain's particular set were variously disposed about the room, which was blue with smoke and cheerful from the blaze of the open fire in the little Franklin stove, and all were rehearsing the exciting events of the afternoon, when Phil walked in on his way to inquire for his friend Hal.

"Speak up, and give an account of yourself, old man," greeted him before he was fairly through the door.

"Give an account, and take an account as well," he replied. "What the dickens is to pay round this college, anyhow ? About eleven o'clock this morning I went down town to mail a letter, and as I was passing the station a small boy stepped up and handed me a telegram signed by Mr. Forster, father's confidential clerk, saying 'Come at once ; your father is just alive.' The train was just pulling out, and I barely swung on to the rear platform. I did not see a soul with whom I could leave any word, and I decided to telegraph when I reached Portland. You can guess how I felt when the first man who met my eyes in that station was Mr. Forster. I rushed up to him and asked for Father. 'Your father sick ?' he said. 'I left him in Boston last night, never better in his life, and have just received a dispatch from him saying he was going to New York this afternoon. There must be some mistake.' I showed him the telegram I possessed, and he said at once it was a forgery. It flashed upon me in a minute that some one had put up this job to get me out of the game for today. I told Mr. Forster of my suspicions, and he was all interest at once. Our first thought was a special engine, and as Forster knew the general superintendent well, he made for his office, to get one for love or money, while I made for the restaurant, knowing I should need a good meal more than anything else just then.

"We hadn't got very far out of the city before I knew what it meant to skim along through the air ; I never shall envy an engineer his work after this ; I felt pretty easy in my mind, and was settled back thinking things over pretty hard, when smash, crash : and there we were in Freeport yard, with a broken driving rod. If it hadn't been for the fact that we were running slow on to a siding for the express to pass us, I might have been worse off, I suppose. Well, thought I, the game is up this time, anyhow. And so was my fighting blood.

AN END PLAY ON THE WHITTIER FIELD.

"My eye fell upon a livery stable ; and I made one more try for Brunswick. The proprietor heard my tale of woe. 'This little mare here,' said he, pointing to a dandy bay in her box stall, 'can take you to Brunswick easy in little over an hour. Take her if you want her.' So off I started once more. I got into Brunswick at just half-past three ; left the mare at the stable, took a fresh horse for the grounds, and raced for Whittier Field, and you know the rest. Now, there is my part of the story, what can you offer to help finish it out ?" concluded Phil.

The boys glanced furtively at one another, as though afraid to offer an opinion.

"Beats me," breathed Kid.

"Mighty lucky Hal Blackford was in fighting trim," hazarded Giant.

"Never saw a chap so tickled as he was when we notified him to take Phil's place," commented the captain, addressing no one in particular. "Said he had been suffering for a chance on the team for weeks, in this particular game," added he, as no one replied to his first assertion.

"None of that," sharply spoke up Phil, "I'd as soon suspect my own brother of double play as to suspect Hal !" and he left the room much disturbed by the implied doubt, the more so because for a moment, and only for a moment, Phil had had the same thought come to him. Hal had envied him his position, he knew, and eagerly longed to be one of the contestants in this, the last game they should play as undergraduates of their beloved college. As he slowly walked along to the room where his friend lay fighting a harder battle than that of the afternoon, with much more at stake, his mind traversed their intimacy of the past four years, and the peculiar circumstances which had linked them together, in spite of much which might have destroyed a less firm friendship than theirs.

Fate had seemingly decreed that he and Hal should be rivals in every important thing through their college course, from the time of election of chairman at the first class meeting down to the Fall term of this, their Senior year, when the rivalry for position of fullback on the team had been the keenest, and he had won only through superior proficiency in punting. Although obliged to admit that his chums had some grounds upon which to base the suspicions they had hinted at, he could not believe that Hal, who had been the soul of honor, could by a miserable trick gain for himself the glory of playing in this game. Banishing this from his mind as impossible and absurd, he stopped at the door of the room where Hal lay unconscious, to be met by Hal's sister Marguerite, of whom he had often heard, but never met. As he saw her sad and anxious face, he thought her the prettiest girl he had ever seen, and as she claimed him as Hal's best friend and told him mournfully of the possible result of her brother's injuries, his suspicion disappeared forever, and only sympathy and grief responded to her wordless appeal for comfort. All that night he watched by the bedside of the injured man, and was rewarded in the morning by seeing the closed lids slowly open, and catching the first faint words : "Did we do them up, Phil ?"

"Yes, and you nearly got done up yourself, old chap ; don't try to talk, but sleep," was Phil's hearty response, and Hal dropped off again as though relieved of his last and only care. The crisis was passed at this time, apparently, and news of one victory seemed harbinger of the other, so much desired; the victory of a sound constitution over almost certain death.

A day or two later, Phil was astounded upon making his call upon his friend, to be met by Rita, with hands outstretched, crying piteously. "Oh, don't tell me that you believe this wicked story which is circulating about, that Hal sent you a bogus telegram keeping you out of the game. You and he have been rivals ; I know the whole story. I know, too, that after you won the $300 mathematical prize, and he would not accept the money you so generously offered him, that it was through your influence he was given that fine position that Summer which helped him so much towards working his way through college. I know your bravery in defending him from the crowd of town boys who laid in wait for him one night, and how you thrashed their leader, and were hurt yourself in the struggle. For that and your other kindnesses, Hal loves you, and if he hears this story, it will break his heart."

What could Phil say ? Simply that the whole thing was a piece of scandal, an outrage, and several other equally decisive denials, and get away as soon as possible to "punch the fellow that tattled," as he wrathfully vowed to himself.

*   *   *   *   *   *   *

The game had been played on Saturday, and since Sunday, Kid, Giant and the captain had not been seen about the campus. It was supposed they had cut college to celebrate over the game.

Wednesday night, Giant sent word to Phil to meet him quietly in the captain's room. He found there with him, Kid and the captain.

"Well," said Kid, "I have been playing the Old Sleuth act, and with the timely aid of these brave lads, have found out who sent you your bogus telegram.

"After you left us, Saturday night, we held a little consultation, and then I went down town after my mail. On the way I met Tom Britton, the tough you will remember who led the yaggers the night they so nearly did up Hal Blackford. As I passed him, he looked up out of the side of his eye and said to me, 'You played a great game, today, Barker.'

" 'We did,' I said coolly, 'but your little trick didn't work to keep Edson out of it, did it ?' He drew back at me, muttering that he knew nothing about Edson, nor any trick, but I smiled and went on about my business.

"You see, we had reasoned it out about this way. Britton is a coward, and a bully, but he is no fool. He has known as the town boys do know, all about the plans for this game, and how we depended on a goal from the field or a place kick to win the game if it came close. Also, that Phil had practiced that particular play for this game, which would be his last, and that he would almost give his right hand before he would lose a chance to play in it. He thought by getting Phil away he would not only revenge himself for the licking Phil gave him on one memorable occasion, but would cause the possible defeat of the team, and the downfall of our hopes, two things which would of all others suit him.

"So," said Kid, in a burlesque dramatic way, "we selected these former knights of Phi Chi whom you see before you, and planned the campaign. It was to be brief and decisive. Tom lives down on the Plains, and last night as he was returning from town about half jagged, a bag was suddenly thrown over his head. I am happy to state that I gave him a solar plexus on my own account which rendered him superior to mundane events for a considerable time.

"I guess you fellows can imagine where Tom found himself when he awoke," continued Kid with a chuckle. "He was in the cave by the sounding sea. He was confronted by the most ghostlike crowd he ever saw, and charged with his crimes. To his credit, though badly scared, he denied the thing in toto. Without further ado, we took the tackle, and after blindfolding him, began to lower him into the Devil's Hole. I happen to know that that hole is fifteen feet deep, for I helped to measure it, but I guess Tom thought it was about fifteen hundred. He begged to be let out ; but we were in for it, and when he was safe at the bottom we pulled off the bandage from his eyes, and set the electrical serpents to running. Gee, wasn't he frightened ! After a while he was pulled out, and he told the whole story.

"He had stolen a telegraph blank, fixed up the message and started a small boy for the college with it. We not only made him confess, but compelled him to sign a written confession, and then left him tied to a tree down below Merrymeeting, and he may be there yet."

A mass meeting was called in Memorial and the whole assemblage was told the story by Phil, who eulogized Blackford and praised his playing, declaring that his work in the first half had really as much to do with winning the game as had his own lucky kick in the second half. Of course, then the easiest thing in the world for college boys to do was to form a procession and march over to the hall where Hal was lying, and he was cheered again and again. While he knew nothing of the suspicions launched against him, the fact that he was thus remembered was more than medicine to the injured man, and each cheer was a liberal dose of a reviving tonic.

As Phil and Hal were walking across the campus, the night after the Dance on the Green which closed the Class Day exercises, Phil stopped abruptly in the shadow of a big tree, and gazing across the enchanted grounds now bathed in moonlight and beautiful to his fond eye as no other spot on earth can hope to be, remarked in a self-conscious manner, "Your sister told me tonight, Hal, that she thought Edson such a pleasant name she might possibly adopt it, about Christmas time."

The two men clasped hands and Hal said with tenderness in his voice, "Dear old Bowdoin never graduated a happier lad than this news makes me."

BOWDOIN'S FIRST GREAT BOAT-RACE

D. A. ROBINSON, '73

BOWDOIN'S FIRST GREAT BOAT-RACE

I T was at the close of one of the Bowdoin banquets, and a number of the younger graduates had remained to smoke awhile longer, sing a few more songs, and tell again the stories of their college days. With them had remained one of the older men, one, though gray and wrinkled, yet who liked to be "with the boys," and tried on such occasions to forget the half a century that had passed since he was young, and to seem, to himself at least, to be a boy again among the rest. They had just finished singing old "Phi Chi" for the "steenth" time, when one of the boys suddenly turned to the Old Grad and said, "It's up to you, old man ; you must sing as a song or tell a story now."

He was pleased at the attention shown him, for it somehow seemed to make him more nearly one of their number, but he modestly said that he could not sing as they very well knew, having heard him try several times; and as for a story, it was much more interesting to him to listen to their songs and hear their fun, than anything he could say would be to them. But they were so persistent and apparently sincere in their desire to hear from him that he finally consented ; and when the cigars had been relighted and the chairs tilted back to the usual angle, he began as follows:

"The first time I walked in through the posts beyond the Church on the Hill and looked upon the Bowdoin campus, way back in the sixties, there was a far different view from what you see there to-day. Old Massachusetts Hall had not been remodelled and its upper story made into a museum as it is now, but it had the same antique and dilapidated appearance as when its walls resounded to the voice of Parker Cleveland. The foundation of Memorial Hall had Just been finished, and the granite for its walls was piled all about that part of the campus. There was no Searles Science Building, no Walker Art Building, no Gymnasium, no Observatory. The North end of Winthrop was closed for repairs. The only entrance to it, as I soon found, was over the 'Tarpeian Rock,' a hole dug through the middle wall from the closet of the inside back room in the upper story. Through this hole, in the dead hours of the night, Sophomores were wont to haul such Freshmen as did not keep fully up to the standard of college ethics as made and provided for their guidance, and bring them to trial in the courts of Sodom, as the North end was called, to distinguish it from Gomorrah, which was the scriptural name of the South end. To have 'Sodom' written in chalk upon his door, or hear the words in sepulchral tones, 'Sodom, to-night,' was the direst threat a Freshman could be subjected to in those days. As I was saying, when I first came upon the campus I was wholly unacquainted with college ways and customs, and knew only two or three of the students. I found a kind-hearted Junior who lived 'up my way,' who allowed me to sleep in his room, until I could take my examinations and procure a room of my own.

"By Saturday night I had collected a few pieces of second hand furniture, sold to me at 'greatly reduced rates' (!) by upper-classmen, and about ten, I went to bed eager for Monday to come when I could begin college work in earnest. I had been asleep about an hour, and was dreaming of the great things I was going to accomplish while in college, when my dreams were suddenly brought to an untimely end by a great noise, in my room and all about me. When I opened my eyes I saw that the room was packed full of students, every one of whom had on a mask and was blowing a tin horn most vigorously ; and one, with a black nose about half a yard long, was holding it close to my face and saying in most peremptory tones : 'Freshie, get up ! Freshie, get up !' I at once obeyed, and was politely handed my pants, and as I balanced myself on one leg to begin dressing, I was unceremoniously toppled over upon the bed in a heap, amid a great tooting of horns and shouts of laughter. I was then hustled out into the other room, and placed upon the top of the stove ; a big flat 'air-tight' that was sold to me at a bargain by a Sophomore, who told me in confidence, it was 'the very one old Prof. Cleaveland used to have in his room !' I found afterwards there were several such about college.

"By the time I was fairly standing upon the stove and the horn orchestra was getting in its work in good style about my ears, I thought the thing had gone far enough, and, having had a good deal of rough-and-tumble experience in the six years I had worked in a crew in a saw-mill, I made a leap into the crowd and was ready for a fight. But fighting was not on the program, and I was grabbed by as many as could get hold of me and put back upon my perch on the stove. Finding that everything was being done in a good-natured way, I subsided at once, and did whatever I was told to do. This spoiled the fun and they soon left me for other classmates.

"This experience seemed to me so different, somehow, from what I had pictured college life to be, that I was at a loss to understand it for some time. There were other things that surprised me as well. When I came upon the campus one of the first things to catch my eye was a long, slim boat, turned over upon some wooden horses under the trees in front of Winthrop Hall. I was told that it was a race-boat, called a single shell, belonging to one of the students. I wondered how anyone could spend the precious time while at college in such a wasteful manner as rowing in boat races. A little farther along I saw a larger boat, which proved to be a four-oared race-boat, called the 'Forget-me-not,'—some of the older graduates will remember that famous boat and it wonderful crews—but I mentally vowed that no temptations would induce me to so far forget what I came to college for, as to take part in any such frivolous sports. But alas for my good intentions, I soon became better acquainted with shells and college rowing than I could ever have dreamed possible in my early Freshman days.

"The next year our class bought a four-oared shell and formed a class crew. The State regatta was to be held that Fall at Bath, and the college entered a crew. But the college crew had such hard luck, the bow oar having to give up on account of boils, and the stroke on account of an attack of whooping cough, that it was finally decided to send our class crew to represent the college in that race, and I was given a seat in the boat. It was only two weeks before the race and though I had had plenty of experience rowing batteaux and running rafts on the river at home, I had never been in a racing shell with outriggers, nor used a spoon oar. But I soon found that I could keep my balance and row quite a stroke, though the oars seemed merely playthings to the big ones I had been accustomed to using. On the day of the race nearly the whole college 'went fluking on the railway down to Bath,' as the old song says, to see the regatta. There were four other crews beside ours, the Longshoremen of Portland, afterwards a famous crew, the Emeralds of Portland, with Pat and Mike Davis for stroke and bow, the Ariels of Portland and the Gleams of Bath. The water was pretty rough down at the start and it was with difficulty that we could get into our boat from the tug and get started.

"We were nearly out to the starting line when a big wave struck my oar, and I caught a crab with such force as to break my oar off at the 'button' We went back to the tug and found that our spare oars had been left in the boathouse three miles away ! The Longshoremen refused to wait for us to get another oar and to our great chagrin and the keen disappointment of the whole college the race was started without the Bowdoin crew !

This was not a very promising beginning for boating at Bowdoin, but it was the beginning of her racing against outside crews. That same year the intercollegiate rowing association was formed and the first race rowed at Springfield, Mass. Only two crews entered, Harvard and the Amherst 'Aggies.' To the surpise of all, excepting those who knew how crews were then picked out at Harvard, the 'Aggies' won. At the next meeting Bowdoin sent representatives to the association and entered a crew for the race.

"To be represented in such an association and to have the prospect of a crew in the race, gave a great stimulus to aquatics at Bowdoin, and the whole attention of the students was devoted to that branch of athletics. Volunteers were called for to begin training for the 'Varsity' crew, and everyone began reading about the Harvard and Yale and Oxford and Cambridge races, and rowing talk was uppermost in all the college clubs. The race was to be in six-oared shells without a cockswain, three miles straight away. About a dozen men began training in the old 'Commons Hall,' then the gymnasium, now I believe the carpenter's shop.

"I did not expect to be a member of the crew, for there were so many others who seemed better fitted for it than I was, but as I liked the exercise, having been used to hard work in the mill at home, I kept up practice with the crew all winter. George Price, the bow-oar of the famous 'Paris Crew'—so called because it had won the races at the Paris Exposition in 1867,—was engaged to train the crew, when the ice should

A CLASS RACE ON THE ANDROSCOGGIN.

The '85 class crew distancing its opponents.

go out of the river, and it could begin work on the water. A new shell was ordered from Elliott, the famous boatbuilder of Greenpoint, N. Y. For practicing, until the crew could sit in a shell, an old six-oared lap- streak was hired from Portland. At length the ice went out and the trainer put in an appearance to pick out the crew, and teach them the racing stroke. You may imagine my surprise when it was announced that I was to be given a seat in the crew ! We found it no easy task to go down to the river before breakfast every morning and again after supper and pull that heavy lapstreak over the two-mile course, half of the way against a strong tide, with the trainer in the stern, keenly watching every motion, and urging us to do a little more all the time. Our hands were soon blistered and every muscle in our bodies lame and sore, not to mention other discomforts caused by sliding on the seats to get a little longer stroke. But our hands soon became toughened, our muscles hardened to the work, our wounds healed, and we 'trained off our second wind,' so that the work became easier each day. Our new shell came at last and to our great disgust we found that an old lady, in examining it while coming down upon the boat ; had punched a hole through the bottom of it with the end of her umbrella ! This meant two more weeks in the heavy lapstreak. Finally we got our new shell and our new spoon oars from Ross of New Brunswick, the famous oarmaker of the Paris Crew, and then we began to find out what we could do. The result of our 'time rows' was very encouraging for a good place in the race. During Commencement week of that year, in order that the crew might not be disturbed by the festivities of such occasions, we were taken to a boarding house down at 'Humphreys Mill,' where the Casino of Merrymeeting Park now stands. Two weeks before the time appointed for the race, which was the second week in July, we went to Springfield.

"We found that quarters had been engaged for us at Mr. Harrison Loomis', in West Springfield, two or three miles above the starting point of the course. After our arrival at Springfield the real interest and excitement began. All the other college crews had arrived before we came and were practicing every day upon the river. We took great interest in watching the other crews row, noting the kind of stroke each used, and reading the newspaper comments about them. As we were so far away from the course, and rowed up river instead of down while practicing, the other crews did not get an opportunity to see us row until a day or two before the race, when we went over the course 'on time.' As we went by the training quarters of the other crews we could see groups of students and their friends rush down to their landings and level their glasses upon us, and we knew that we were for the first time being 'sized up' by all our college rivals. The next day the most important headline in the Springfield papers was, 'Bowdoin Goes Over the Course for the First Time' ! Then followed columns of comments upon our crew, our stroke, our speed, and speculations about our probable position at the finish. All of this was of course intensely interesting to us, but the paragraph that pleased our trainer the most was the one that contained the comments of John Biglin. He was a famous oarsman in those days and was there looking after one of the college crews. As we went by he was standing on the shore, with a reporter of one of the Springfield papers and a group of college men about him. 'There goes a crew on time,' said the reporter. 'Who are they?' Biglin looked at the crew a moment, and then recognizing the familiar swing of the old 'Paris Crew' stroke, he said, 'That must be the crew that George Price is training.' 'Then it is the Bowdoin crew,' said the reporter. 'What a queer stroke,' said a Yale man who was in the group. 'Isn't that what they call rowing in a circle' ? Biglin, whose eyes had not been taken from the crew since it came in sight, turned to the students about him and said, 'Well, boys, you may call that stroke rowing in a circle, or what you like, but if they can make their boat go like that over the whole course on the day of the race, that's the winning crew.' We were naturally much elated at such praise from a professional oarsman, and the betting fraternity evidently took the tip from this remark and from that time to the day of the race the Bowdoin crew was the favorite against 'the field.'

"For several days before the race I had noticed that when we came to the last half mile in our practicing, especially if we had an unusually hard spin, the boat would have such a 'list to port' that I could not feather my oar clear of the water. I spoke of this several times to our trainer, who did not appear to take any notice of it ; but the night before the race he went with me out to the boathouse and taking out his pocket-knife he cut the 'gunnel' of the boat, where the handle of my oar came over it, clear down to the short ribs. 'There,' he said, 'I think that that will help you.' Then he told me in confidence that one of the men had 'gone a little stale,' and when hard pressed at the end of the course would 'ease up' on his stroke, which would throw the boat over to the other side. 'But I think you will be far enough in the lead when this happens,' he said, 'that no one will get by you before he catches on again.'

"The morning of the long expected day at length dawned upon us. We had retired somewhat earlier than usual the evening before, but could not go to sleep quite as readily, for visions of the morrow's events would keep crowding in upon our minds, no matter how hard we would try to keep them out. As the race was not called until afternoon, we lounged around during the forenoon, trying to appear as indifferent and calm as possible. We put the finishing polish upon the boat, roughened the handles of our oars, tightened our foot-straps, and did many little things of this kind, in order to have everything in perfect readiness for the race but more especially to keep from thinking too much about it. After a light lunch we launched our boat and paddled down to the starting point. All along the way we could see the roads on either side of the river filled with crowds of people, hurrying to get places where they could see the race. There was an observation train on one side of the river near the starting point loaded with an excited throng of students from the various colleges and their lady friends. Along the other bank stretched a fine carriage road which was lined with all kinds of vehicles, from a hayrack to a tally-ho, each carrying its load of eager sightseers. And every jutting point of land along the course was crowded with groups of college men ready to cheer their respective crews to victory.

"We didn't see many white flags displayed, for Bowdoin was too far 'down East' for many of her students to attend the races there ; but old Mike Harrigan, the captain of the river steamer, saluted us as he swept down the course, his boat loaded down with passengers, and he was proudly carrying the Bowdoin flag at his masthead. We drew lots for places at the start and found that we came between Harvard and Yale. Beginning from the western shore the boats lined up as follows : Amherst 'Aggies,' Harvard, Bowdoin, Yale, Amherst, and Brown. So we had a good position near the middle of the river. The tide was pretty strong that day, and it took a long time to get the boats into line for the start, for it is no easy matter to handle one of those long racing shells in a swift current.

"After a good deal of floating down past the buoys and backing up again, the line was formed, the starter dropped the flag and shouted 'Go !'

"A great shout went up from the crowds on either shore. We dug our oars into the water with the short starting stroke we had practiced, the next a little longer, the third a full stroke pulled with all the strength that three months of hard and faithful training had given us, and our boat went jumping through the water with a speed to delight the heart of the most critical oarsman. So intent were we upon our work that we did not notice for some little time that all the other crews had stopped rowing, and the referee was firing his pistol and shouting for us to come back. It seemed that Yale and Brown were not ready for the word and did not start at all, so we had to go back and try again. This was exasperating to us, but we came into line again with renewed courage, for we had seen that we could get away as quickly as any of them.

"It didn't take so long to get into line this time, for everyone was ready and eager for the race. At the word we were off again ; our oars went into the water together, came out without bucket or hang at the finish, were feathered flat ; just skimmed the surface without touching it, and went in again in perfect time. The boat rode on an even keel, and we could feel it jump ahead at every stroke, as the six brown backs bent with all their power upon the oars. After a few moments had gone by I ventured to look about me, and to my great satisfaction, I could count five boats behind us, so we were surely in the lead. We kept up the spurt with which we started until the nearest boat was several lengths behind, and then settled down to our regular racing stroke. So determined had we been to get the lead that, as we learned afterwards, we had rowed the first half-mile in two minutes and two seconds and had passed the first mile flag inside of five minutes, making a record, both for professionals and amateurs, for a mile with a six-oared boat.

"When about half way over the course, the boat that was nearest to us, which I could tell was Harvard from the crimson oarblades and sliding seats, began to slowly lessen the gap between us. Seeing this, a group of Harvard men upon the shore began to cheer most lustily. As the 'Rah !

Rah ! Rah! Harvard !' was roared from a hundred throats, we could see the crimson oars flash more quickly to the stroke, and then their boat came dashing through the water, lessening the space between us every moment. When only a boat length separated us, we quickened our stroke to a spurt and soon saw them fall astern.

"We had hardly dropped back to our regular stroke, when looking farther out on our port side I could see another boat, already ahead of Harvard, and coming very fast. Suddenly 'Amherst ! Amherst ! Amherst !' came across the water from the shore in shrill and frantic tones, and then this other boat came tearing after us like a race horse under the whip. Again we quickened up our stroke and soon had the satisfaction of seeing Amherst drop astern as Harvard had. We passed the two-mile flag, and had entered upon the last mile of the course, when again the snappy Harvard cheer was heard, this time louder and fiercer than before. The Harvard crew again responded gamely to the call and came on as if bound to win or die. But we were equal to the task and gave them spurt for spurt and kept the lead.

"So we went rushing down the course. Bowdoin in the lead, Harvard a few lengths behind on the starboard side, Amherst the same distance to port, and the others trailing farther back. As we drew nearer to the end the crowds became greater and more excited. Our exertions had begun to tell upon us, and though the stroke was kept up there was not quite so much driving power behind it, but we were still ahead and felt certain we would win. The cheering kept growing louder and more prolonged, the 'Rah ! Rah ! Rah !' from hundreds of enthusiastic Harvard men kept their crew up to their work in splendid style. Amherst, encouraged by the good race they had already made, kept up the killing pace with most persistent and seemingly untiring energy. So we fought it out, length by length, with Bowdoin still ahead. A crashing Harvard cheer again rang over the water, at once joined and made louder and more thunderous by the shouts of those who were urging Amherst on. The two boats seemed suddenly to take on new life and the gap between them and us was rapidly closing. Our stroke went up from 42 to 44, but still they gained. We quickened to 46, which seemed to barely hold them where they were. Just then above the din of cheering came the piercing blast of a steam whistle, which was so loud and shrill that for the moment all other noise was drowned. Mike Harrigan had pulled wide open the whistle valve, to cheer us on. This friendly signal acted like an electric shock upon our crew. The stroke went up to 48, clean and strong as at the start, the boat shot forward with increasing speed, and our hottest rivals began to fall astern again. Suddenly I felt a shiver in the boat, followed by that fatal 'lurch to port.'

"The handle of my oar struck the 'gunnel' with a bang and the blade was buried to the button. While the port oars were thus dragging in the water the starboard oars were waving in the air. We struggled hard to right the boat and get the stroke again, but so great was the list to port that the oars of that side would not clear the water, while the other side could barely touch the water with their blades. The boat rocked from side to side and fast lost her headway. Amherst came steadily on, and now her bow lapped our stern. In a moment more she had passed as if we lay at anchor. Harvard lapped us next, and as she was going past we made a desperate effort to prevent it, but without success. How long we labored thus I do not know, for seconds seem hours at such a time. To have the victory that seemed so surely ours thus snatched by accident away when almost in our grasp was hard to bear. But still we struggled on, trying to keep defeat from being too disastrous, and crossed the line the third instead of first, with almost broken hearts."

As the Old Grad neared the end of his story, the incidents he was relating came so vividly to his mind, the cheering crowds, the flashing oars, the flying boats, that he unconsciously had risen to his feet ; his tall form was drawn to its full height, the muscles of his sinewy arms could be seen working, as if in remembrance of the events of that day, his eyes shone with excitement, his face flushed, and his breath came quick and heavy as if again he had been actually rowing in the race. When the end came he dropped into his chair and remained for some moments in silence. His auditors knew that although that first great race had been thus lost, the crews of Bowdoin in the next few years had won races over these same rivals and others. At length, with a sigh, he arose to his feet, and saying with a saddened voice, "I hope I haven't wearied you," went slowly out, without another word.

The younger men sprang up and cheered him as he left, and then cheered again for Bowdoin pluck, and for the Bowdoin spirit which is the same inspiring force today that it has been through all the glorious history of the college.

A COLLEGE GIRL'S
BELATED IDEAL

FRANK WARREN HAWTHORNE, '74

A COLLEGE GIRL'S BELATED IDEAL

And, last, to you, whose dainty shoe
Imprints the pathways classic,
O Brunswick girl, Romance's pearl,
I drain a cup of Massic.

P ERCIVAL Jason McMillan sat alone at a little table in the grill of the University Club. But for his own presence and a group of attendants in a farther corner chatting and gossiping for the most part inaudibly, the room was deserted, quiet. It was still too early in the afternoon for up-town New York to drop in at its clubs on the way home to dinner. It was much earlier than McMillan's wont. If asked, he couldn't have told exactly why he was there at 3 o'clock. Why, the market had barely closed, and it would be an hour and a half yet before any of his friends was likely to put in an appearance ! How did *he* happen to "blow in" so early ?

McMillan had a sort of half-way consciousness that the day, the weather perhaps, had had something to do with it. The month was October, and October had always been a more or less eventful month in the forty odd years of his life. It was in October that he had first met the girl whom he made his wife ; they had become engaged in October—not the same October, of course not; their wedding day was in October ; in October their boy had been born ; in the same month McMillan had "pulled up stakes" and gone into the Southwest with a vague idea of knocking a fortune of some sort out of that region ; in October, thirteen years later, he had returned, moderately successful, and made a home in New York ; and only a year before—almost the same date, in fact—he and the son had taken a desolate journey up into Maine to bury the dead wife and mother—and here was another October rolled around again !

And what a glorious Indian Summer day it was, too ! Just like those which had made so deep an impression upon his boyhood life in Maine ! And what a flood of reminiscence it called up !

McMillan had had a noon engagement to lunch and talk over some business with a friend on the upper West Side. It was all over by 2 o'clock, so he had walked through Seventy-second street to the Park, thinking to take a car there down town to his office. But the day, the bracing air, the resplendent foliage in the Park had somehow conspired to lure him inside, and he had zigzagged leisurely through it, coming out at the Fifth Avenue plaza, and thence the walk down to his club was only a matter of a few minutes.

Why go down town ? There was really no pressing reason why he should. The day had already been knocked into pieces, so far as doing any more business was concerned—so into the grill he had gone.

But still the "King William high-ball" stood untasted on the table with its little cube of ice rapidly melting away ; the cigar, with half an inch of ash on it but no suspicion of smoke about it, protruded over the edge of the little bronze tray ; the top coat, hat and walking-stick lay in orderly fashion in the recess of the open window ; and McMillan, well-preserved, rather stout, well-groomed, with the fingers of his left hand straying occasionally through his grayish-and-brown hair, sat thoughtfully with the October spell on him.

Then a dignified mulatto in liveries, with a letter on a salver, appeared at the open door and, with his face and eyes discharged of all expression, announced perfunctorily :

"Mr. Percival Jason McMillan !"

The owner of the name started out of his reverie, made a motion of acquiescence, and the waiter advanced and placed the missive in his hand, retiring in perfectly conventional order.

McMillan would have known the sender of the letter if he hadn't recognized the writing. Nobody but Thorneleigh, his boy, ever addressed him by his full name like that. Thorneleigh had early discovered the two dactyls and the one spondee composing it and had insisted that even half a hexameter line shouldn't be wasted ; so for a long time before that was the mode the father's cards had borne all three names—and, if only it pleased Thorneleigh, it "went" in the McMillan family.

The father's manner had changed instantly on the calling out of his name, and now he stood up, tossed off the stale high-ball not without a grimace, re-lighted his cigar, tore the note open and read :

PHILADELPHIA, October 19.

My Dear Father :—

Why can't you take a run over here to-morrow and spend Sunday with me ? I can't get away myself, or I wouldn't ask you. But I'm very anxious to see you, and besides, I've something particular to talk over with you. You see, I sort of feel that I shouldn't have done it without first consulting you, and I want to ease my conscience—there, I've said that much, and I may as well tell the whole thing, right here !

I'm engaged. Of course, she's the sweetest girl in the world—but not the handsomest, if I do say it, who shouldn't. But you come over and see her for yourself. You'll fall dead in love with her, I know, right in the first act. I did. Met her only a week ago out at the Brandywine Links; have seen her four times since—and here I am, landed ! I, only four months out of college, and less than three weeks in business ! Is it all very foolish ? You won't say so when you see the girl. Suzanna's "the whole thing"—and how does that name strike you ?

You see, her father, Surgeon Pearston, died out in the Philippines two years ago, and her mother is now on her way home from there. Suzanna's just out of Bryn Mawr. I can't tell you any more about her here. We've been swapping biographies, but her's doesn't come on very well—I interrupt her too often.

But I'll tell you what I'll do : Meet you at the train to-morrow afternoon, turn you over for a while to Col. Jack Potter or some other of your old friends here, then take you with me to call on Suzanna ; then I'll "blow" you both to a good dinner out at Wissehickon. We'll let Sunday take care of itself.

Thanks for my November check so long in advance—and more for the extra fifty in it. You're a peach. Sincerely,

THORNELEIGH.

McMillan wasn't surprised. He never expected the boy would become engaged according to rule. But he had read the letter over for the third time before something in it set him to thinking hard again. Then he called a waiter, had his hat and other belongings checked at the coat-room, ascended to the library, hunted up a copy of Curtis' "Prue and I"—which always had a sort of soothing effect on him—retired to a quiet corner and let the afternoon shadows gather slowly about him as he read and thought.

The October spell was on him again.

*   *   *   *   *   *   *

Yes, it was on him fast and deep. It took him back thirty years or more to a time when he was a boy fitting for Bowdoin and planning to enter there the next year. And it was a bright, crisp, clear October afternoon, too, an inspiriting scene that came up before him.

College baseball was at that time in its infancy in New England. Even Harry and George Wright and the old "Red Stockings" had only just appeared on the professional horizon. Bowdoin had organized a good nine, but Harvard's was the nearest team in the college world, and the Bowdoins were thus forced to confine their contests to such clubs as the State furnished. There were the Cushnocs of Augusta, the Eons of Portland, the Live Oaks of Bath, in all of whom the college boys had found "foemen worthy of their steel" ; and latterly, up in Oxford county, the Pennesewassees of Norway or Paris Hill or some other old hill, had entered the lists for the Maine championship and the trophy—a huge solid silver ball made to order in Boston and encased in a truly magnificent silk-lined jewellers' box. These farmers were playing "phenomenal ball" even at that early day, had wiped up the earth with all ordinary comers, and on the afternoon that came so vividly back into McMillan's memory they were playing the last game in a three-cornered series, being tied with the Bowdoins, and the championship—not forgetting the silver ball—was hinged on this contest.

What a scene ! A regular Donnybrook Fair in miniature ! And what a crowd, too ! They had come from all over. The whole town and a good part of Topsham had turned out, of course, and it seemed as if every livery team in Bath, Lewiston and Freeport had been called into commission for the occasion, with nearly all the farm-wagons in the intervening country thrown in for good measure. On both sides of the Delta the Bath road and the Harpswell road were jammed full of teams— many of them gay turnouts, with gay young men and women occupying them—and the cavalcade stretched away down into the pines and opposite the Dunlap monument ; the grand-stand was filled to overflowing with students and the "college girls" of Brunswick ; every window in the Medical Hall had been preempted, and "yaggers" swung from the branches of every near-by tree.

Into all this mix-up McMillan, with his plump cousin in a brand-new gown and jacket at his side, had steered her black mare and phaeton. They had driven from their home in a neighboring town and had come upon the scene just in the middle of the third inning, the game being temporarily stopped in order that Dr. " Johnny" Lincoln might examine the eye of "Sile" Burnham of the Pennesewassees to learn if it had been seriously injured by a hot "liner" struck by Bill Perley of '69. The "Oxford Bears" were one ahead on the score, and the excitement was intense. Blithecock of '68, only just graduated, with a couple of Dartmouth Seniors, who had come down from Hanover to arrange for a Bowdoin-Dartmouth game if possible, approached the phaeton to greet the plump cousin (it was for this—not the game—that she had come) ; so McMillan left her in their company and mingled with the excited crowd.

He had a slight acquaintance with two or three undergraduates, and after some difficulty managed to find Witchell of '72, who took him in tow and steered him onto everything of interest, taking advantage, now and then, of the opportunity to do a little quiet "fishing."

"Fifty cents he don't make his second !" came in a shrill, thin voice from near the posts on the Harpswell-road side of the Delta. There stood a short, slight fellow in very light trousers, the "bobbiest" of bob-tail cutaways, a black derby hat cocked over on his ear, a red neck-tie, and bunches of greasy "scrip" held between his fingers, while he gesticulated wildly with both arms and kept repeating his offer in the sharpest *crescendo*. (This was long before the resumption of specie payments, and our only fractional currency was paper and pennies).

It was Goodwin of '72, and close by him was his *Fidus Achates*, Ireland, of the same class, somewhat similarly attired, but towering fully a foot above him in height.

Price of '71, with a most disreputable-looking "stovepipe" perched on the back of his head and a long-stemmed German pipe held between his teeth, took the bet, after rolling his *r's* a good deal in discussing the terms of it. As a sport, Price was much inclined to look too long for a sure thing. "Bob" Robertson, the tailor, standing close by with his Scotch-plaid trousers, as usual, guiltless of belt or "galluses," held the stakes, remarking to Goodwin as he took the money, while caressing his drooping red moustache with the back of his hand : "You'll never see the color of that fifty again, Frank !"

There was betting of a similar sort going on all around the diamond. All the college sports were in it, with not a few yaggers and other outsiders. They all held their "scrip" between their fingers counting it occasionally, after the manner of a side-show hawker at a circus ; sometimes the stakes would mount up to a dollar or two, which would be the signal for a good deal of crowding and pushing around the betters, and then "Old Pot" and Townsend, the two town constables, would have to "move-on" the crowd and threaten dire things for disobedience. The betting was going on constantly—fresh ones its often as a player went to the bat, and a good deal of wild hedging and doubling up whenever a base runner chanced to reach third safely.

It was a Norway lad, "Jud" Parrott, who was spitting on his hands at the home plate and trying the bat in all sorts of positions, when Goodwin made his bet. "Jud's" uniform was not a uniform at all—it was *sui generis* on that diamond : A coarse-ribbed grey undershirt, with the sleeves rolled well up above the elbows ; a visorless red cap ; a pair of "pants" cut off square at the knees ; red stockings that didn't come quite up to the "pants," thus disclosing a good bit of intervening white cotton flannel ; and for shoes a pair of old rubber boots cut off at the ankles. No two of the Pennesewassee "uniforms" were alike except in the one feature of abbreviated leg gear, and one of the nine invariably went to the bat barefooted, while others ran their bases in long-legged boots.

But "Jud" was onto Perley's curves in great shape. He sent the ball spinning way down among the pines and went sprawling onto third with both hands in front of him just a second before the Bowdoins' centre fielder got the ball up there. He was safe, and the yelling and excitement became intense, while the bets were multiplied furiously.

"Toot" Carr, asleep on the box of his hack with four smartly dressed Portland fellows inside, woke up at the noise, blinked sleepily around, borrowed a fresh chew from a bystander, and then lapsed promptly again "into the arms of Morphine," as Melcher of '71 put it—whereat the assembled students laughed inordinately, and little McMillan thought it must be a fine thing to be an undergraduate at Bowdoin.

In front of the south steps of Adams a bit of a town-boy whom everybody called Herbert was selling molasses candy, and another little sawed-off yagger called "Ratzy" was peddling cheroots. "Pure Havanas !" he kept shouting, "Pure Havanas ! Cut off at both ends so't I could get 'em into the box !"

Over in the rear shadows of the old, low-studded gymnasium across the Bath road, Ackley of '72 was showing the abnormally developed muscles of his right calf to an admiring crowd, when "Prof" Dole appeared on the scene, coming through the Appian Way, and dispersed the sightseers, the whole party rushing pell-mell over into the Delta, where pandemonium had broken loose.

"Jud" Parrott had been put out trying to steal home, "Wally" Hooker of the Bowdoins had made a home run in the last half of the fifth, and the score was now tied on even innings. In all the buggies and barouches the occupants were standing up cheering lustily for Bowdoin or the " 'Wassees" and waving handkerchiefs, hats, canes and improvised flags. The college girls kept up an almost continuous hand-clapping, and as often as it subsided somebody would call for "three cheers for Hooker !" which would be given with a "tiger" on the end that awoke the echoes. Bowdoin, like most of the American colleges, had not yet, in the autumn of 1868, arisen to the dignity of a college yell.

A party of Gleam Boat Club men from Bath, standing on the seats of an open carriage, were offering all sorts of wagers on the college nine, with few takers, when a humpbacked sport from Portland elbowed his way through the surging crowd and, flashing a crisp, new bill on the Bath enthusiasts, shouted :

"A hundred dollars even that the farmers win the ball !"

That feazed the Bath boys for a minute or two, especially as the hunch-back kept repeating the offer. But, after a whispered consultation, Frank Russell, two of the Houghton boys and Frank Joslyn-Ricker came up with the "century." "Bill" Field held the stakes, and the backers of Bowdoin took heart again as news of the $200 bet flew over the field.

The game moved along with varying fortune for the two teams through the sixth and seventh innings—a whole game used sometimes to occupy four or five hours in those days—and McMillan, strolling about among the onlookers with now and then an introduction from his undergraduate friend to some well-known college character, was at length attracted by a smart basket phaeton outfit, with two young girls on the seat, one of them holding a whip in her right hand while with the left she managed the reins as dexterously as a track expert.

She was a picture—an oval-shaped, rather thoughtful-expressioned face, with blueish hazel eyes and dark brown hair ; a gown of some soft black, dinging material unrelieved by even a bit of color or other adornment ; a big, broad scarf of white India mull about her neck crossed demurely in front like a nun's *amice* and caught and held together with a college society pin ; a big black hat flaring up on one side and topped with two great ostrich feathers, white and black ; her black kid gloves fitted a pair of plump hands as perfectly as those on the store models ; and a short black-cloth jacket, perfectly plain, completed a costume that was not fashionable or even conventional in those days ; and the figure was all the more striking in its picturesqueness because of its contrast with the handsome, stylishly dressed girl at her side.

"That's Miss Halsey, the most popular college girl in Brunswick," whispered Witchell. "All the best fellows know her from Seniors down and a half dozen of 'em are in love with her, so it's said. She knows everything that's going on in college, all the college secrets, all the little love affairs and flirtations ; but she never gossips, never gets anybody in trouble, and never makes an enemy, they say. And the girls all like her, too. She treats a Freshman or a Medic just as nicely as she does a Junior—and I guess that's the secret of it."

But Witchell, unfortunately, didn't enjoy an acquaintance with this picturesque paragon of a girl—so little McMillan was unhappy for the moment, as there was no chance of being presented to her then.

The game went furiously on into the first half of the ninth inning— but McMillan had lost all interest in it. The basket phaeton with the calico mare kept moving all about, always with a group of students about it, and sometimes it disappeared altogether from the scene ; but wherever it stopped about the Delta, McMillan somehow found himself near, with his eyes fairly livened on the black-gowned driver. His student escort had left him, and he was just beginning to wonder if it wasn't time to look up his plump cousin, when loud shouts, angry protests and a bit of profanity intermingled suddenly drew his attention, and pushed along by the crowd he found himself near the home plate.

"Sile" Burnham had struck a "grounder" down past the first base, and followed it himself as if shot out of a cannon's mouth ; the ball had been stopped by the Bowdoins' right fielder, who sent it in to the first baseman in fine form just as "Sile's" rubber shoe landed on the bag. Was he "out" or not ?

"Judgment ! Judgment !" went up from all over the field. The umpire hesitated, and players and spectators all crowded up about that official to proffer advice and give information. A hundred or more were talking, shouting, protesting, arguing all at once—and the excitement was at an almost riotous pitch, for the Pennesewassees had a good lead in the score, there were two men out already, and the Bowdoins had only half an inning in which to catch up ; besides, there was more or less "scrip" up on the game and on this particular play. "Sile" Burnham couldn't resist the temptation to join in the angry debate, and he started to run up to the umpire.

"Hold your gool, 'Sile' ! Hold that gool, Silas ! Get back there, you d—n fool !"

The "Wassees' " captain had a voice on him like a hired man's and his warning came none too soon, for the first baseman, who had also been off the bag, was already bearing down on Silas to clap the ball on him, in which event he would have been out anyway, much to the umpire's relief. Silas obeyed in time, but "Hold your gool !" from that moment became a college byword and went down securely in Bowdoin baseball traditions.

At length came the decision —"Out at first ! Three out ! Side out !"

And the Bowdoins, not altogether cheerful or hopeful, went back to the bat for the last time, with the odds heavily against them.

A whitewash was their record for that inning.

Then the riotous element broke loose again. They yelled, hissed, hurrahed, "groaned" for the umpire and did all sorts of things to stir up the excited crowd and add to the general confusion. Skittish horses reared and backed, wheels got interlocked, there were one or two upsets and half a dozen incipient fights stopped promptly by the long-bearded "Pot." On top of it all a chorus of horns swelled up from over on the campus, the big Phi Chi drum boomed a thunderous bass, the "ponderous hewgag that had made Gomorrah hum" for five years back added its notes to the din, and then twenty odd Sophomores, in battered "beavers" and skull-and-cross-bones togas, and led by Charlie "Shep" came trooping into the field. Eye-glassed Seniors and smartly dressed Juniors were carrying members of the defeated nine about on their shoulders just as if they were victors; the president of the baseball association had made a little speech formally surrendering the silver ball to the Norway boys ; their captain had replied in an acknowledgment that comprehended little more than "Thank you. By gawd, Silas, we've got that ball!"; the early evening shadows were already gathering, and the crowd was beginning to scatter.

Then "Mose" Owen of '61, who had been in the company of the Gleam Boat Club boys all the afternoon, and under the influence of their hospitality had felt the *afflatus divinus* gradually moving him to composition, stood up on the box of "Ant" Hall's hack and read dramatically to the multitude, now hushed into semi-silence, these lines scrawled in pencil on a glazed paper cuff—an apostrophe to his home ball nine:

> "Majestic Live Oaks ! Your names shall stand
> When broken noses adorn the land,
> And forth, next Spring, at your Ricker's call
> May you strike a blow for that silver ball
> Which now reposes, 'mid cows and bosses,
> Up with the gentle Pennesewasses ;
> For, though Bowdoins swore they would never yield,
> They were "choked" to death on their chosen field—
> They got dismayed, and could not rally
> At the cry of 'Out !' instead of 'Tally !' "

Thus ended the famous Bowdoin-Pennesewassee game.

Little McMillan had never lost sight of the basket phaeton. But now he rather reluctantly hunted up the plump cousin, who promptly substituted him for the Dartmouth man at her side, the striped, crocheted lap-robe was tucked in at the sides of the buggy, and they were just about to take the road for home when the plump cousin whispered :

"Why, there comes Suzanne Halsey ! Just the sweetest, sensiblest girl! I've been trying all the afternoon to get a chance to speak with her. You ought to know her, Percy. Whoa !"—and the introduction was over in half a minute.

It was merely a well-bred nod, a hurried chat with the cousin, and then : "I hear you're to enter Bowdoin next year, Mr. McMillan. I hope I shall see something of you and that we'll be good friends. Good night !"

And the picturesque paragon in black gracefully waved her whip with the Bowdoin ribbons tied on the handle, and whisked out of sight in the early twilight.

McMillan had met his fate—but it took him a long, long time to find it out.

   *   *   *   *   *   *   *

"Wake up there, Fleecie ! Break away there, old man ! We've been looking all over for you for the past three hours." (Early in his college days McMillan's middle name had easily suggested Jason's voyage in search of the golden fleece—and thenceforward he was known as "Fleecie" and so addressed by everybody).

It was a trio of '75 men who thus aroused him from his reverie in the library corner. "Bodine of '73," they continued almost in concert, "has just blown in here from Minneapolis and we're going to give him a dinner up at the Claremont. Brace up and come along ! We're none of us going to dress for it. The carriage is down at the door now"—and they fairly pushed McMillan along and out onto the sidewalk.

At the dinner he was a little moody at first. When he asked if any of them recalled who it was that Miss Halsey had married, Curtman was quite sure that it was a doctor—but nobody recalled anything further. There was some chaff over the college girls and the query "Are we so soon forgotten ?" but even when the little company of diners were at their gayest McMillan found himself wishing that the morrow would come and speed him to Philadelphia.

On the train for there next day he recalled a thousand and one of the incidents that clustered about his association with Suzanne Halsey, in college and afterward. She was a bright, thoroughly original girl, thoroughly independent in all her ideas and ways, and could do the most unconventional, almost outrageous things even, without provoking criticism or barely comment from the townsfolk or the little college world. She was only eighteen years old, but well-educated even then, a lover of books, extremely well bred, with a vein of humor that never ran out, and a kindly disposition toward everybody in the whole wide world.

It was Suzanne who flew in the face of college and town social traditions by engineering the famous Freshman sleigh-ride to Lisbon Falls in the Winter of 1869-70. On that occasion eighteen or twenty '73 men took as many "Senior girls" on a ride and hop without even letting the ladies' men of '70 into the secret, whereat there was wrath in upper-classdom and a tornado of gossip in town, until it was known that Suzanne had negotiated many of the preliminary introductions that had been necessary, and had infused enough enthusiasm and courage into the other girls to get them to accept invitations from Freshmen. Then the affair took on another aspect—it was all right.

It was Suzanne who, in male attire and mask and with dark lantern and hatchet, had "gone the college rounds" one Winter midnight with the "Omicrons" and refused to faint when the uncovering of a barrel on the top floor of the Medical hall had disclosed the head and face of a corpse floating in alcohol.

She never danced—never so much as attended a college hop or German—but she always knew exactly what girls had been invited, and she somehow managed to bring the disengaged students and the uninvited girls together before the night of the function.

So secure was she in the college friendships that she formed that, when she took a notion that she would like to go here or there, or to this or that entertainment, she felt perfectly free to ask any one of her young men friends to take her or to permit her to act as escort herself.

One soft Indian Summer day in McMillan's Junior year he had gone to the club to dinner and found there under his plate a business-looking note, which read :

"This will be a glorious afternoon for a drive, Fleecie. I'm afraid you won't think to ask me—so I'll call around at Sodom in the phaeton at 2 o'clock for you. If you can't go, come to your window and say so ; if you can, why, come down and jump in."

And Suzanne did the thing up right with a pocketful of cigars and a box of confectionery—but hadn't thought of toll to pay on Bay Bridge, and was mortified beyond measure to have to borrow it of her companion.

It was Suzanne who sent flowers and delicacies to sick undergraduates whom "the girls" didn't know, simply because "there was nobody else to do it." She it was who wrote comforting letters to the sisters and mothers of suspended Sophomores so that they would be "let down easy at home." She knew all about the plot to steal the chapel bell in the Fall of 1870, for a month before the actual theft, and had measured the mouth of nearly every reservoir and well-platform in town to see if it was big enough to take the bell in—that was to divert suspicion from any of the thieves who might be recalled afterward as having measured these things. She made the foul flags for the ball grounds, embroidered the big "B" on the boat club's colors, and when the crews were in training down at Humphreys' Mill used to drive their "best girls" down there to see them, because the oarsmen couldn't get up to town themselves. She could skate like a professional, could paddle a canoe safely through the Hog Island rapids, and once when an oarless skiff with two small French boys in it was about to be carried over the upper falls she had waded out with Layton, of '69, into the still, shallow waters above the dam and caught the boat with the crooked end of an umbrella-stick just in time.

There were lots of fellows who used to get devoted to her—but never engaged. Brimley, of '69, for a long time after he had graduated, used to come back to Brunswick often to see her, and as McMillan's own Senior year was waning he couldn't quite decide which she cared for the more, himself or Brimley. But one May afternoon, just as the dandelions were the yellowest and the syringas were beginning to bud, she was sitting with him on her back porch, and looked so irresistible that McMillan, after due deliberation, was just on the point of settling the thing right there and then, when she broke in with :

"Don't look at me in that tone of voice, Fleecie. It doesn't become you. And it sort of frightens me, besides. Do you know what I was thinking of ? No, of course you don't, or you wouldn't have looked that way ! Well, it was this : If ever my ideal should stumble along and find me, and want me to marry him, I should insist, as a prerequisite, that the marriage ceremony should take place on the steps of the south wing of the Chapel, on an October afternoon when the maples are the most gorgeous and the hedges still in leaf. You're pretty near my ideal, Fleecie—only just a little 'shy.' But I'm young yet."

Then he was almost dead-sure that Brimley was "it."

But nearly four years later, during which time he had seen much of the girl at intervals, he met her one morning at a florists' exhibition in New York, and, as they walked up town together, he announced his own engagement and approaching marriage. She was radiantly effusive in her congratulations, assured him, however, that she had long foreseen the outcome of what she was pleased to term his "little affair," and then informed him serenely that Brimley was engaged, to——

"Oh, no ; not to me—for I know you were going to ask it—to an army officer's daughter now at the post with her father at Fort Pembina. But I've an inspiration, Fleecie. 'Brim' is in town here now. Suppose you both dine with me at the Brunswick tomorrow—a sort of parting feast from a bachelor girl to two 'shy' ideals ? Drop in here with me, and I'll get 'Brim' on the telephone."

If the idea of the dinner was an inspiration, the dinner if self was a poem. All three were at their very best and very brightest, and when the white Burgundy was being served McMillan imparted to Brimley his Senior-year secret :

"If you hadn't been in the way," he said, "I know I should have lost my heart to Suzanne, here. I came desperately near it."

"Holy corner-lots ! By all the first liens and second mortgages !" (Brimley was in real estate) "It was you, man, that saved me from making myself ridiculous ! If I hadn't firmly believed that she was dead in love with you, I should have proposed a dozen times !"

But the pair had finally to admit that it was Suzanne herself who had saved them both from making fools of themselves.

And as they both escorted her from the carriage and up the steps of her brother's home to say good-night and goodbye, the older of the two couldn't resist the temptation to recite somewhat dramatically, with apologies to Thomas Bailey Aldrich—

> "And if, perchance, again we meet
>   On this side or that of the equator,
> If then I have not turned teetotaler,
>   And have wherewith to pay the waiter,
> To thee I'll drain a modest cup,
>   Ignite with thee the mild Havana,
> And we will waft, while liquoring up,
>   Forgiveness to the coy Suzanna."

McMillan had never seen either Suzanne or Brimley, after that parting—twenty-three years ago.

Thorneleigh boarded the train twenty miles east of Philadelphia, very much excited.

"I couldn't wait for you, Pop," he explained. "My Suzanne's mother has come—Mrs. Pearston, you know—come unexpectedly from 'Frisco. In the very deepest of deep mourning. And, but for her white hair, she wouldn't look a day older than her daughter. And, oh, my, but she's a beauty ! She was 'easy,' too—never even protested or looked me over, but told Suzanne she rather liked me ! How's that for a 'mother-in-law-elect' ? And in half an hour she had told me more about *you* than you had ever told me yourself in all your life !"

*   *   *   *   *   *

There were four plates laid at Thorneleigh's little Wissehickon dinner—and somehow McMillan didn't get back to his club for a full week.

Nearly a year later the Union Square stationer protested that the wording of these cards was in shockingly bad form, but he had finally to give in, and the engraver nearly had a fit when the copy came into his hands :

335

It would please Mrs. Thomas Telfair Pearston exceedingly to see you on the turf by the south wing of the Chapel, Bowdoin College, at 4 o'clock, on the afternoon of October 20, next ; on the steps her daughter, Savanna Halsey Pearston, will be married to Mr. Thorneleigh McMillian, of Philadelphia.

[Over.]

At the same place, fifteen minutes later, Mr. Thorneleigh McMillan would be pleased to have you witness the marriage of his father, Mr. Percival Jason McMillan, of New York, and Mrs. Thomas Telfair Pearston, of Washington, D. C.

Rain or shine.

All four at home, Montclair, N. J., Thursdays in December.

Mrs. Pearston-McMillan explained to anybody rude enough to comment on the cards that the scheme saved envelopes, postage and a good bit of fuss and feathers—she was under contract to marry that way whenever her ideal happened to stumble along.

ONE NIGHT IN JUNE

JOHN CLAIR MINOT, '96

ONE NIGHT IN JUNE

AFTER the crowd had cheered the ends and given the final cheers for the college and the Senior class in front of the Chapel, most of the fellows started for the Art Building steps, just for a song or two ; but with a common impulse the half-dozen boys of the Senior delegation lingered behind.

"We've sung enough for one night," declared Tucker, and the hoarseness of his voice, whatever the cause, seemed to vindicate the assertion. "Let's stay here and listen. It will sound great across the campus."

"We are out of the active ranks now, anyway, and we might as well get used to the sensation," said Macfarlane in a tone which indicated that to him, at least, the sensation did not bring much joy.

And, indeed, it was a solemn, rather than the usual joyous, gathering which the old fraternity hall had witnessed that evening: The farewell supper to the Senior delegation is apt to be such, for the shadow of the approaching parting is heavy upon all hearts and the severing of the ties of active membership is not a cheerful process. The Senior whose throat does not fill when he gets upon his feet to speak after the spread is either a hardened wretch with little feeling, or a man of great self-control. And few college boys belong to either class. So it was with natures tuned in a minor key that these boys watched their brothers of the lower delegations hurry across the campus to the Art Building while they remained behind and seated themselves upon the Chapel steps.

At first there was little said. It was a glorious night in early June. Through the foliage of the trees the full moon made its witching, wavering tracery upon the campus paths. From the resonant loggia of the Walker Art Building, sung with the spirit and harmony that only undergradute voices know, softened in volume by the distance, yet marvellously clear on the air of the solemn midnight, came the old songs of the college and the fraternity.

Big Mosher was the first to break the silence. He had less sentiment than the other fellows, possibly due to the fact that he had played football, four years. "Say, Tom, do you remember the first time we walked up this central path to the Chapel ? O, but I was verdant then. Still I wasn't frightened, while you were morally certain you'd be killed in the rush after chapel. It seems only yesterday, but in a few weeks more we'll be parading down this same path, togged out in caps and gowns, right behind the band, the heroes of Commencement week. Can you realize it, Tom ?"

Tom Winslow realized it keenly enough without the aid of the slap which Mosher gave his shoulder. "It's all right being a Commencement hero and following the band, but what about next year, when we come back and are dropped clear to the tail of the procession ? There's no fun or glory in being alumni. I'd like to start my course over again."

"O, well, we all would, in a way," said Tucker, "and then again we wouldn't. It is up to us to get out and hustle, and do something so that Bowdoin won't be ashamed of us."

"You are cut out for a preacher, no doubt," interposed Macfarlane, whereat the group laughed softly. "But you can't make us feel really reconciled to the prospect of leaving here. I tell you, boys, now that we are just ready to graduate we are beginning to appreciate life here and to realize what it means to touch shoulders as chums at this old college. I wish somebody would write a book of Bowdoin stories so that a youngster about to enter here could get some conception of the good things in store for him. It would take more than one book, though, to do the subject justice."

"What is the matter with Kellogg's Whispering Pine stories?" suggested Winslow.

"Nothing, of course. They are the best ever written in their line, but they touch only on life and pranks here sixty years ago, and lots of things worth writing about have happened around here since then. They are not the oldest Bowdoin stories, by the way, for Hawthorne's first novel, 'Fanshawe,' published the year after he graduated, dealt with college life, and the scenes and characters are plainly those of early Bowdoin, thinly disguised. One scene is a student revel in the old Tontine, interrupted by the President. The villain is an ex-pirate who tries to capture the

President's fair ward. The hero was soulful and studious, too good to live long. It is quite a yarn, and told in splendid English, though the style seems a bit heavy and old fashioned now. They say that Hawthorne regarded it as a youthful effort and wasn't particularly proud of it, though since his death it is included in his works. It isn't much read. Even Prof. Harry admitted to me, the other day, that he had never seen the book. But what we want is a book of Bowdoin stories of recent years and today. Think of the unlimited amount of good material that is waiting to be used,—and there are scores and scores of literary men, some of them winners, too, among the alumni."

"You are right, Mac," said Tucker, "it ought to be done and probably will be, some day. Why, I know enough good stories myself, if I could only tell them well, to fill a small library, and I don't pretend to know much of the college before our day, either. Just think of the days when Phi Chi was young, and when the great drill rebellion was on, and when there was a girls' boarding school just across from the campus, and when they had yagger wars, and when they buried 'Anna,' and when—when lots of things happened," he concluded lamely, stopping rather on account of the great possibilities presented than because he had exhausted his list.

"Speaking of 'Anna,' " broke in Mosher, "do you know that when Lieutenant Peary was here at the '97 Commencement, just before starting for the Pole, he and a dozen of his classmates took the '77 'Anna' gravestone from the terrace at South Appleton where it had been transplanted, and dragged it out into its first resting place in the pines beyond the Observatory ? They had a lot of fun over it."

"I should think the most interesting stories could be made out of the old days," observed Winslow. "The planting of Thorndike oak, for instance. You know that George Thorndike, who buried the little acorn over beside the steps of Massachusetts, was in the first class and he died in Russia, I believe, the first graduate of Bowdoin to die. If that old oak could talk, as Tennyson's did, what tales it could tell us, tonight. In those first years the whole college was housed in Massachusetts, and Prexie McKeen used to call the boys to prayers by rapping with his cane on the stairs. The first Commencement was held in September, and I've read that it was postponed one day on account of the rain. Commencement was always held late in the Summer, and in the early times it was more or less like a circus, I judge, and everybody drove in from miles around and made a day of it with peanuts and red lemonade, or their equivalents."

"It is something of a circus now," remarked Mosher, thinking of three girls, in Bath, Lewiston and Portland respectively, all of whom were eagerly counting on being his guests when the great occasion came.

But Winslow refused to heed the interruption and went on: "There ought to be a ghost story or two, or at least some wild larks, in the old tumble-down, deserted tavern that stood for years on the corner of the campus, near the church. But I suppose the real Bowdoin ghost stories could be found in some of the grave-robbing episodes that were more or less frequent when the Medics had harder work to get subjects for dissection than now. There has also been a suicide or two, if a grewsome theme were wanted. There might be material for a good yarn in the burning of Maine Hall, 'way back in the 'twenties and again one night in the 'thirties, or the burning of the President's house after they had had a big row over his resignation. And think of the chance for a story in that meeting on the coast of Africa between Commodore Bridge and his former college mate, Russwurm, I think his name was,—the only negro who ever graduated from Bowdoin, and who had become a dignitary of importance, possibly a king, among his own people. And there was the outbreak of the war—"

"O, that's all ancient history," interrupted Macfarlane. "The best Bowdoin story would be one of today with the hero winning the Worcester meet or a big football game, and his girl in the grandstand holding her breath all the while. There is no story to wake up a college man like one in which a fellow wins glory for the old college by lining out home runs, or bucking the line for a touchdown or breaking the tape at the finish. That sort of thing, with a vivid picture of the big crowd going wild as the plucky hero snatches victory from defeat, makes the Old Grad's blood tingle as nothing else will. And I guess the outside public likes it as well as any kind of a college yarn, though it gives the impression that college life is about all athletics."

"If anybody writes about Bowdoin athletics," said Winslow, "they mustn't forget the days of rowing. There are some great stories told of

THE WALKER ART BUILDING.

those victories on the water, between the time when Tom Reed rowed on the Androscoggin and the last class race when '96 beat '97 in the Spring of '94. Some of the intercollegiate victories when Bowdoin beat even Harvard and Yale resulted in celebrations here that make present jollifications seem pretty tame. It is a pity that boating had to be given up, and the old boathouse and the shells go to wreck and ruin."

"Well, football and field sports have more than taken rowing's place in college life," said Macfarlane. After a pause he continued, "Next to athletic stories, I think the story of undergraduate pranks and deviltry is most appreciated by college men, though this kind also is likely to give a false impression to those outside the pale. Now, for instance, there is a splendid chance for a storiette in that episode of a recent Ivy hop when a Junior brought his girl over to the Chapel here at intermission, to show her the picture of an angel that he declared was the exact image of herself. Some of the boys were onto it, and—well, I'll tell you the whole story sometime, if you have never heard of it. The painting is that of the Baptism, third one on the left ; and just notice that dark-haired angel in the lower part, the next time any of you forget yourselves and go to chapel. Or, if a prank story is wanted, it might deal with that affair when a few '96 fellows locked up two Fseshmen in the tomb down in the cemetery, after taking them down to the river. It made a lot of trouble, but probably the hazing sounded worse than it was. Then I've heard an alumnus up home tell how '80 lost the Y. M. C. A. presidency by winning the annual Fall field day. You see, they had only one man really eligible to that office and when they celebrated their field day victory, somebody accidentally doctored the new cider which they used, and they over-celebrated. But the man who thereby lost the Y. M. C. A. presidency was game, and declared he had rather have his fun with his class than hold any college honor. And I've heard about a fellow in '75 who fell off the roof of Maine Hall—"

"Now wouldn't that jar you !" murmured Mosher.

"O, it's no joke," continued Macfarlane. "His name was Hewes. He is now a lawyer over in Washington county, and a good one. Workmen were repairing the roof and he was up there looking around when he slipped and rolled over the edge to the ground. Never fazed him, and he was as good as new in an hour or two. Nobody has tried to duplicate the feat, though. I met him once, on a Glee Club trip."

"Was that the trip when you were jugged, over in Bangor?" inquired Tucker.

"That wasn't Bangor ; it was in Bath that I joined Bowdoin's immortal Convict Club to which so many good men have belonged. It wasn't my fault the cop was fresh, you know."

"O, that's always the way of it," assented Tucker.

"But, to continue," said Macfarlane, "there would be a chance for a great story on the days when it was fashionable for fellows in different colleges to send bell tongues, chapel Bibles and such things, back and forth. Once the Colby Sophomores sent a bust of one of their Presidents, Chaplin or Champlin, down here to Bowdoin. Our Prex didn't see the joke, and accepted the gift in a nice little note of thanks to the Colby Prex. Then the Colby Prex didn't have the heart to tell him that it was only a piece of Sophomoric skylarking, and so the bust remained here and it is here now over in Memorial, I think."

"It strikes me that you are wandering into ancient history, yourself," said Winslow. "What do you think of this idea of a book of Bowdoin yarns ?" he added, turning to Larry Howard who had been lying back against the Chapel doors, listening to the distant singing and taking no part in the chatter of his companions. Perhaps, under the influence of the moonlight which affects the tides of the heart as it does those of the sea, his mind had wandered back to that memorable day during the previous Summer's vacation, when he had induced a fond and trusting mamma to allow her daughter to accompany him from a not far away shore resort for a day's inspection of the campus, deserted but never so attractive as when in the luxuriance of its midsummer foliage. Perhaps he was thinking,— who could blame him ?—of that tour of the Art Building when, in the seclusion of the Assyrian Sculpture room, the bold Junior had poured into the ears of the maiden, pink ears as willing as they were dainty, a story, not a college story, but one older far than the inscriptions on the unheeded tablets around them. Perhaps —.

"What do I think of it ?" he repeated, slowly coming out of his trance, "Why, I think it is a great idea that somebody ought to act upon. But if you fellows talked all night you couldn't mention one in a thousand of the things in Bowdoin's history around which good stories of the past or present could be written. There is simply no limit to them, no college is so rich in opportunity for the story-teller, and the man who tries to get up the book will probably find himself buried under an avalanche of desirable contributions. "But I also think," he added, getting up with a yawn, "that it is time we all turned in. This is their last song."

True enough, the boys on the Art Building steps, having sung themselves out, were giving as their last selection before coming over to the End, that favorite by Harry Pierce of '96, he who could make the claim, and justify it, of kinship with Bowdoin's greatest singer :

BOWDOIN BEATA.

When bright skies were o'er us,
And life lay before us,
'Neath Bowdoin's pines we gathered far and near,
So filling our glasses,
And pledging all classes,
We drink a health to *Alma Mater* dear.

CHORUS.

Clink, clink, drink, drink, drink !
Smash the glass in splinters when you're done.
Bowdoin Beata, O dear *Alma Mater*,
There is no fairer mother 'neath the sun.

When manhood has found us,
And children surround us,
Our college days and friends we'll still recall.
With heartfelt emotion,
And deathless devotion,
We'll send our sons to Bowdoin in the fall.

CHORUS.

When age, gray and hoary,
Has filled out our story,
The tender mem'ries swelling back again.
Loyal forever,
Until death shall sever,
One glass to *Alma Mater* we shall drain.

347

CHORUS.

So, comrades together,
In fair and foul weather,
Your glasses fill to Bowdoin and her fame.
For where e'er we wander,
Stronger and fonder,
The tend'rest ties shall cling about her name.

CHORUS.